Ink on the Tracks

Ink on the Tracks

Rock and Roll Writing

Edited by Andrew McKeown and Adrian Grafe

BLOOMSBURY ACADEMIC

NEW YORK · LONDON · OXFORD · NEW DELHI · SYDNEY

BLOOMSBURY ACADEMIC
Bloomsbury Publishing Inc
1385 Broadway, New York, NY 10018, USA
50 Bedford Square, London, WC1B 3DP, UK
29 Earlsfort Terrace, Dublin 2, Ireland

BLOOMSBURY, BLOOMSBURY ACADEMIC and the Diana logo are trademarks of
Bloomsbury Publishing Plc

First published in the United States of America 2024

Copyright © Andrew McKeown and Adrian Grafe, 2024

Each chapter copyright © by the contributor, 2024

For legal purposes the Acknowledgements on p. vii constitute an extension of this
copyright page.

Cover design: Louise Dugdale

Cover image © OlgastockerAdobe Stock

All rights reserved. No part of this publication may be reproduced or transmitted in
any form or by any means, electronic or mechanical, including photocopying, recording,
or any information storage or retrieval system, without prior permission in writing
from the publishers.

Bloomsbury Publishing Inc does not have any control over, or responsibility for, any third-
party websites referred to or in this book. All internet addresses given in this book were
correct at the time of going to press. The author and publisher regret any inconvenience
caused if addresses have changed or sites have ceased to exist, but can accept no
responsibility for any such changes.

Whilst every effort has been made to locate copyright holders the publishers would be
grateful to hear from any person(s) not here acknowledged.

A catalog record for this book is available from the Library of Congress.

ISBN: HB: 979-8-7651-0195-7
ePDF: 979-8-7651-0197-1
eBook: 979-8-7651-0196-4

Typeset by Deanta Global Publishing Services, Chennai, India

To find out more about our authors and books visit www.bloomsbury.com and sign up
for our newsletters.

Contents

Acknowledgements	vii
Editors	viii
Contributors	ix

Introduction: A lover's discourse? Rock and roll writing
Andrew McKeown   1

Part 1   Come Writers and Critics

1   'I read the news today . . . oh boy': Taking the pulse of UK popular music journalism *Simon A. Morrison*   9

2   Lester Bangs and the great American mythos *Maud Berthomier*   24

3   Rock and philosophy: From Adorno to the anti-Adornian generation? *Cristina Parapar*   35

4   The concert: Creation, re-creation and the writing of popular music *Julie Mansion-Vaquié*   49

5   Class and race in popular music history *Jon Stratton*   64

Part 2   Every Day I Write the Book

6   All the years combine: Digital media, the Grateful Dead archive and the wheel of time *M. Cooper Harriss*   81

7   'I obliterate myself in song': Music, selfhood and discovery in YA fiction *Ben Screech*   93

8   Rock music and the contingencies of history: Dawnie Walton's *The Final Revival of Opal & Nev* *Adrian Grafe*   106

9   Writing into the canon: Women and music memoir *Lucy O'Brien*   119

10   Rock obits: Patti Smith and the deceased *Janneke Van Der Leest*   133

Contents

11 'The magic runes are writ in gold': Writing mythology, transcendence and faith in rock *Simon McAslan*   146

12 Paul is dead . . . long live Paul: Reinventing Eden in rock and roll writing *Charles Holdefer*   159

13 Something up their sleeve? The doubtful art of liner notes *Andrew McKeown*   172

General Bibliography   187

Index   191

Acknowledgements

The editors are grateful to Leah Babb-Rosenfeld and Rachel Moore and the Bloomsbury editorial board for welcoming our project and for their patience and professionalism throughout the editorial process. We also express our thanks to all the contributors who made this volume possible.

Editors

Adrian Grafe, BA Hons (Oxon), English professor at Université d'Artois in Arras, France, has published widely on the connections between popular music and literature, and written for *TLS* (on Dylan), *Essays in Criticism* and *The Spectator*. He co-edited and contributed to *21st-Century Dylan: Late and Timely* (2021). His novel *The Ravens of Vienna* was published in 2022.

Andrew McKeown teaches English at the University of Poitiers, France. He has made several contributions to scholarly works on poetry and popular music. He co-edited and contributed to *Edward Thomas: Roads from Arras* (2018) and *21st-Century Dylan: Late and Timely* (2021). He has also published poetry, *You What?* (2017), and fiction, *Spurts* (2022).

Contributors

Maud Berthomier (PhD Université de Poitiers, France, and Concordia University, Canada) is the author of three books: *Encore plus de bruit: L'âge d'or du journalisme rock en Amérique par ceux qui l'ont inventé* (2019), *The Clash: L'Expérience* (2021) and *Very Good Trip: Une histoire intime de la musique* (2022).

M. Cooper Harriss, associate professor in the Department of Religious Studies at Indiana University, in Bloomington (USA), teaches American religion, literature and culture. He is the author of *Ralph Ellison's Invisible Theology*, a founding editor of the journal *American Religion* and is completing a book provisionally titled *Double Cross: Muhammad Ali and the Irony of American Religion*.

Charles Holdefer is a writer based in Brussels. His latest novel is *Don't Look at Me* (2022).

Janneke van der Leest, curriculum developer at Radboud Academy (Radboud University, Nijmegen, The Netherlands), is currently working on a PhD project entitled *Rock and Romantic Mourning: Presentation and Representation of Young Deceased Rock Stars*.

Julie Mansion-Vaquié, specialist in popular music, is a lecturer in musicology at the Université Côte d'Azur in France and a composer. She is interested in scenic re-creation, interpretation and creation, as well as the multiple forms of existence of music and the relationship between sound, image and narrativity. She is a member of CTELA and IASPM-bfE.

Simon McAslan teaches in the English Department of Vanier College, Montreal, Canada. He has published essays on Bob Dylan in *21st-Century Dylan: Late and Timely* (2021) and *The Politics and Power of Bob Dylan's Live Performances: Play a Song for Me* (2023) and has presented conference papers at Université d'Artois, France (2018) and the MLA Annual Convention (2021).

Simon A. Morrison, writer, academic and programme leader for Music Journalism at the University of Chester, UK, has reported on music scenes everywhere from Beijing to Brazil, published books including *Discombobulated* (2010) and *Dancefloor-Driven Literature* (2020) and contributed to many international books and journals. He has presented his research at conferences in the UK, Portugal, Holland, Germany and Australia.

Lucy O'Brien (PhD), writer, academic and broadcaster, has published *Lead Sister: The Story of Karen Carpenter (2023)*; *She Bop: The Definitive History of Women in Popular Music (1995)*; *Dusty: The Classic Biography (1999)* and *Madonna: Like an Icon (2007)*. She co-authored *The Liverbirds* (2024) and *It Takes Blood and Guts (2020)* with Skin. She teaches Music Industry Management at London College of Music, UWL, UK, and once played in all-girl punk band The Catholic Girls.

Cristina Parapar, PhD candidate in Aesthetics of Music at Sorbonne University, France, educated at Salamanca and Paris Universities, has been a visiting researcher at Duke (USA), Columbia (USA) and Berlin Humboldt (Germany) Universities. Her research focuses on the critical theory and philosophy of popular music. She has notably contributed to *Pearl Jam and Philosophy* (2021) and *The Marcusean Mind* (2024).

Ben Screech, senior lecturer in Education at the University of Gloucestershire, UK, has recently completed a three-year ERASMUS+ project piloting approaches to raise the profile of literacy in three European contexts of disadvantage. In summer 2023, he was Visiting Fellow at the International Youth Library in Munich, where he researched environmental trauma in young adult literature, in preparation for a monograph on this topic. His recent publications include: 'The Oxford Museums and Storytelling for Young People' in *Museums in Literature* (2023) and 'Depression in Florian Zeller's *The Son*' (2022) in *FRAME*.

Jon Stratton, adjunct professor in UniSA Creative at the University of South Australia, has published widely in Popular Music Studies, Cultural Studies, Media Studies, Jewish Studies, Australian Studies and on race and multiculturalism. Jon's most recent book is *Spectacle, Fashion and the Dancing Experience in Britain 1960–1990* (2022).

Introduction

A lover's discourse? Rock and roll writing

Andrew McKeown

Language is a skin: I rub my language against the other. It is as if I had words instead of fingers, or fingers at the tip of my words. My language trembles with desire. (Barthes 1978: 73)

Roland Barthes's description of the language of love contained in this fragment offers interesting parallels for the writers in this volume in their accounts of the words that translate – just as they embody – the experience of rock: a lover's discourse rubbing up against its readers and turning them on (maybe) just as the music turned them on.

Simon Morrison opens the discussion with an assessment of the relations between print and digital media in the new millennium. While it is clear that rock journalism has moved online to a large degree, and that certain of the print giant bywords are now bygone (Q, for example), it is by no means certain that the shift is one-way traffic, or that things are irreversible. Morrison argues that the assumed antagonism between print and digital media is in fact abating, perhaps mirroring the moving tides that have seen the return of vinyl – print's analogue brother – in spite of the apparent universality of digitized formats.

Rock and roll journalism has a rich history marked by famous scribes and iconic publications. Maud Berthomier's interviews conducted with the likes of Peter Guralnick, Jon Landau and Dave Marsh (*Encore plus de bruit: L'âge d'or du journalisme rock en Amérique, par ceux qui l'ont inventé*, 2019) provide the groundwork for her discussion of one of the genre's leading writers: Lester Bangs. For Berthomier, Bangs is not to be understood as a music journalist, in the sense that his reviews are not about the music itself, but (in addition to Bangs's own self-mythologizing) about the myths of Americana which underpin the music – the quest for innocence, for example. To read Bangs's journalism, argues Berthomier, is to adhere to an ethos. The writing is the voice of the musical experience – hence the 'gonzo' and the 'bozo' tags that accompany this writing's rough and rowdy ways. Rock writing is about the 'party', not the 'tradition', shouts Bangs's 'barbaric yawp'.

Bangs certainly had his acolytes. Step forward Nick Kent:

> I wasn't writing about rock as an idea: I was writing about it as a full-blown, flesh-and-blood reality – surreal people living surreal, action-packed lives. From what I'd learned coming up, rock writing was fundamentally an action medium that best came to life when the writer was right in the thick of that action. (Kent 2010: 149–50)

But the 'gunslinger' approach – while it suited Garage and Punk – does suggest that scholarly and *post-intuitive* writing misses the point, or is simply not allowed because, well, it's just *no fun*. In this volume that point is challenged by Julie Mansion-Vaquié and Cristina Parapar who, from differing perspectives, discuss writing with a more scientific approach to rock and roll: scenography and philosophy. Parapar examines the German philosopher Theodor Adorno's belief that *leichte Musik* (in this case, rock) is fettered to commercialism and consumerism and as such is incapable of intellectual effect, that is to say, it can only procure *divertissement* and consolation. Parapar shows how some contemporary French philosophers have challenged Adorno's anti-rock philosophy by focusing on the technological nature of rock, its existence as a recorded product. This means, so the argument runs, that rock and roll is a 'multilevelled collaboration', containing its own 'plurality, progress and complexity' which resists the 'ubiquity of commercialism'. These philosophers locate the ontology of rock and roll within the means of production.

Coming at the subject from a different angle, Julie Mansion-Vaquié shows how concert structuring, the *writing* of stage space through lighting, sound, stage clothes and set design, creates a performance *text* which renews the music and how it works on the auditor/spectator, organizing and structuring *affect*, in a way analogous to scripted accounts of music. The idea that a parallel should exist between written text and spatial discourse is an original, semiotic point of view, opening up new ways of thinking about rock and roll.

The current volume also embraces a sociological perspective on rock and roll writing. Rock writing in the United States, Jon Stratton contends, is bound up with notions of race, while rock writing in the UK is tied to issues of class. Stratton looks at exemplars of this cleaved model – Garofalo/LeRoi Jones and Cohn/Frith – and traces its persistence through to contemporary sociology.

That popular music should have a social determinism is no doubt a challenge to Adorno's snubbing of *leichte Musik* and adds further weight to the belief which underpins this volume, that rock and roll writing is more than just 'dancing about architecture', as one wag – Frank Zappa, if indeed it was he – once observed.

In 1996, Simon Frith stated the role of rock writing as follows: 'creating a knowing community, orchestrating a collusion between selected musicians and an equally select part of the public – select in its superiority to the ordinary, undiscriminating pop consumer' (quoted by McLeod 2001: 50). That kind of exclusiveness, which may – or may not – have been the aim of rock writing in print, has been challenged by the development of online platforms; if only superficially, these facilitate greater connectedness between artists and fans. Cooper Harriss explores this new development in rock media through the specific case of three Grateful Dead archives providing access to recordings of their concerts: an online radio station, a Facebook page and an iPhone app. According to Harriss, this content curation – in tandem with the write-ups from archivists and subscribers alike – establishes a new paradigm of fan experience, where the exclusiveness indicated by Frith is replaced by something less hierarchical; a looping, infinite return of music, written in digital form – in ones and zeros – echoing one of rock's oldest myths: that rock and roll – gratefully *undead* – is here to stay. And stay, and stay.

A further, expanding field of rock writing is to be noted in the world of fiction. In this volume, Adrian Grafe and Ben Screech offer two accounts of rock novels. The latter explores how rock and roll is integral to the genre of young adult (YA) fiction. Musical experiences in YA novels, Screech proposes, are key to the adolescent preoccupations of school life, love and friendship formation. Through readings of Foucault, Screech argues that music acts as a 'limit experience' providing an antidote to the homogenizing effects of language, while Adrian Grafe's essay on Dawnie Walton's first and prize-winning novel, *The Final Revival of Opal & Nev*, embraces the notion of rock fiction as a socio-historical document. Here the focus is the United States, specifically a docufiction/autofiction account, conducted largely through oral interviews, of the career of a fictional African-American female rock musician which nevertheless recalls the lives of Grace Jones and Tina Turner. Following on from Jon Stratton's chapter on the centrality of race in North American writing about rock and roll, Grafe argues that through the characterization of Opal and her confrontations with racism and sexism, rock music – and rock writing – can be seen to be something more than mere 'commodity culture' (Babae and Silva 2014: 191).

4   *Ink on the Tracks*

That Dawnee Walton, a woman, should be the voice behind rock and roll writing, at least a slice of it, is testimony to a wider development that this volume seeks to embrace, namely the place of women in the conversation about rock and roll. Lucy O'Brien's chapter on female memoir challenges the notion of a male canon about rock writing, specifically in the field of biography. Her discussion provides an overview of recent and contemporary music memoirs by women writers – an indication of a certain levelling-up of *gender* within the *genre* – and concludes with her work as ghost writer on the memoir of the Liverbirds – the other, *female* Fab Four from 1960s Merseyside.

Music writing, it could be argued, is a second-hand art: a tale about something happening somewhere else. But it is also possible to conceive of things differently. Janneke van der Leest does exactly this in her discussion of Patti Smith's poems and lyrics where rock writing exists *first-hand*. Van der Leest presents Smith's work in the context of the elegy and examines the relationship between the elegist and the deceased in the art of necrology. In so doing she raises the problem of hagiography that rock writing can fall prey to.

In their respective chapters both Simon McAslan and Charles Holdefer pursue this question of religiosity in rock and roll. According to McAslan, rock and roll works very much like a myth: a supernatural narrative assimilated by its audience in a manner akin to religious faith. To illustrate his point, the author analyses four rock texts: a 'how-to-be-in-a-band' guidebook, a short story, a rock hotel travel guide and an album review. These works – nay, gospels – cultivate a form of religious practice, says McAslan, through superficial tricks like Bible-type fonts and more pervasive effects such as the encouragement of ritual and repetition. But they also lovingly mock the urge to spiritualize, deify and mythologize, through auto-derision. Rock as religion? You must be kidding! Charles Holdefer pursues the problem of fabulation tending towards mythical status by examining the story of Eden in rock and roll writing: the idea of roots and beginnings which rock and roll replicates from generation to generation. Holdefer's argument draws its originality from the belief that this narrative is a collective one, orally transmitted for the most part, in which artists and audiences – and, of course, journalists – participate, not to say conspire. Writing is collective. We are all rock and roll writers, one might say, the moment we enter the rock and roll universe.

From the spiritual to the commercial: Andrew McKeown brings the volume to a close with an overview of the art of record sleeve writing in the rock and roll era. At times light-hearted, at others in deadly earnest, sleeve notes have accompanied rock releases through thick and thin, surviving the minimalism of the CD format and digital compressions. While their value as writing space has sometimes been squandered, and even if their teleology is commercial, liner notes have worked a curious fascination on music lovers – haters, too, no doubt – ever since those anonymous lines about Elvis Presley's 'belting style' and his 'universal popularity' on his 1956 debut album sleeve. Who can resist the urge to read what it says on the back? Not Andrew McKeown, at any rate, who takes us on a tour of sleeve writing highs and lows from the 1950s to the 2020s, from the glib to the Grammy-Award winning and back again.

In the discussions which follow, the contributors to this volume evaluate the many ways in which rock writing has embraced its subject. Whether that connection is scientific, fictional or mythopoeic it ends up as an agent of the music, transmitting its effect along a chain of meaning – *trembling* with Barthes' desire – which very often, if not always, brings us back to the music.

References

Barthes, Roland (1978). *A Lover's Discourse*. Trans. Richard Howard. New York: Hill & Wang (2010).

Kent, Nick (2010). *Apathy for the Devil*. London: Faber & Faber.

Part 1

Come Writers and Critics

1

'I read the news today ... oh boy'

Taking the pulse of UK popular music journalism

Simon A. Morrison

Pop's first literary attendant was journalism, which to this day remains its acolyte and accomplice. (Kureishi 1995: xix)

Front cover

Throughout the history of popular music, music writers have been tactically positioned just to the side of the stage. Indeed, as soon as young people began producing 'pop' music, other young people were critiquing it and reporting it. The negative reaction in the US mass media to the emergence of Elvis Presley, for instance (reinforced by *Melody Maker* in the UK), was equalled by the fans themselves, in their own mediated responses. From the emergence of the countercultural music press in 1960s America with *Rolling Stone* and *Cream*, to the power of the weekly 'inkies' in the UK in the following decade, to the explosion of colour in the 1980s 'glossies', the key moments in popular music history have been matched and mirrored by media reaction and deconstruction. However, more recently, the emergence, then dominance, of the digital sphere has changed, irrevocably, the media landscape. It was already navigating that challenge when Covid-19 fell as a further hammer blow, for example taking down established British music titles such as *Q*. Already overwhelmed by the digital imperialism of the internet, it would seem music journalism is in grave peril.

Or at least it would 'seem'. This chapter will analyse the current state of popular music journalism in a specifically post-Covid UK context, but also argue for a more positive picture than the one put forward in recent writing on the subject. The year 2022 alone saw the publication of the memoir of Ted Kessler, the last editor of *Q*, entitled *Paper Cuts: How I Destroyed the British Music Press and Other Misadventures*, alongside Paul Gorman's latest overview of the music media, *Totally Wired: The Rise and Fall of the Music Press*. It is telling to note such pejorative barbs often come from ex-music journalists, as indeed do the counterattacks, such as Dave Simpson's 2018 *Guardian* article 'What Crisis? Why Music Journalism Is Actually Healthier Than Ever' and Ellen Peirson-Hagger's 2020 response to the closure of *Q*, 'The Music Press Isn't Dead', published in the *New Statesman*. With that sense of the fourth estate in mind – and in terms of a methodology – this enquiry will reach for the trusted tool of all seasoned hacks and venture out to talk to people, utilizing primary research to test the hypotheses that the music media has either 'fallen' or indeed been 'destroyed'.

In 2002, music academic Roy Shuker commented:

> Rock critics perform an influential role as gatekeepers of taste and arbiters of cultural history, and are an important adjunct to the record companies' marketing of their products. [. . .] Given this role, the music press has received surprisingly little attention in the writing on popular music. (Shuker 2013: 78)

Since Shuker's comment, music journalism has, in fact, grown as an area of academic enquiry, within the field of musico-literary intermediality, and an area of H.E. study, with degree courses appearing (and regrettably disappearing in some cases). In the last twenty years there have also been various 'state of the union' insights, paying that 'attention' to music journalism (Hearsum 2013; Warner 2014; Hearsum and James 2020) alongside books, journal special editions and symposia. This chapter is intended to contribute to that ongoing discourse, although possibly more concerned with defining the current state of the industry than offering a historical overview. Unusually, perhaps, it will also start with its conclusion: that the future of music journalism is *there is* a future for music journalism, a point that will be reinforced, ultimately, by an unlikely ally: AI.

Alongside Shuker's commercial function of driving consumer choices, there remains a deeper, ontological function of music journalism – placing text within *context* – glimpsing meaning, importance and significance in what may seem, at first glance, rather ephemeral pop music. As a UK example, consider the intimate relationship of the band Joy Division and the emerging music critic Paul Morley, and the romantic purity he perceived in that band. As Paul Crosthwaite remarks (Crosthwaite 2014: 19): 'Enter the pop critic, free to interpret, speculate and invent at will. Or as Morley puts it: "Just because the group didn't know what was lurking inside their music didn't mean it wasn't there". On the other side of the Atlantic, rock star Bruce Springsteen registers the importance of music critics in his own career, from the moment in 1974 when a local Boston music critic, Jon Landau, was sent to review a Springsteen gig, famously witnessing 'rock & roll future'. Springsteen expands on this in an interview ('Bruce Springsteen Says Rock Critics Were "Incredibly Influential" in His Career', *NJArts*, May 2021) conducted during the pandemic:

> We were supported primarily by rock writers, for the first two albums. The first two albums we made bombed, they didn't go anywhere. And so the only support we had was . . . we had some radio support, but we had a lot of critical support, and that was really, really essential at that time.

A little later in the interview he adds:

> You know, it really was an enormous part of the conversation of music, at that time, and was incredibly influential in my work life. I ended up with a rock critic (Jon Landau) as my manager, you know . . . and really, it was a lot of rock writing that pretty much kicked off a certain part of my work life, you know. So, it was very, very influential. Dave [Marsh] and Jon, and Bob Christgau, and Lester Bangs, and Greil Marcus. They were all incredibly influential at that time.

To offer some context, then, almost as soon as the white hot elements of popular music criticism began to solidify, then codify, into the discipline we now understand it to be, people have sought to announce its demise. These announcements have been regular and usually premature. As one example, each generation has considered the *NME* (*New Musical Express*) both Bible and guidebook, and then inevitably grown away from it, as the years pass. Anecdotal reports recall a letter to its famous letters page, for instance, that complained this venerable bastion of UK music journalism had lost its way and was not as good as it used to be. That letter was sent in 1953, a year after the title first came into circulation. The current perceived crisis in music journalism is therefore neither new, nor novel. We are in another such moment of the reading of last rites, and rumours of a demise have, once again, been greatly exaggerated.

Digital love

When commentators such as Ted Kessler and Paul Gorman pronounce the decline or indeed demise of music journalism, they are really talking about a certain branch of music journalism – largely, the printed music press. The printed page was where music criticism began, of course, dating back to organist Charles Avison publishing his 'Essay on Musical Expression' in 1752, and it is easy to understand a sentimental attachment to print, and to mourn the loss of key titles such as *Melody Maker* and *Q*. However, that presents a rather limited definition of what music criticism might entail, and what platforms it might utilize, in this third decade of a new century.

Even a cursory overview of the so-called golden age of music journalism in the 1970s will reveal three principal places, a holy trinity of inkies, where young music critics could be published – *NME*, *Melody Maker* and *Sounds* – along with *Record Mirror* and *Disc & Music Echo*. An early thread of this chapter must be to debunk, to a certain degree, any sense of this decade being a 'golden age' because if, as a young music fanatic, you were not able to write for one of these titles you were likely not writing at all, at least until the advent of punk and the fanzine. Now consider the digital landscape and – notwithstanding the issues inherent in the internet – we can see that the limits of publishing now extend as far as the outer boundaries of the web itself. Beyond the digital adjuncts to established music titles we will shortly consider, there are also brands that have evolved entirely in a digital space. In the United States, we can locate *Stereogum* and *Pitchfork* (the latter turning over an estimated $5 million annually); in the UK, *The Quietus* stands as an important home for all matters of music and culture, alongside other titles such as *Pop Matters* and *Drowned in Sound*. With free content management platforms such as WordPress and Wix, no one need wait to get a commission – that DIY punk ethos extends from the music to publishing as well – with intriguing and innovative personal blogs allowing new journalistic voices to emerge, such as Lizzy Goodman and Laura Snapes.

Two examples, one from each side of the Atlantic, will help trace the evolution of off-line music journalism into the online sphere. In the United States, Jann Wenner established *Rolling Stone* in 1967, following a trip to the UK and meetings with the magazine *Melody Maker*. Wenner headed up the massively influential title for fifty years before finally selling it on. In that time it also developed an online adjunct, *rollingstone.com*, and in a rather neat generational twist, that website was headed up by Gus Wenner, Jan's son, now of a generation more immersed in the digital sphere. If we now turn to the UK, and to *Melody Maker*'s great rival the *NME*, what would that angry letter writer of 1953 make of this title now? 'Now the *NME* has gone,' concerned parents may ask at open days for the Music Journalism programme at my institution, 'what future is there in music journalism?' True, it has disappeared as a print proposition but it lives on, and is *functioning*, in the digital environment, serving consumers of pop music by utilizing the medium they – predominantly young people – use: the internet. Owned for many years by publishing giant IPC, the title is now operated by BandLab in Singapore. Further, it is, for the first time in many years, returning a profit in its current form and indeed has been hiring. Far from 'gone', the *NME* now resides in the phone at the end of your fingers, closer to hand, literally, than it has ever been, certainly closer than the Thursday dash to the newsagents to buy the latest print edition.

When surveying the current field of music journalism, we need, therefore, not to look down and into the page but out across the digital landscape. Indeed, these are the sunny climes where some of these older print journalists have migrated – for instance, Ted Kessler himself starting *The New Cue* (a pun on the original intention to title the old *Q, Cue*) via the Substack platform, also disseminated as 'The World's Greatest Music Newsletter' (following the print magazine's perhaps precipitous claim to be 'The World's Greatest Music Magazine'). We also need to consider the energy and activity in music criticism that lies beyond the written word entirely. Radio was always the perfect medium for music – an audio platform for an aural art form – and that synergy extends into areas such as podcasting, whether musicologically geared podcasts such as *Song Exploder* or *Sodajerker on Songwriting*, or more traditional interview-style podcasts that seek to place text within context, such as *The Rockonteurs*. David Hepworth and Mark Ellen – founders and editors of magazines such as *Q* and *The Word* – also continue to work via new media platforms, with their podcast, *Word In Your Ear*. The internet further allows for a horizontal page to become a vertical screen, with YouTube vloggers such as *Needle Drop* evolving a way to present music journalism *visually*. With over two million subscribers, *Needle Drop*'s Anthony Fantano – the self-styled 'internet's busiest music nerd' – leads a field of critics using YouTube as their chosen platform. Marshall McLuhan was right, of course: the medium is the message. And whether long-form print or TikTok meme, the medium now shapes the musical message.

14 Ink on the Tracks

Take the case of the brand *Louder Than War*. Established by punk musician and music writer John Robb, *Louder Than War* began as a website, but then reversed that proscribed print-to-digital trajectory to evolve into a print magazine, as part of the Big Cheese stable (along with titles such as *Vive le Rock* and *Fistful of Metal*). Robb's first editorial, in issue 1 of the print edition, was headlined 'Print's Not Dead'. As someone who grew up with punk, ran his own fanzine (*Rox*) and conducted the first UK interview with Nirvana (for *Sounds* magazine), you might imagine Robb fetishizes print media, but in fact quite the opposite is true. When interviewed by the author, he bemoaned those 'older people who think, because they're not engaged in the culture anymore, there is no culture'.[1] (Robb 2023) *Louder Than War* takes in a website, a magazine (when conditions allow – the last print iteration was also a victim of the pandemic), social media outlets, a YouTube channel and has extended into hosting a music literature festival, Louder Than Words. Like punk itself, in fact, Robb considers the internet a liberator, a disruptor and a space where new voices might emerge. Ploughing all profits from *Louder Than War* (50 per cent from advertising and 50 per cent from subscriptions) back into the brand, Robb is committed to the Manifesto published on the website and the need, constantly, to bring young people, and young energy, to the fore, arguing: 'Music is like air, it's not owned by anybody, it's all out there and anybody can engage with it any way they want.' (Robb 2023)

And what of those brands that reside in both the off and online worlds? Even *Pitchfork* understands the power of print, publishing longer form pieces in their attractively produced *Pitchfork Review*, seemingly incapable of abandoning, completely, the pejoratively labelled 'dead tree media'. Meanwhile *Vice*, founded in Montreal, Canada, but based in the United States, has become a global digital behemoth that has notably turned to video as a medium to tell music stories. And yet the brand, perceived by millennials (if perhaps not by all Generation Z) as the definitive way to *do digital*, also sees value in print, acquiring UK-style Bible *i-D*. Staying in the UK, an interesting title is *Dork* (a title much loved by younger music consumers, with a strapline 'Down With Boring'), which provides readers with the choice to access content on the site for free, or pay for a physical copy of their monthly magazine, allowing *Dork*, in turn, to pay contributors. The internet is now part of our lives, of course. And the capability

[1] See 'References' section for details of this and two further interviews, one with Tim Bell, one with Paul Benney, conducted by the author. Unless otherwise stated, all quotations from these three sources are taken from the interviews.

of the internet to allow content and opinion to be instantly shared; for the conversation to be joined 'below the line'; for music videos to be embedded; and for the possibility to purchase music immediately is all-engaging, infectious and undeniable. Certainly, you cannot 'out internet the internet'. But maybe, after this step change revolution in media and tech, it might just be possible for both worlds to exist, alongside one another, just as the digital streaming of music has not subsumed, completely, the world of vinyl.

Let's get physical

This story, then, might be a little more complex than one that traces the clearly signposted trail of a perpetually forward technological determinism – that vinyl will inevitably be obliterated as a means of music consumption by first the CD, and then a digital stream; or that print will be consumed entirely by the inexorable, voracious rise of the internet. No, you cannot 'out internet the internet', but equally you cannot curl up in bed with a good screen, safe from pop-ups and paywalls. And, yes, with the internet the horizon is endless. But sometimes that is too much; it can be overwhelming, almost, like a listicle with no end. Sometimes the finite, hermetic properties of a magazine can be reassuring, where everything is contained within the physical liminality of the front and back cover. The online world can be as dangerous as it is alluring: a digital maelstrom when set against the calming aesthetics of the physical page. We are now adjusting to a world of Artificial Intelligence (AI) and Virtual Reality (VR), but that does not negate the existence, and resistance, of what might be called AR (for *Actual*, not Augmented, Reality). Print is the 'best it's been in years' reports Stephen Ackroyd, the co-founder of *Dork* in Laura Snapes' 2020 *Guardian* article, 'Like a Tap Being Turned Off: Music Magazines Fight for Survival in UK'. Merlin Alderslade, editor (at the time) of the print magazine *Metal Hammer*, comments in the same article: 'The huge drop-off that most magazines experienced in the early 2010s has, relatively speaking, flattened out for many brands. [. . .] Most of our issues in 2019 were actually up year on year.'

That is not to say it has been easy for these magazines – especially during the pandemic – but more to point out that the print sphere exists, persists and indeed is bolstered by new entrants to the newsstand. If the *NME* was, then, Exhibit A in the first section of this chapter, then let us label the 2020 closure of *Q* Exhibit Q. Notwithstanding the context of a business decision

16   *Ink on the Tracks*

made during a global pandemic, an argument can also be made that these magazines were, in any case, failing creatively. Rather like 1970s *NME* journalists such as Mark Ellen joyously 'barbecuing the dinosaurs' of their perceived 'dad rock', it might be argued that it was also time to call a meteor strike on some of these big beasts of monthly music publishing, with the same cycle of cover stars, the same (arguably) stale music featured within. Magazines such as *Q*, and perhaps also *Mojo* and *Classic Rock*, are servicing an older readership now fading at the same rate as their favourite concert-going jeans. Reports from an alleged crisis meeting at *Q* as the meteor drew so close it was visible to the naked eye show that the best idea proposed to avert certain disaster was to put Paul Weller on the cover (*Mojo* have indeed done that, since). John Robb is in agreement: '*Q* was terrible. It's a better world now we don't have *Q*. It was boring, it was so dry. There's no love for the music or the culture.' (Robb 2023) And yet Exhibit Q is further evidence, medical evidence, waved accusatorily as proof positive of the ill health of the patient. Certainly it drove Ellen Peirson-Hagger to pen her very persuasive riposte in the *New Statesman*, 'The music press isn't dead.'

However, to write off music journalism because *Q* has closed is short-sighted. simply lazy. One imagines the claim on the cover of Ted Kessler's memoir – *Paper Cuts: How I Destroyed the British Music Press and Other Misadventures* – is more a matter of book marketing rather than anything else. There are, evidently, music magazines in print, and this chapter will now subdivide such titles into a topography of three areas.

First, there are more traditional music magazines, as we would know them, that remain current and, it seems, viable. *Rolling Stone* is now owned by Penske Media in the United States and following a brief UK existence between 1969 and 1972, the new owners evidently felt the conditions were right to return, publishing the first new UK edition in September 2021. At the time of writing, we are up to the ninth edition of the UK magazine, with a pagination of 162 pages, an impressive range of content within and Sam Smith on the cover (one hopes Smith recalls Dr Hook's paean to the importance of that achievement, in their track 'On The Cover of the *Rolling Stone*'). There are, then, titles recognizable from their mastheads, old survivors like *Kerrang!* and *The Wire* joined by resurrected titles such as *The Face* and new entrants covering all music niches, including *Rock Sound*, *Clash*, *Planet Rock* and magazines from indie publishers such as Big Cheese. Just within the electronic dance music world older brands such as *DJ* have been joined by newer titles such as *Electronic Sound*, founded by

'I read the news today . . . oh boy'

Push (previously of IPC's club culture title *Muzik*), which evolved from an app to a multimedia offer.

The rather too staid and stale positioning of older newsstand titles has also opened up a space for new entrants in what, taken together, can be considered the second area of music criticism in print – actually a reappearance of an old format that we will call the 'new inkies'. Such titles operate on a completely different business model: printed on cheaper paper, entirely free, distributed on a sometimes local, regional or quasi-regional basis around accommodating venues such as bars and record stores and sustained on ad revenue, alongside brand partnerships and sponsorships. Taken together, these titles form an intriguing, innovative and most welcome wing of the music publishing scene, tending to focus on young, new music, with content written by young, new writers, as much a breeding ground for the next, diverse generation of music writers as the underground press and fanzine scene once were. Here we are considering local magazines like Liverpool's *Bido Lito* and Scotland's *The Skinny*, but also semi-regional magazines such as *Loud and Quiet* and, indeed, the re-emergence (occasionally) of that old inkie *Sounds*, as *New Sounds*, in Manchester. There are also national successes like *Crack* magazine, published in Bristol and distributed to five hundred outlets in the UK, with the brand statement 'New music in a free magazine'.

Such titles can come and go but what remains, and endures, is the authenticity in the process and pleasure of reading about music in print; the same authenticity and romance that is derived by placing a vinyl record on a turntable. And that is precisely why music, and its attendant literature, go together so well in independent record stores: vinyl stacked in racks, the magazines just to the side, in stacks. So finally, as well as authenticity we must also consider the *aesthetic* qualities inherent in print magazines: a desire to create something beautiful. That is what inspired Paul Benney who, along with John Burgess, published *Jockey Slut* in Manchester between 1993 and 2004, as well as running the electronic event Bugged Out! that brought their interview subjects to 3D life. After *Jockey Slut* closed, Benney moved into the digital sphere, with *Dummy*, latterly *DMY*, but in 2022 was compelled to return to magazine publishing, following a successful crowd-funder, with the biannual *Disco Pogo*. Benney decided there was a space to publish something for the people that shared the dance floor with him, as well as inquisitive more recent entrants to that scene, divining 'a market out there for quality journalism, quality physical products, quality photography and design'. The mission was relatively straightforward, as Benney details:

It's aimed at our generation. That's the beauty of it, you know. We're not trying to appeal to 20-somethings. We're aiming at a 30, 40, 50-somethings. 60-somethings even. We're very comfortable with that because that's a market that we can have access to easily, whereas *Mixmag* and *DJ* are probably pretty obsessed about trying to hit 20-somethings and find new readers. We're not. We're trying to connect with old readers. You know, the people that used to read *Jockey Slut*. (Benney 2022)

Issue 2 features producer Daniel Avery on the cover and a variety of content that is indeed relevant for participants of the UK club scene in the 1980s and 1990s, as well as *new* music within the electronic sphere that might be of interest to such readers.

The quality of the product, and the pleasure to be derived in reading it, is indeed akin to the experiential process of buying and consuming music in the physical realm:

In the *Jockey Slut* days, you'd read a magazine and that would mean you'd then go to a record shop and buy some vinyl. And that's all a beautiful thing. But it was quite a long, extended process, wasn't it? So there's lots of elements of online that's a wonderful thing. Read something. Click on a video, click on a streaming link. So I love all that. But it's not special anymore. You know, it's so much a part of our lives and so much part of our work lives as well. But there is something special again about print, having that physical product in your hands. (Benney 2022)

That romance touches on both consumption and production of the magazine:

You ascribe some value to a physical product that they [the readers] can see has been lovingly put together, but also is full of journalism where the journalists have been thinking, 'I'm writing something that's going to be in a print magazine', and a photographer who's taking photos, thinking, 'I'm taking photos that are gonna be in a print magazine'. (Benney 2022)

Crucially, the magazine is less interested in text than it is with *context*. With only two issues per year, there is no real consideration for reviewing new releases, for instance, as traditional music monthlies would do at the 'back of the book'. Instead, towards the back of *Disco Pogo*, the feature 'How I Made . . . ' invites producer Laurent Garnier to revisit his track 'The Man With The Red Face', while there is also an in-depth consideration of the seminal Manchester nightclub The Haçienda, with contributions from old *Jockey Slut* writers, and indeed, John Burgess himself. Such content has the twin appeal of both time-travelling significance for those who were there originally and educational intel and importance for younger readers keen to know what it was like. Despite his earlier protestations, Benney is certainly also appealing to 'people in their 20s that are buying this magazine because younger people are also interested in how we got to this point musically. They want to read about what happened in the 80s or the 90s'. (Benney 2022) These magazines physically exist and move around the planet, and that physicality in the analogue, in the *actual*, also results in the pleasure of seeing people post (online, of course) stories about *Disco Pogo*, everywhere from Scandinavia to Toronto. When we talk about *Pitchfork* and its founder Ryan Schreiber, Benney comments: 'Ryan got in touch with us recently, actually. He sent us a message saying he absolutely loved what we were doing with *Disco Pogo*.' (Benney 2022)

New music magazines such as *Disco Pogo* are divining and discovering new spaces for publishing, exploring frequencies that place them somewhere between a magazine and a book – not as ephemeral as a magazine but perhaps less permanent than a book – something 'twice yearly, heavy weight, with really good looking quality' (Benney 2022) The difference is immediately discernible, from the thickness of the spine, from the quality of the paper and from the pagination of 232 pages, plus covers. The aesthetics of print allow the reader to indulge fully in the process of reading, of absorbing the photos and reading long-form pieces that are really able to dig into a subject, areas the internet is not able to do well, or certainly not satisfactorily. Benney describes it as 'an analogue product', amusingly detailing 'we've got a website but the purpose of the website is to sell print magazines. It's not to grow millions of unique users to sell banner ads'. (Benney 2022) A cover price of £15 is also a divergence from the normal positioning of magazines but enables the writers to be paid, and for the licensing or commissioning of quality photos, often running over a dps (double-page spread). Benney claims: 'There is something special about print, having that physical product in your hands', (Benney 2022), and *Disco Pogo* is, certainly, a title designed to be lived with; more likely to be displayed on a coffee table than hidden away in a magazine rack.

Disco Pogo is by no means out on its own. After a stint publishing monthly with Big Cheese, John Robb also feels the time is right for *Louder Than War* to return to the physical realm, possibly biannually. Robb explains: 'That's what we'll probably do in the end. We keep talking about it. We just need to get round to it.' (Robb 2023)

Back cover

More and more independently published music magazines are appearing from all around the world, such as *Rodeo* from Manchester, *Zweikommasieben* from Switzerland, Germany's *20 Seconds*, *We Jazz* from Helsinki, *Little White Lies* in London and niche titles such as *Synth History* (perhaps a niche price, too, at £25 per copy) and many others. The difference may be scale, and the thorny subject of monetization, as these fiercely independent magazines eschew corporate publishers such as IPC, EMAP and Bauer, feature artists that equally eschew the major labels such as Sony BMG and Universal and are unlikely to be sold in the main UK retailer WHSmith. Instead, independent magazine stores are appearing, a network of retailers to support and sell these titles. Even within Greater Manchester we find Rare Mags in Stockport, Village Books and a relatively new entrant, UNITOM, situated in the equally, and fiercely, independent Northern Quarter area of the city (stocking all the magazines listed above). Store manager Tim Bell argues that younger people are actually turning away from screens and returning to the page:

> People want to break free from it; they want to retaliate against it. [. . .] Young people, absorbing all their information online. I think they're waking up to the fact that it's a distorted reality. Algorithmically you're fed stuff and then you're blinkered to all this other stuff that's out there. (Bell 2023)

Far from opening up horizons, the digital state, and its algorithmic enforcers, can work to imprison music consumers in echo chambers of similar opinions and options. As Bell argues: 'The internet promises everything but actually precludes you from discovering any of it.' (Bell 2023)

One suggestion might be to appreciate, not denigrate, Gen Z, and instead celebrate the continued desire in young people to seek out the music, and the media, that work for them. UNITOM (which also functions as a bookshop and visual arts space) is popular with young people. This is by no means to demean the value of the internet or to suggest we should try and force it back into some sort of Pandora's box; rather, it is to encourage a relationship with the physical and digital realm that is more harmonious than contrapuntal, to borrow musicological terms. Both can coexist and indeed play to their own strengths, with some print titles including digital playlists, for instance, to form a soundtrack to the reading process. Bell sees a divide between the magazines that 'play it fairly safe and produce something fairly generic, a bit vanilla, but they know they're going to sell' and 'the other end – the indie mag end – where the innovation is, where they push boundaries'. (Bell 2023) These magazines consciously reject much of the theory of magazine publishing, in terms of format and indeed frequency; they can be biannual, quarterly, infrequent or indeed publish at a rate that shows no form or pattern, while others describe themselves as 'bookazines'. But they look good and they sell, Bell commenting: 'What you get as a contrast is true innovation, true passion, true desirable interesting content.' (Bell 2023) And in UNITOM, rather than shelved in the newsagent style that concertinas one on top of another, the magazines are proudly displayed, either vertically on shelves or indeed laid out on tables, as though art. Bell explains: 'We were conscious when we opened that we wanted to display them. [...] The photography is beautiful, the design is beautiful, it becomes a desirable object in its own right.' (Bell 2023) There is even a snug, where Bell encourages visitors to pick the magazines up, to read them, to fall in love with them.

The actuality, then, is not the decline, destruction or demise of the music media but rather the fact that, once you take time to look around, there is actually more music, and more *interesting* music journalism, than ever before, across print, online and broadcast mediums. From the (by turns vicious and hilarious) pen of Mr Agreeable writing for *The Quietus* (the enraged, irradiated persona of celebrated music writer David Stubbs) through to the lyrical and elegantly constructed music writing of Kate Mossman at the *New Statesman* and Jude Rogers (various) to YouTubers such as Needle Drop, the landscape has never been as varied or verdant. Streaming platforms allow instant access to new music in a way that would have been unimaginable even a few years ago. With so much access to this music, we need, more than ever, that critical assistance in cutting through the noise in order to get to what is worth listening to. Ironically perhaps, after all these years and all the industry has been through, such important decisions are best left to human agency, to organic judgement and taste. That notion then brings us circling all the way back around to where we started: the fundamental role of the music critic in creating and curating opinion.

There is a battle, no doubt, and the lines are already drawn between the fronts: between words and numbers, between human agency and digital algorithms, between organic culture and digital data. But music is not merely data, and criticism of that music is not the preserve of machines. It sometimes feels we are already surrendering to the supremacy of the algorithm, as though it provides perfect, unchallengeable logic. Yet even this week, in setting a task for my first year Music Journalism students, I invited them to review John Cage's experimental composition *4'33"'* – 4 minutes and 33 seconds of silence. Ironically, the track is on Spotify. Perhaps more ironically, Spotify's algorithms deduced that after '*4'33"* I 'might also like', for my next listen, the soundtrack to the Netflix film *Glass Onion*. There is, then, a much more positive picture for music journalism than has been suggested by these recent books, and a more positive future picture for the industry. Neither AI nor its algorithms are the perfect pure science they are sometimes perceived to be, and we should not succumb to their corrosive effect; not while our own random tangle of tympanic membrane, neurons and synapses has something to contribute.

References

Bell, Tim. Interviewed at UniTom, 8 February 2023.

Benney, Paul. Interviewed via Microsoft Teams, 20 December 2022.

Crosthwaite, Paul (2014). 'Trauma and Degeneration: Joy Division and Pop Criticism's Imaginative Historicism', in Rachel Carroll and Adam Hansen (eds), *LitPop: Writing and Popular Music*, Farnham: Ashgate.

Gorman, Paul (2022). *Totally Wired: The Rise and Fall of the Music Press*. London: Thames and Hudson.

Hearsum, Paula (2013). 'Music Journalism', in Barry Turner and Richard Orange (eds), *Specialist Journalism*, London: Taylor and Francis.

Hearsum, Paula and Martin James (2020). 'The Rock Press', in Allan Moore and Paul Carr (eds), *The Bloomsbury Handbook of Rock Music Research*, New York and London: Bloomsbury Academic.

Kessler, Ted (2022). *Paper Cuts: How I Destroyed the British Music Press and Other Misadventures*. London: White Rabbit.

Kureshi, Hanif (1995). 'Introduction', in *The Faber Book of Pop*. London: Faber and Faber.

Peirson-Hagger, Ellen (2020). 'The Music Press Isn't Dead', *The New Statesman*, 27 July. https://www.newstatesman.com/culture/2020/07/the-music-press-isnt-dead (accessed 20 February 2023).

Robb, John. Interviewed at the Creative Futures Event, University of Chester, 17 January 2023.

Shuker, Roy (2013). *Understanding Popular Music*, 4th edn. London: Routledge.

Simpson, Dave (2018). 'What Crisis? Why Music Journalism is Actually Healthier than Ever', *The Guardian*, 24 October. https://www.theguardian.com/music/2018/oct/24/the-crisis-in-music-journalism (accessed 31 January 2023).

Snapes, Laura (2020). '"Like a Tap Being Turned Off": Music Magazines Fight for Survival in UK', *The Guardian*, 24 May. https://www.theguardian.com/music/2020/may/24/like-a-tap-being-turned-off-music-magazines-in-uk-fight-for-survival-covid-19 (accessed 7 March 2023).

Springsteen, Bruce (2021). 'Bruce Springsteen Says Rock Critics were "Incredibly Influential" in his Career', interviewed via Zoom, *NJArts*, 9 May 2021. https://www.njarts.net/bruce-springsteen-says-rock-critics-were-incredibly-influential-in-his-career/ (accessed 8 March 2023).

Warner, Simon (2014). 'In Print and On Screen: The Changing Character of Popular Music Journalism', in Andy Bennett and Steve Waksman (eds), *The Sage Handbook of Popular Music*, London: SAGE.

2

Lester Bangs and the great American mythos

Maud Berthomier

Introduction: A sense of belonging

In a music review, one might expect to find musicological discourse that would require specific skills both of the writer and the reader. In the early American rock press, however, Lester Bangs chose not to explore the subject of music per se, preferring instead to foreground a non-musical language. His idiosyncratic and at times outlandish comparisons and metaphors beg a serious question: Does Bangs obscure, perhaps even eschew, a descriptive approach to music in order to promote only his *style* of writing and the musicality of *his* words?

Lester Bangs does not seek to describe music. His approach in his record reviews is neither musicological nor historical. By detailed semantic analysis of the content of his texts, what we discover is the systematic use of the greatest narratives of American literature, which – although they are extra-musical – give American music its full meaning. This idea is crucial. All Americans are familiar with the American Dream, the quest for wilderness and innocence: they are collective and national myths. Inspired by America's popular history, they don't require any technical discourse on music or any particular skills. Moreover, through the prism of memory, music written about in this way 'gains meaning' (Grassy 2010: 50), making it accessible and understandable to a mass audience (Rudent 1993: 244), as other academic studies have also shown in their works on the links between the press and music. The issue at stake is simply to make music significant.

This chapter will therefore explore how Bangs understands music not as music per se, but in relation to 'non-musical themes' (Rudent 1993: 244). Music for Bangs reflects the world. Music is that window through which we see. Music, in short, is always more than music – American music, at least. The latter enables us to maintain a sense of belonging in a typically American quest. This is why music in his articles is rarely discussed in its own right. Music is only a pretext: a pretext for literary writing and a pretext for writing about other subjects (Berthomier 2019, 2020b), such as American myths. 'Nothing was more relevant than the apparently irrelevant' (Bangs 2003: 22), writes Lester Bangs ironically and wittily in one of his articles, since writing about music according to him should remain an open field, full of promises.

The quest for innocence versus youth culture

The most often repeated and easily identifiable American myth in Bangs's texts is the quest for innocence. This myth transposed to rock refers to adolescence and its purity. It is an age that Bangs has lost and that he tries to relive eternally in his texts. Its occurrences are therefore nostalgic but also joyful and delightful:

> Rock is mainly about beginnings, about youth and uncertainty and growing through and out of them. And asserting yourself way before you know what the fuck you're doing. [...] Rock is basically an adolescent music, reflecting the rhythms, concerns and aspirations of a very specialized age group. It can't grow up. (Bangs 1987: 45)

If Bangs talks about teenage rock, it is because he spent his adolescence from 1964 to 1968 listening to music. By reviving this period in his texts, he also tells readers the story of his youth: his own story, in fact. Still, time has passed: when he starts writing in 1969, he is in his twenties. He is already well past the age of puberty and, on paper at least, has attained the age of reason. Similarly, the 'Youth Culture' (Bangs 2003: 44) of his adolescence has aged: it has become adult culture. To combat this double ageing (of himself and of youth culture that used to be his), he proceeds to perform a reversal. He decides to stay the teenager he was in the mid-1960s through his *persona* in his texts. Embodying this return to origins (this age of spirit and not of flesh), he not only creates a gap with the present time of his writing, but he also makes room in his non-musical analyses for a human and most amusing personification: the retarded adolescent.

It is important to understand that for Bangs, music expresses a way of life, more precisely 'a sort of metaphor for [a] life-style' (Bangs 1987: 51). This state of mind is juvenile (like the bands whose oldest musicians are only nineteen) and this is what he wants to focus on: 'I [am] more interested in talking attitudes than music' (Bangs 1987: 180). More precisely, if this 'spirit of some kid' (Bangs 1987: 18) means searching for lost innocence, it is because it follows a necessarily contradictory movement. It implies metaphorically both a retreat to a point of origin and a progression towards a future. Returning to a state of mind younger than youth culture (which has been ageing since the end of the 1960s) is simply regressing in order to evolve better. The name Lester Bangs gives – not without a certain sense of humour – to this behaviour is 'that nth devolution' (Bangs 1987: 85). He himself embodies it in his persona in his texts. Because rock 'can't grow up' (Bangs 1987: 45), the rock fan that he is shouldn't either.

Bangs develops this notion of 'infantilism' (Bangs 1987: 182) further in his texts, an idea he elsewhere describes as 'unschooled ignorance' (Bangs 1987: 45). For him, it is a means to oppose in his texts two major ideas in rock history: youth culture and teen culture. That said, the meanings he gives to these two labels are new. First of all, Bangs links youth culture with the vocabulary of loss. 'Count-out culture' (Bangs 1987: 115), he dubs it, thinking specifically of the hippies, playing on and debunking the revolutionary pretensions behind the term 'counter-culture'. The hippies are out of date, Bangs believes, tracing the roots of their demise as far back as 1966 with the release of the Beatles' album *Revolver*. For him, the Beatles' following albums, *Sgt. Pepper's* in 1967 and *The Beatles* in 1968, only sadly confirmed this trend. Having become competent and intelligent, they had lost their ingenuity, the very virtue that made them great. Above all, what Lester Bangs reproaches the Beatles for is their self-importance, their vanity. That they turned their backs on what he calls 'a good-humored sense of style' (Bangs 2003: 45) is an unforgivable act in his eyes. Youth culture voices this loss of innocence.

On the other hand, teen culture would enable a return to the original spirit of youth – a rebirth of the innocence lost since the last days of the Beatles. The remedy is simple: it consists in adopting a 'bozo' lifestyle (Bangs 1987: 99). According to Collins dictionary, a bozo is a 'funny guy', and for Bangs, more precisely, he is an extravagant, eccentric, clumsy, silly and immature character. He is a retarded teenager, the one we referred to earlier in this chapter. Although his attitude evokes the theme of stupidity, the lexical field that Bangs attaches to this character is always laudatory. To summarize, the bozo (by his deviant behaviour) captures some of the original naivety of the Beatles. Bangs sees no other solution to fight the virus of the 'post-hippie' society (Bangs 1987: 38) – that end-of-decade disease that youth culture spread – than to treat evil with evil. As a simple curative treatment and to recover some of the lost energy and innocence, he advocates a greater pathology: the bozo is not only a moron, a cretin, he is also triumphantly 'pathophile' (Bangs 1987: 146), with Lou Reed, in Bangs's point of view, offering a fine exemplar.

What strikes Bangs and even enthuses him (because it becomes a driving force for his writing) is the ageing of youth culture. The bozo typifies the emptiness of existence since the fall of the Beatles. He *is* adolescent boredom, suburban depression. In Bangs's texts, it's recurrent: we often see a young teenager listening to rock music, languishing in a building on the outskirts of the city, a handful of painkillers in his hand, about to swallow them. The bozo is a fan who isolates himself from the rest of the world. Instead of joining others in community gatherings (as in the former spirit of youth culture), he withdraws from society, curls up in a shell, a world he constructs for himself outside the world in autarchy. Alone, cloistered in his room, he listens to records and no longer goes out into the streets to make friends. Lucid about his condition, he knows that the concept of 'group' is no longer relevant and unifying. The metaphors Bangs uses are unequivocal. 'Joining together with the band merely [means] massing solitudes' (Bangs 2003: 135). He also speaks of fans as 'sequestered suburbanites' (Bangs 1987: 143), confined in suburbs like prisons, fans as 'people by the air conditioners' (Bangs 2003: 79).

To convince his readers, Bangs presents another argument. For him, the loss of adolescent innocence is also due to the end of the notion of 'group' both on the part of the musicians – 'a homogenous group' (Bangs 2003: 44) – and on the part of the public – 'Our Generation' (Bangs 1987: 65). Indeed, we understand from his texts that when the Beatles broke up in 1970, the solo artist (as the new entity) suddenly replaced the band: each Beatle started a solo career and at the same time, within the public, nothing remained of the spirit of union. The hippie community became fragmented into thousands of pieces. The picture looked sad, but in Bangs's eyes it was not. In Detroit, for example, 'where the kids take a lot of downs and dig down bands' (Bangs 1987: 69), the bozo remedy works very well, he says. 'If you happened to be a sixteen or seventeen-year-old male sagging in the rubberband scrotum of suburban America it braced you' (Bangs 1987: 58).

In short, because music opens up the boundaries of existence and briefly suspends (or even erases) the psychic collapse of kids, it carries a positive message. It saves souls. Moreover, Bangs does not hesitate to use the vocabulary of dreams, myths and light in their full religious sense, not hiding the link he wants to make between the role played by music and the idea of providence and salvation. He openly damns the consumerist version of America, the 'bogusly suburban [myth]', and alludes mystically to its musical antidote: 'a glow that touches' (Bangs 2003: 83). However, as Bangs admits, such musical salvation is rare, with the exception of Iggy Pop whom he introduces in these terms:

> Iggy: a pre-eminently American kid, singing songs about growing up in America, about being hung up lotsa the time (as who hasn't been?), about confusion and doubt and uncertainty, about inertia and boredom and suburban pubescent darkness. (Bangs 1987: 33)

In these lines, isn't Bangs attributing to music what isn't musical? This portrait of Iggy Pop is symptomatic of Bangs's non-musical analyses. For what we read instead is a metaphysical and literary description of a nation, America, where growing up has become synonymous with alienation, derealization, a social withdrawal specific to an age group. Indeed, America in the late 1960s for Lester Bangs is mainly teenagers, who are overwhelmed by melancholy, overwhelmed by 'the worst personal, interpersonal and national confusion we've seen' (Bangs 1987: 33).

Thus, even though the notion of 'band' disappeared historically (which is true for the Beatles), Lester Bangs's portrait of the bozo remains literary and non-musical. It connects to the theme of problematic selfhood which traditionally runs through American literature: in other words a narrative in which the main character obscures his past and instead cultivates a fantasy about origins, as seen in Stephen Wright's *Going Native* or Fitzgerald's *The Great Gatsby*. This narrative expresses above all an amalgam between American history and rock history. The bozo, as a rock music fan, takes refuge within himself, embarking on a romantic journey. His path drifts towards a fictionalization of rock history.

A return to the wilderness and the 'punk cry'

If we continue to read the story of the bozo as told through Bangs's texts, what happens next to this unconditional rock fan – that is, Bangs himself as embodied through the persona in his texts – is that he becomes a cliché. The bozo ends up being nothing more than a simplistic and narrow-minded teenager, turned towards an absolute quest for innocence. However, Bangs makes him drift towards another self too. This second metamorphosis, just as caricatured as the first, consists in a 'return to the wilderness'. In order to maintain a sense of belonging and origins, Bangs develops the metaphor on a larger scale: rock music no longer merely reflects adolescence; it also reflects the 'stone age'. The reader needs to understand that Bangs rewrites the history of music on the scale of the human species.

How is this possible? From the retarded teenager, Bangs simply makes his persona evolve towards the 'savage', namely a 'troglodyte', a 'caveman', and this new figure invades his writing. The music he is interested in and which he talks about becomes 'prehistoric': musicians (in addition to taking on the role of the suburban teenager) wear a warrior's outfit: 'loincloths and bones in their noses' (Bangs 1987: 84). Lester Bangs makes full use of humour and metaphors here. He imagines, for example, the English 1960s rock band the Troggs 'skulking through the gutter' (Bangs 2003: 197), or 'squatting around the cannibal fire' (Bangs 2003: 85), in the form of a 'dog man' (Bangs 2003: 85) or even 'in the form of a naked mangy teenager [. . .] covered head to toe in grime and filth and shit' (Bangs 2003: 53–4). Here is a full extract:

> What did happen was that the kave kats became the namesake for the Troggs, who undoubtedly played in some fairly grottolikle or grottotious clubs in their coming-up days. [. . .] They did have extremely analogous elements in their music that gave listening to it all the appeal of riding a Jo mad bull elephant. (Bangs 2003: 55)

In other words, teenage rock is turning into 'a primitive rock 'n' roll' (Bangs 2003: 51), and Iggy Pop (according to Bangs) is still the archetype. His cry is 'animal, warlike'. Distorted and piercing, it oscillates between croaking, bleating, yelping and squealing. It is self-fulfilling: 'Iggyish' (Bangs 2003: 57). This neologism refers to the logic that Bangs followed in his texts from the very beginning to describe music. For him, bands like the Troggs, the Fugs and the Godz do not sing but 'groan and gurgle' (Bangs 2003: 88). Their music is not music but 'noise' (Bangs 2003: 43), 'goony fuzztone clatter' (Bangs 2003: 8), 'unmistakable stunning blare' (Bangs 2003: 43). Iggy Pop would thus be their descendant in a long 'punk' tradition.

Bangs's onomastic analysis is not without its blind spots, however. True, the Stooges and the Troggs share a kindred, primitive-sounding name. But 'Love is All Around' and 'Dirt' are worlds apart, lyrically and acoustically. Yet Bangs doesn't hesitate to associate the two groups, and doesn't let the occasional contradiction get in the way of the big idea: that the Troggs, like the Stooges and the Fugs and the Godz, starting from their very names, have come to stand for an 'original' noise: 'the very first grungy chords' (Bangs 1987: 55), 'the antique moan' (Bangs 1987: 61), 'the primordial rock and roll drive' (Bangs 1987: 41). For him their music embodies the ancestral, quintessential noise of rock, what he calls a 'punk' noise.

It should be noted here how Lester Bangs develops an idea which is central in rock history: the opposition between 'Art-Rock' (Bangs 1987: 42) and 'Primitive Rock' (Bangs 1987: 51). Like the opposition between youth culture and teen culture considered above, the art/primitive cleaving is perfectly antonymic. Art-Rock, on the one hand, is based on the isotope of delicacy. It is synonymous with intelligence, subtlety and preciousness, but Bangs finds these qualities suspect. In strict contrast, in Bangs's eyes, Primitive Rock refers to the isotope of barbarity, coarseness and heaviness but also to simplicity and instinct. This cartography, as in the case of youth culture versus teen culture, is therefore a change of tastes where what is bad is good, and what is good is bad. It is necessary, writes Lester Bangs, that 'everybody realize that all this "art" [. . .] is just a joke and a mistake' (Bangs 1987: 74). We must also realize – Bangs definitely liked contradictions – that 'grossness [is] the truest criterion for rock 'n' roll, the cruder the clang and grind the more fun' (Bangs 1987: 10).

These two quotations underline an opposition between good taste and bad. In Bangs's terminology, if good taste is bad, it is because it is not authentic in his eyes. Conversely, if clumsiness and bad taste are more authentic, it is because they are sincere. There are many passages in his texts that confirm this opposition. He describes 'raw' rock – 'utter lack of imagination' (Bangs 2003: 38) – as honest and direct music: it is 'no-jive' (Bangs 1987: 55) but 'a happy highho' (Bangs 2003: 37). It is even a 'joyful churning'. Its lack of sophistication, 'ineptitude of any kind in music' (Bangs 1987: 18), its musical 'illiteracy' (Bangs 1987: 89) are sure signs of quality and greatness from his point of view. This way, music can always please him as long as it fulfils this contract of a return to the wilderness. Bangs even alleges that 'there is a certain quality in the approach of a musician not totally familiar with his instrument' (Bangs 1987: 88). He went so far as to imply that the more 'crass and artless and young' musicians are, the better their music will be (Bangs 1987: 68).

Obviously, with Bangs this triumph of bad taste over the usual standards of good taste is subversive. It is a positive regression: like in the quest for innocence, it is an 'nth devolution' (Bangs 1987: 85). Once again, Bangs is reluctant to use music to support his judgements. What he believes in instead is the style of life that gives music all its value. 'The real artifact, of course, is not the record. It's the mood' (Bangs 2003: 45). In other words, rock music must offer an ethos. It is a mode of behaviour and brings with it a vision of the world.

The American Dream and the 'dissipation of rock'

Curing evil with evil, producing deviant music that can be judged as good. As we have just seen, there are plenty of remedies to fight the virus of post-hippie society according to Bangs, and the Stooges are always there to demonstrate it. Moreover, Bangs adds that we must identify the evil more rigorously, that is to say, identify its origin, to understand its mechanisms, the better to counter it. Rock must be adolescent and primitive, he explains, but what is its target precisely? To answer that question, Lester Bangs introduces a third myth: 'the new Age of Implosion' (Bangs 2003: 222). It is based on another well-known fact in rock history: the precise moment in the late 1960s when rock music became fragmented into a multitude of standardized musical variations.

This idea of the loss of cohesiveness in rock has a historical context. This myth consists of thinking that the sudden irruption of a multitude of genres within rock somehow signalled the end of an age. For Lester Bangs, citing Jethro Tull's LP *Aqualung*, rock had become 'heterogeneous': 'rock, Rock, a bit of rock and roll, a lot of mostly borrowed jazz, and folk strains both British and American, as well as the odd "classical gambit"' (Bangs 1987: 128). More importantly, these heterogeneous influences have made rock 'arty', that is 'more melodic and complex stuff' (Bangs 1987: 128). Plus, this narrative of an 'Age of Implosion' is also metaphorical, as always with Bangs. Its function is to enlarge the mythological space. Indeed, it is no longer just a question of teenagers, nor the human species, but cosmology.

This is when the reading of Bangs's texts becomes particularly vertiginous and jubilant, since a billion years becomes the unit of reference for measuring the age of the rock universe and the gap that separates it from its origin. In fact, in this space of infinite dimensions, a new scenario is written by Bangs: that of an inverted Big Bang, in other words, the apocalyptic implosion of a music world shattered into an infinite number of pieces: pieces that pile up in a detonating mixture. This image of an implosion in rock is operative because it relies on one of America's oldest myths: the American Dream. The fall of the American Dream can be read metaphorically as the source of an infinite fragmentation:

a fragmentation of society, of time, of space, of the self, of music, of wealth, of mentalities, of human faculties. It is this American myth that Lester Bangs refers to when he uses the term 'fragmentation' in his texts (Bangs 2003: 134).

To underpin this third and final major idea, Lester Bangs invents two new major themes: the 'Party' and the 'Tradition' (Bangs 1987: 72). What connects them is a cyclical, back-and-forth movement. For a time synonymous with Party, rock always becomes Tradition in the course of its history: 'Rock 'n' roll is only a moment' (Bangs 2003: 157). In other words, it is only a temporary, joyful and recreational awakening of consciousness that is eternally interrupted, segmented in repetitive cycles by interminable phases of waiting and silence: Lester Bangs speaks of episodes of 'rock drought[s]' (Bangs 1987: 114) and 'musical recessions' (Bangs 1987: 5). The isotopes of scarcity for the Tradition and of explosion for the Party are explicit. What they indicate is a return, at more or less regular intervals, of two types of rock: music without initiative, without invention, which is standardized, impeccably made and boring (that of Tradition); and music that is crude, unrefined, but original and invigorating (that of the Party).

We find again the oppositions previously mentioned between youth culture and teen culture, later between Art-Rock and Primitive Rock. Tradition in short designates the episodes of good taste that Bangs hates: 'the Right Way' (Bangs 1987: 72), followed by the 'nice and careful and positive-thinking' (Bangs 1987: 66), the 'technically impeccable' (Bangs 1987: 180) in music. Conversely, the Party designates the periods of bad taste that Lester Bangs is particularly fond of, a 'gutter pure' (Bangs 2003: 50) version of rock to be found, for example, in the Count Five track 'The Hermit's Prayer', 'a prototype slab of gully-bottom rock 'n' roll' (Bangs 1987: 17); or, in Iggy Pop's 'I Wanna Be Your Dog', taken from the Stooges' first album released in 1969.

Conclusion: A pact with the reader

It is clear that Bangs is obsessed with one era: the middle and second half of the 1960s. More than just a setting, it is in his texts a stage for experimentation, the theatre of his life, where he can explore new selves as he pleases: a 'retarded' self, a 'wild' self and a 'fragmented' self, in the footsteps of rock. His persona takes refuge in rock to the point of seeking tangible proof of his own existence.

What is striking also in reading his texts is the extent to which his rather non-musical analyses construct a Manichean vision of the world. Lester Bangs's

Lester Bangs and the great American mythos 33

writings are very normative and offer a resolutely binary vision of rock: in short, for him, a fan is either openly 'for' or 'against' rock; a supporter of 'teen culture' or 'youth culture'; an adept of 'primitive rock' or 'art rock'; a great defender of the 'Party' (and its associations with politics and radicalism) or the 'Tradition'. No intermediate position is possible, because Lester Bangs leaves no room for a nuanced discourse on music (which would be more characteristic of a rock critic today, no doubt).

This leaves us with a question: If it is difficult to agree with Bangs's peremptory assertions, how did he manage to convince his readers? What reading pact did he construct in his texts to make his ideas (the 'Party', 'primitive rock', 'teenage culture') heard and understood? How did he even succeed in faithfully reflecting the concepts that would be defended after him in popular music studies?

To define music, Lester Bangs used a system of values inspired by American myths and fictionalizations through his own persona and other major rock musicians and singers such as Iggy Pop and Lou Reed. For him, rock is 'theme music' (Bangs 1987: 31) and is experienced directly: 'this is a kind of party you LIVE' (Bangs 1987: 73). There are countless examples in his texts. From 'bozo' behaviour to 'wild' behaviour, through his literary persona and rock idols, Lester Bangs relives the big moments of rock history as an actor would. He not only documents but also *stages* rock and internalizes its values. In short, once again, for him rock is an ethos.

Why, then, does he always implicitly refer to the American mythos? It is because when they are made entertaining by a writer like Bangs, American myths, both literary and national, make it easier for the reader to adhere to the ideas expressed in his texts. In the end, their use has a communicative and playful purpose. Their fictionalization imposes a particular reception of the texts, in which the reader temporarily forgets the rational and intelligible readings of history and instead accepts the hypothetical and the conditional, delivered with a sharp sense of humour (Berthomier 2013). Through the use of American myths, fiction accompanies rather than replaces music history in Bangs's texts. Its purpose is to communicate more, by engaging the readers' imagination and intuition. It is this 'Moralism in the very best sense' that fellow rock critic Greil Marcus points to with admiration in Bangs's texts and which Marcus defines as 'the attempt to understand what is important, and to communicate that understanding to others in a form that somehow obligates the reader as much as it entertains' (Bangs 1987: xiii).

References

Bangs, Lester (1987). *Psychotic Reactions and Carburetor Dung*. New York: Knopf.

Bangs, Lester (2003). *Mainlines, Blood Feasts and Bad Taste: A Lester Bangs Reader*. New York: Anchor Books / Random House.

Berthomier, Maud (2013). 'What if Writing About Rock Criticism was Also Writing with "ifs"?', *Transatlantica*. http://transatlantica.revues.org/6329 (accessed 31 May 2023).

Berthomier, Maud (2019). *Encore plus de bruit : L'âge d'or du journalisme rock en Amérique, par ceux qui l'ont inventé*. Auch: Tristram.

Berthomier, Maud (2020a). 'Points de rencontre entre nouveau journalisme et critique rock', in Timothée Picard (ed.), *La critique musicale au XXe siècle*, Rennes: Presses Universitaires de Rennes.

Berthomier, Maud (2020b). 'La genèse de la critique rock américaine : Entre presse et littérature', in Timothée Picard (ed.), *La critique musicale au XXe siècle*, Rennes: Presses Universitaires de Rennes.

Grassy, Elsa (2010). *Le lieu musical: Du texte à l'espace, un itinéraire sémantique. Poétique des catégories géographiques dans les musiques populaires américaines (1920–2007)*. Doctoral thesis. Paris: Université Paris-Sorbonne.

Rudent, Catherine (1993). *Le discours sur la musique dans la presse française: l'exemple des périodiques spécialisés*. Doctoral thesis. Paris: Université de Paris IV.

3

Rock and philosophy

From Adorno to the anti-Adornian generation?

Cristina Parapar

Roger Pouivet has written 'Someone once told me that he couldn't distinguish between the music of Jimi Hendrix and the sound of a broken washing machine' (Pouivet 2010: 85).[1] The French philosopher deconstructs such assertions in order to define rock music philosophically. He took rock seriously from a philosophical perspective. He was preceded and succeeded by other philosophers, such as Max Paddison or Frédéric Bisson. All of them had to face the implicit or explicit legacy of Theodor W. Adorno (1903–1969).

Philosophy has traditionally vilified popular music in general, and the first philosopher to inaugurate this persecution of *leichte Musik* was Adorno. At first, the author of *Minima Moralia* condemned jazz, which he described as a musical commodity and mere entertainment, but soon his animosity towards jazz extended to popular music in general. His earliest writings on popular music date from the 1920s and his later ones from the 1950s, and he did not even take an interest in the numerous musical genres and sub-genres that emerged up to 1969, the year of the philosopher's death. He never reconsidered his ideas about popular music. He never went back on them. This was Adorno's mistake.

The aim of this chapter is precisely to reflect on why rock matters philosophically, at least for some philosophers. First, I will try to explain Adorno's animosity towards popular music. Being a chapter focused on philosophy and rock music, it may seem strange to spend a part of it on the relationship between Adorno and jazz. Nevertheless, this explanatory prelude is necessary in order to understand his legacy in the philosophy of rock. It is because his method of analysis of jazz (immanent critique) set a precedent for the rock philosophers of

---

[1] All quotations from Pouivet and Bisson have been translated by the author.

the future.[2] Second, I will present two philosophical currents of the late twentieth and early twenty-first centuries that share the same objective: to rethink rock from, with and against Adorno. They are the philosophers of rock par excellence. I will examine their approaches and how they confront or embody the Adornian legacy. In conclusion, this chapter seeks to answer the following questions: Is it possible to think philosophically about rock? Is there an aesthetics of rock? Does an anti-Adornian generation of philosophers of rock spontaneously emerge in the realm of aesthetics?

Adorno: Popular music and deception

Adorno died just ten days before the Woodstock festival, so he never heard Jefferson Airplane's *Volunteers* live. Nor did Adorno experience the live performances of the Ramones or Misfits at CBGBs. Nor did he hear *Bohemian Rhapsody* or see Pete Townshend destroy guitars on stage. Nor see Jimi Hendrix set them on fire. Adorno didn't get to hear PJ Harvey evoke passages from the Bible in *Dry* or MIA criticize American immigration policy accompanied by a sampler of the Clash in *Paper Planes*. However, even if he *could* have seen and heard all this, it is likely that he would not have chosen to do so.

The author of *Minima Moralia* was the first to write about popular music philosophically.[3] His 'meditations' do not take the form of scattered, inconsistent and anecdotal writings; rather, he forges a genuine philosophical corpus on popular music. Paradoxically, Adorno missed the great (r)evolution of the forms and genres of mass music, and yet his texts are still relevant today. Why did popular music arouse Adorno's 'interest' and what made him distrust it? Is there an Adornian heritage that has survived to the present day?

In 1938, the philosopher came to New York to participate in the Princeton Radio Research Project at the Institute for Social Research, a study directed

---

[2] The immanent critique was the philosophical method used by Adorno to analyse culture and society. The German philosopher starts from the very phenomena of society (art, thought, etc.) in order to criticize it. He pushes the real to its limits in order to show its fissures. Therefore, with regard to jazz, Adorno studied the musical material or the techniques employed by the composer to demonstrate its non-truth content. In this way, the immanence of immanent critique refers to the analysis of the things themselves. In other words, the immanent critique of popular music is a method of reflection that does not use external elements to demonstrate its commercial, non-musical or entertainment character, but does so from the musical material itself.

[3] Adorno uses popular music, light music (*leichte Musik*) and mass music interchangeably, and in most cases, he refers to jazz. He does not include folk music in the category of popular music.

Rock and Philosophy 37

by Paul Lazarsfeld. A sort of memorandum of this experience has survived. It was reconstructed and published under the title *Current of Music*. Adorno's conception of this light music he listened to on American radio is clearly revealed in this passage:

> Good hits are by no means those which borrow heavily from the higher musical language. [. . .] Any evaluation which would simply measure popular music by standards of the serious style would not only be unrealistic but also aesthetically superficial by applying criteria utterly alien to the ones inherent to the composition itself. (Adorno 2006: 327)

This music is simple entertainment or *divertissement*. According to the philosopher, it is light music (*leichte Musik*). It is not serious music; it is a commodity, a product to entertain the public. Therefore, its sound must be familiar, accessible and easily consumable. It should prevent any kind of innovation and/or evolution in the musical material because 'mass listening habits today gravitate about recognition. [. . .] The basic principle behind it is that one need only repeat something until it is recognized in order to make it accepted' (Adorno 2006: 299).

In addition, Adorno was particularly worried about popular music's social function because 'the commercial character of culture causes the difference between cultural and practical life to disappear' (Adorno 2001: 61). This means that the critical distance between society and art is erased and thus the critical power of music is annihilated. The negative character of music is transformed into a mercantile character. In other words, popular music reproduces the pleasures of the affluent society, forgetting the disasters and fissures of the reality from which it distances itself. For this reason, Adorno states clearly that:

> The thought that after this war life could continue on 'normally', or indeed that culture could be 'reconstructed' – as if the reconstruction of culture alone were not already the negation of such – is idiotic. Millions of Jews have been murdered, and this is supposed to be only the intermission and not the catastrophe itself. What exactly is this culture waiting for anyway? (Adorno 2005: 58)

Popular music is a deception, a substitute for the real, a veil that disguises reality and catastrophe. Popular music is part of the 'administered world'. However, Adorno denounced not only the ideological and commodity character of popular music that he analysed during his American exile, but also the jazz that emerged in the Weimar Republic. This jazz was the target of his criticism in *On the Social Situation of Music* (1932), *Farewell to Jazz* (1933), *Music in the Background* (1934) and *On Jazz* (1936).

As Jonathan Wipplinger explains, in its early days the word 'jazz' was a label for a new dance, not so much a type of music. In the 1920s, the definition of jazz in Germany was fuzzy. It could be said that jazz represented music that was considered modern and with exotic overtones. Therefore, the label 'jazz' was like a marketing brand whose origin and political dimension were not taken into account. In short, jazz was 'the newest fashionable dance' (Wipplinger 2017: 27) that was intermingled with German salon music, that is, the light music generally played by pianists in salons to entertain the nineteenth-century bourgeoisie. Consequently, Adorno considered that jazz is 'the amalgam of the march and salon music [and] is a false amalgam: the amalgam of a destroyed subjectivity and the social power which produces it, eliminates it, and objectifies it through its elimination' (Adorno 2002: 491).

It could be said that this popular music is the 'art' of pseudo: pseudo-democratic, pseudo-individual and pseudo-liberating. In short, the popular music that Adorno is familiar with in the United States and in Germany is musical merchandise destined for consumption. For this reason, this music predisposes the subject to similar reactions. In the philosopher's terms, it is pre-digested music. The bourgeoisie and the proletariat dance and enjoy themselves to the same music. For the upper class, jazz is primitive, original, 'natural'. The bourgeoisie 'take pleasure in their own alienation'. For the proletariat, jazz is urban and therefore modern (Adorno 2002: 474). From this it follows that the function of popular music is somehow (or for a while) to erase class barriers, to standardize thinking and to show a false totalizing reality. *Ergo*, popular music participates in a mechanism of deception.

Adorno never reconsidered his assertions about popular music, not even in the face of the (r)evolution of rock. He closed his eyes and covered his ears. In fact, he only commented superficially and almost anecdotally on popular music from the 1950s onwards on two occasions. First, during an interview with Peter von Haselberg (1965), Adorno criticized the regressive character of the Beatles whose musical pieces, he believed, were the result of the degradation of traditional forms. In 1968, he also succinctly mentioned Joan Baez during another interview for German television. He states that the mere attempt to link political revolt with popular music is a failure, since the very ontology of *leichte Musik* does not allow it to go beyond consumption and entertainment in such a way that it is not possible to attribute such a critical function to it. In short, the very category of protest song is *contradictio in adjecto*. With reference to Baez, he confesses that he finds it unbearable to witness how the horrors of Vietnam are turned into sweet, consumable melodies. What would Adorno say about John Lee Hooker's *I don't want to go to Vietnam*, Jimi Hendrix's *Machine Gun* or King Crimson's *21st Century Schizoid Man*?

Adornian legacy: A contribution to the philosophy of rock

Adorno died in 1969, and since then, his work on music has perished and been revived at the same time. On the one hand, Hullot-Kentor claims that Adorno's philosophy of music reveals 'the most contemporary issues of aesthetics, perception and politics' (Adorno 2006: 15). On the other, he states that 'radio music in its early decades offered itself to such an interpretation in a way that it no longer does, or certainly not too insistently' (Adorno 2006: 18). It is therefore worth asking whether Adorno's philosophy of music responds to the reality of popular music today or whether it has become obsolete. This dilemma unleashes the wrath of many rock philosophers whose activity lies in large part in demonstrating that rock deserves to be taken seriously. Thus, the stigmatization of popular music in the field of philosophy has led them to rethink rock philosophically from, with, against and/or on the basis of Adorno.

Many philosophers have reacted to Adorno's inquisitiveness, but this chapter will simply focus on two currents of the philosophy of rock that have arisen perhaps spontaneously, but which undoubtedly present consistency and coherence. I have observed that from 1990 onwards a series of texts have been published that question the aesthetic and ontological value of rock from, with and against Adorno. On the one hand, Max Paddison promoted an attempt to re-evaluate rock using Adorno's own categories. Instead of completely discarding his observations on popular music, the British philosopher attempts to deconstruct them by returning to Adorno's texts on serious music. He applies the properties of serious music to his philosophical analyses of rock. Paddison inspires later philosophers such as Stefano Marino or Marco Maurizi and Agnès Gayraud, among others. From the Adornian philosophy they rescue the work of Frank Zappa, Radiohead or Pink Floyd. On the other hand, in France, a kind of generation of authors was born who think about rock from an ontological point of view. They gravitate around Adorno's philosophy of music but in order to discredit it. They are Roger Pouivet and Frédéric Bisson and Agnès Gayraud (the latter straddles both currents). From the 2000s onwards, French philosophers have taken the definition of rock succinctly enunciated by Theodore Gracyk in *Rhythm and Noise: An Aesthetics of Rock* (1996), and considered rock as a new ontological reality that overcame the limits imposed by Adorno's theory of popular music. For these authors, a rock song is an '*artefact-enregistrement*' (recording-artefact). In the following discussion, I will look more closely at the difference between the two perspectives mentioned above (the current that starts from Adorno and the current that revolts against Adorno).

As previously suggested, Max Paddison starts from Adorno's immanent critique of music to reflect on the subversive potential of rock. For this purpose, he reflects on why Adorno 'never allowed for the possibility that popular music in certain of its manifestations might be able to change its function' (Paddison 1996: 94). Paddison recovers Adorno's philosophical categories to justify the aesthetic value of what he calls 'radical popular music', that is, 'groups working in the general area of avant-garde rock and jazz in France, Italy, Germany, Holland, Scandinavia, America and Britain' (Paddison 1996: 102). He suggests that there is at least some popular music which meets the criteria of serious music evoked by Adorno and which comes paradoxically from the sphere of the *Kulturindustrie*. He mentions almost exclusively rock music, namely Frank Zappa.

In order to defend this position, he adopts a strategy that is divided into two moments. First, Paddison explains the differences between uncritical music and critical and reflective music in Adornian theory. The former 'encompasses all music which is unable to resist exploitation as commodity' (Paddison 1996: 89). This category includes popular music, as well as notational or 'classical' music that has been perverted by radio broadcasting and the development of the culture industry. Likewise, 'classical' music that continues to employ obsolete techniques and laws that come from outside the musical material also falls into this category. So uncritical music is opposed to critical and reflective music. This category includes serious music because it opposes the reification of art. According to Adorno, popular music could never be part of this category because critical and reflective music 'strives, through negation, to retain a necessary tension between Subject and Object, individual and collectivity' (Paddison 1996: 89). It is critical and reflective music because it reveals fissures, flaws and cracks in the 'false totality'. It does not reproduce the 'administered world'. It does not imitate it. Its meaning is non-meaning, that is it denies the dominant meanings. Adorno evidently never envisaged the possibility of the culture industry promoting 'music through which that which is not yet identical may still be glimpsed' (Paddison 1996: 89). However, Paddison does, and argues that radical popular music is critical and reflective music.

How does Paddison connect popular music with the sphere of serious music? To begin with, he quotes the ninety-eighth aphorism from *Minima Moralia*. From this, he deduces that music 'can exist meaningfully outside the historical dialectic and the dominant system itself – or rather exist within that system but escape being embraced by it' (Paddison 1996: 98). It seems to contradict Adorno, but Adorno himself mentions certain composers who don't reveal the historical dialectic of material and who make serious music compositions, namely Satie, Mahler and Weil. Paradoxically, these composers 'work meaningfully with regressive tonal and formal material – within the sphere of serious music' (Paddison 1996: 100). Their compositions reveal the contradictions of this obsolete material. It is critical and self-reflective music.

Paddison suggests that 'it now merely remains to consider whether the same possibility also exists within the sphere of popular music' (Paddison 1996: 100). According to the philosopher, avant-garde rock of the 1960s is critical reflective music because it can reveal the fissures of the culture industry, that is, it accepts its fate as commodity and at the same time opposes it. It is radical popular music. This rock shows contradictions and neutralizes the effects of the culture industry. Thus, he inserts rock into Adorno's philosophy of music by drawing on the writings on serious music. It is a way of revisiting Adorno's philosophy, but without denying it. In conclusion, Frank Zappa's Mothers of Invention music from the 1960s has a critical and self-reflexive attitude because it reveals the contradictions of *Kulturindustrie* from or inside the culture industry.

Later, a group of rock philosophers emerged in France. They reacted against the Adornian theory of popular music, basing their work on the 'ontology of rock'. They were in turn inspired by Theodore Gracyk, the first philosophically to suggest a discourse on the aesthetics of rock as such. The American author states that rock is 'popular music of the second half of the twenty century which is essentially dependent on recording technology for its inception and dissemination' (Gracyk 1996: 13). Gracyk notes recording technology is the raison d'être of rock. In short, recording becomes the condition of possibility for rock, and it is this outline of the ontology of rock that will inspire future French rock philosophers, as I explain below.

The question now is twofold: how does Gracyk weave his ontological argumentation of rock, and what is his relationship with Adorno? The author of *Rhythm and Noise: An Aesthetics of Rock* goes back to 1954. According to Gracyk, the aesthetics of rock was born with Elvis at Sun studios (Memphis) in 1954 because for the first time he 'employs recording as its primary medium'

(Gracyk 1996: 13). Rock and roll became rock. This means that Sam Phillips, Elvis's producer, used the studio as an instrument to give corporeality to Elvis's voice. He uses the studio to make Elvis be Elvis. So the work in the studio technologically sculpts the rock sound, and the rock sound acquires the ultimate independence from rock and roll. This corporeality, this presence and this unique sound is the raison d'être of Elvis's rock music. It is not his voice or his guitar, but how they sound. In Gracyk's terms, these recordings at Sun studios 'epitomized rock and roll as a performance style, but they also embodied a new sound as an essential quality of musical work' (Gracyk 1996: 15). *Ergo*, the vocals, the dizzying rhythms and the reminiscence of the blues style of Elvis's music were inseparable from the techniques employed in the studio.

Elvis's music is rock because of the processes, decisions and techniques employed in the studio. This constitutes 'how it sounds (e.g., the echo, the "presence"). [. . .] These qualities are expressive elements and relevant features of the musical work' (Gracyk 1996: 16). It follows that neither performance nor a particular instrumentation defines rock, but that rock is essentially dependent on technology and recording for its inception. Gracyk also refers to the Beatles', the Rolling Stones' and Bob Dylan's albums released in 1965 as authentic rock-works because 'as composers, they composed with sound, not in notation' (Gracyk 1996: 12). They demonstrate that recordings are the 'primary texts' (Gracyk 1996: 21). In other words, rock can only be accessed through the album, not through scores or performances. The rock album is an indiscernible whole. It is the musical work.

Gracyk also states that 'offering recordings as primary texts, rock emphasizes multileveled collaboration and negates the same conventions' (Gracyk 1996: 173). The American philosopher assumes that the emergence of rock denies the conventions of popular music, but to which conventions does he refer? This brings us to the second question: What is the link between Gracyk's aesthetics of rock and Adorno's philosophy of music? In contrast to Adorno's stigmatization of popular music, the recordings and multileveled collaboration of rock reveal the plurality, progress and complexity of its musical material. This means that rock can assert itself against the ubiquity of commercialism and resist the conventions about the unchanging and mercantile character of popular music established by Adornian criticism. Moreover, Gracyk suggests that the Adornian legacy in the philosophy of music is binarism. In other words, he blames Adorno for the theoretical division or polarization between popular music and serious music, artistry and commercial entertainment, affirmation and negation of the administered world and so on. This radical binarism ended up taking away the aesthetic value of popular music.

In the 2000s, Roger Pouivet, Frédéric Bisson and Agnès Gayraud followed and took over from Gracyk's ontology of rock. They published *Philosophie du rock* (2010), *La pensée rock* (2016) and *Dialectic of Pop* (2019), respectively (the latter is not limited to the study of rock, as I will explain below). These authors were inspired by Gracyk's definition of rock, pushing it forward to its limits. They start from the idea that rock's identity is ontological and construct an ontology of rock as such. What does this mean? What is the relationship between this current and Adorno's philosophy of music?

The precursor of ontology of rock in France is Pouivet. He declares that he does not want to define rock from a sociological, musicological, historical or political point of view, because the core that unites all rock groups and sub-genres of rock is philosophy, specifically ontology. For this reason, Pouivet recalls that rock was born in the heart of the mass cultural industry in the 1950s, and these conditions make it an ontological novelty. Thus, 'rock is the creation of musical works as recordings within the framework of the mass arts' (Pouivet 2010: 11). Recording is *conditio sine qua non* of the rock-work. In Pouivet's terms, the rock-work is a fabrication of a recording. *Ergo*, the recording and/or technological character of rock is not simply a means to large-scale dissemination (a fundamental characteristic of rock); it is the end in itself.

In contrast to Gracyk, Pouivet does not refer to rock music as songs. He uses the term 'recording-artefact' (*artefact-enregistrement*), and he also suggests that these songs are rock-works (*oeuvres-rock*) within the *Kulturindustrie*. Correspondingly, Pouivet's philosophy of rock can be considered as a critical reaction to Adornian thought for several reasons. First, he elevates the rock song to the status of a work of art (*oeuvre-rock*/rock-work). One could even say that he also elevates the status of the rock-work to the category of serious music. The rock-work is not conceived on a rigid musical scheme where the parts of the piece are contingent, like ornaments. According to Pouivet, the rock-work is produced as an organic whole, as part of a closed process of musical mixing that means that the rock-work is constituted by parts (*les instances*). These layers of sound and the whole are perfectly related thanks to the recording process. In short, each part is indispensable to form the musical work, so that if a sound layer is suppressed, the *oeuvre-rock* is annihilated. Doesn't this definition remind us of the Adornian ideal of serious music?

Interestingly (and paradoxically), Pouivet shares Adorno's view of the psychological function of popular music. In fact, Pouivet states that 'rock-works do not have an important cognitive role' (Pouivet 2010: 241) and asserts that their artistic value is inferior to Bach's *St Matthew Passion* (unfortunately he does not justify such an assertion). It seems that finally the French philosopher also attributes to the rock-work properties such as *divertissement* and consolation, as Adorno claimed in *Funktion* in the short essay 'Dissonanzen'. This leads him to consider that rock has an instrumental function, that is the provision of a kind of psychological comfort that he calls 'control of our everyday emotions' (*le maîtrise au quotidien de nos emotions*) (Pouivet 2010: 241).

To sum up, although Pouivet disavows classical ontology and only refers (superficially) to Adorno on two occasions, it is striking that he partially agrees with him about the function of mass music. From his references to the German philosopher, a certain sense of distrust of Adorno and continental philosophy emerges. In fact, Pouivet considers that traditional aesthetics fails fully to reflect on rock as an ontological novelty, and yet he returns (consciously or not) to the immanent Adornian critique in order to reveal the psychological function of rock.

Based on Gracyk and Pouivet's ideas, Bisson also insists that recording has transformed the ontological status of rock music, but he mainly studies the affects produced by rock-works as recorded works. In other words, the rock effects of the recording itself elicit certain emotions, and the affects produced by these effects are the ultimate reality of rock. Thus, Bisson approaches rock from the affects resulting from the effects inherent in the phonographic nature of rock. To appreciate the subtlety of Bisson's rock philosophy and his differences with Pouivet, I will take a musical example that the author himself gives in *La pensée rock*. He explains that *Heroin*, by Velvet Underground, expresses drug addiction through the effects of/in the phonographic musical material itself. To this end, the American band compulsively repeats the chords of D major and G major, increasing the *tempo* without varying the harmonic modulation and indulging in *accelerando*. The listener captures this effect, this concrete reality of rock, and it arouses certain emotions (compulsion, addiction). Hence, 'musical affects are beings, they are ultimate ontological components, the atoms of music' (Bisson 2016: 60). In essence, phonography does not express itself. It is the effects of recording and its particular qualities that produce the affects, that is, the ultimate reality of the rock artefact.

Bisson's ontology of rock differs slightly from Pouivet's, also in metaphysical terms. In fact, Bisson accuses Pouivet of relying on 'the substantialist nature of

Aristotelian realism' (Bisson 2016: 45) in order to define the rock-work (*oeuvre-rock*). To put it simply, Bisson wants to go beyond the object (*oeuvre-rock*) to delve into the process that gives rise to that object (the process of recording/the technology moment). He leaves the apparent substance of rock music in order to justify that the *oeuvre-rock* is and exists as the result of a process of constitution (effects) that has shaped it. He properly analyses the formation of these effects and their affects and insists that 'processes are not merely realities alongside other substantial realities, but the ultimate reality of which substances are made' (Bisson 2016: 48). This is Bisson's processual, non-substantialist and pragmatist ontology, which, like Pouivet, moves away from classical aesthetics to analyse the new ontological reality of rock.

The importance of this process of constituting rock music contributes to Bisson's thinking not only in/from philosophical concepts, but also musically. What does this mean more concretely? According to the philosopher, 'the richest appreciation of a musical work does not require categorical knowledge' (Bisson 2016: 55). Rock music does not require an absolute understanding and respect for the composer's intention because the effects of the rock-work may arouse affections or appreciations different from those intentions. Therefore, Bisson praises 'inadequate listening' (*écoute inadequate*) and error. This does not mean that he denies the value of proper listening, but that inadequate listening and error have a source of creation in the rock experience. It would seem that in this 'error' the listener also becomes a creator. This is profoundly anti-Adornian because Adorno insisted on the passive attitude of the popular music listener. Finally, he also reacts against Adorno because he appreciates the idea of repetition in popular music. As is well known, repetition, familiarity and standardization are ideas castigated in Adorno's theory of popular music. Bisson not only values the power of rock repetition, he even differentiates between 'mechanical repetition' and 'complex repetition' (*répétition mécanique et répétition complexe*). Consequently, this repetition becomes a source of creation and discovery of the phonographic work as well.

In summary, Bisson appreciates the functional character of rock, repetition, error and inadequacy in the appreciation of the rock artefact. However, it is not surprising to read these reflections gravitating towards (and opposing) Adorno's philosophy since Bisson explicitly alludes to *The Form of the Phonograph Record* (1934). His comments on that text are numerous, but his essential criticism of Adorno boils down to his stubbornness in judging popular music from the perspective of classical aesthetics. It prevents him from discovering the aesthetic potentialities and new ontological properties of the phonographic work of art. The author of *Minima Moralia* bases his thinking on the idea that the form of the phonographic record leads to the reification of music, both popular and serious, and to this end, Bisson argues, 'he relies on strong concepts (*concepts qui sont de plomb*): the culture industry, "regressive or atomized listening", standardisation, etc.' (Bisson 2016: 83).

Agnès Gayraud also reacts to this Adornian conceptual cage. In 2018, she published *Dialectic of Pop* and established herself as a *rara avis* among what I define as the French philosophers of the rock generation. Like Gracyk, Pouivet and Bisson, Gayraud also understands that rock is a new musical reality whose material is determined by the recorded-form and this requires thinking of it differently. However, she suggests that phonographic raison d'être is not unique to rock, but to a musical totality. This musical totality is called 'popular recorded music' (*les musiques populaires enregistrées*) or '*la pop*'. Gayraud defines this notion as 'the globalised phenomenon that fuses black American influences, remnants of European folk music, African drums, and Indian sitars, all captured by the technological means – electrification, amplification, studio production – of recorded music' (Gayraud 2019: 19). Of course, '*la pop*' includes rock, but also rap, R&B, heavy metal, and so on.

Although Gayraud does not speak exclusively of rock, it seems pertinent briefly to mention her philosophical work because she directly challenges and criticizes Adorno's aesthetic categories by using many examples of popular music, including rock music. This explains why Gayraud values the technical reproducibility of '*la pop*' and its contradictions, but also its ambivalence and the imbalance of the pop form that generates new styles and authentic works of art. In addition, she connects pop with notions of critical theory such as negativity, historicity and progress. These terms articulate her discourse on pop in order to revalue it. For example, she explains that pop is constituted negatively, an Adornian philosophical method. This means that the form of pop has 'a broken form, dislocated by these tensions that inscribe it into a very particular historicity' (Gayraud 2019: 122). In short, pop is constituted from what it is not. Pop music has to be thought of dialectically with 'anti-pop'. The French philosopher also observes that the musical material of pop music progresses and also ages. Here is another reference to Adorno, namely to his theory of the historical dialectic of the musical material. Finally, she asserts that there is no standardization or *Zeitlose Mode* (timeless mode/style) that responds to the pop form, as Adorno says. In conclusion, Gayraud affirms the expression of singularity and subjectivities that pop expresses and reclaims a kind of *Zeitgeist* of '*la pop*'. This is the definitive proof of the Adornian mark on her work.

Hence, Gayraud thinks with, against and from Adorno as she reformulates the limits of rock philosophy, namely the work of Pouivet and Bisson. She carries out the philosophical task by confronting and relying on Adorno from the beginning to the end of *Dialectique de la pop*. This is why, at the beginning of his book, Gayraud defines Adorno as 'a most curious hater' (Gayraud 2019: 19), and she describes the philosopher as an 'intransigent modernist, apostle of a hermetic musical avant-garde regarded as the exclusive model of authenticity' (Gayraud 2019: 19). Nevertheless, this brutal critique contrasts with the last pages of her work when she finally appeals to Adorno's *Introduction to the Sociology of Music* in order to endorse the uniqueness of '*la pop*'. It seems that it is difficult to escape Adorno's influence.

Conclusion: An anti-Adornian generation?

Gayraud's insightful philosophy invites us to conclude this chapter with a question that may not be answered: Are these generations of rock philosophers a reaction, a replica or a continuation of Adorno's work? Do these authors form one (or maybe two) currents of Adornian, anti-Adornian or post-Adornian rock philosophers? Only one thing is clear, and that is that Adorno's philosophical legacy is more alive than it seems. In Bisson's own terms, the rock philosopher can only rethink Adorno's philosophy of music 'by opposing it with other concepts, another finer or lighter division, another enhancement of truths' (Bisson 2016: 83). And this is exactly what Paddison, Gracyk, Pouivet, Bisson and Gayraud have done. They opposed the cage of Adornian concepts with a more critical spirit, with more enlightenment (*Aufklärung*). Since it seems difficult to escape completely from Adorno's musical aesthetics, these rock philosophers respond to the philosopher of enlightenment with more enlightenment. Hence, Adorno's legacy in the philosophy of rock is simply enlightenment, more enlightenment.

It could be said that both Adorno's brutal critique of popular music and his reflections on serious music have proved to be an invaluable contribution to the philosophy of popular music and particularly to the philosophy of rock. The author of *Minima Moralia* has provided the necessary tools and aesthetic categories to define the concept of rock and to take it seriously. At the same time, he has forced later philosophers to be demanding about the music played on the radio (and now also on streaming platforms). Admittedly, the 'Adornian aesthetic pessimism' has become a commonplace of philosophy and the German author's Achilles' heel, but this 'pessimism' is nothing other than an invitation to pursue enlightenment. Maybe this Adornian aesthetic pessimism has somehow pushed Pouivet to explain philosophically what difference there is 'between the music of Jimi Hendrix and the sound of a broken washing machine' (Pouivet 2010: 85).

References

Adorno, Theodor W. (2001). *The Culture Industry. Selected Essays on Mass Culture*. London and New York: Routledge Classics.

Adorno, Theodor W. (2002). *Essays on Music. Selected, with Introduction, Commentary, and Notes by Richard Leppert*. Oakland: University of California Press.

Adorno, Theodor W. (2005). *Minima Moralia. Reflections from Damaged Life*. London and New York: Verso Books.

Adorno, Theodor W. (2006). *Current of Music*. Cambridge: Polity Press.

Adorno, Theodor W. and Peter von Haselberg (1965). 'Über die geschichtliche Angemessenheit des Bewusstseins', in Walter Höllerer and Hans Bende (eds.), *Akzente Zeitschrift für Dichtung*, 487–97. Munich: Carl Hanser Verlag.

Bisson, Frédéric (2016). *La pensée rock. Essai d'ontologie phonographique*. Paris: Questions Théoriques.

Gayraud, Agnès (2019). *Dialectic of Pop*. Falmouth: Urbanomic Media.

Gracyk, Theodore (1996). *Rhythm and Noise. An Aesthetics of Rock*. Durham and London: Duke University Press.

Paddison, Max (1996). *Adorno, Modernism and Mass Culture. Essays on Critical Theory and Music*. London: Kahn and Averill.

Pouivet, Roger (2010). *Philosophie du rock*. Paris: Presses Universitaires de France.

Wipplinger, Jonathan O. (2017). *The Jazz Republic: Music, Race, and American Culture in Weimar Germany*. Ann Arbor: University of Michigan Press.

4

The concert

Creation, re-creation and the writing of popular music

Julie Mansion-Vaquié

From Alvin Lee's guitar solo on 'I'm Going Home' at Woodstock in 1969 to TuPac's appearance as a hologram at Coachella in 2012, concerts have embodied music in contemporary history. This chapter aims to define this constitutive object of popular music by addressing its existences, practices and contents in a theoretical and analytical way, with specific reference to writing and how concerts contribute to the writing – in the broad sense – of history.

On stage: Definitions

Popular music: A theoretical reminder

Popular music has an intrinsic link with recording. This link gives it a multiple mode of existence, a specific ontology. Referring to Gérard Genette (1994), Serge Lacasse (2006) proposes the following tripartition of recorded music: composition, performance, phonography. The distinction of this division is based on the regimes of immanence developed by Nelson Goodman (1976): allographic art versus autographic art. Thus, composition is associated with allographic art, performance with autographic art and recording, according to Gracyk (1996) and Lacasse, with a multiple autographic object.

> A recording has its own production history, which is impossible to recreate exactly. More precisely, the production history of a recording, as found on the market, is twofold: in the first stage, a master tape is produced, which has its own production history, usually consisting of the capture (simultaneous or successive) of one or more performances that will then be edited, mixed and

50   *Ink on the Tracks*

> matrixed, a complex process impossible to reproduce exactly. The second stage
> of this double production history consists of the duplication of the content of the
> master tape on new supports in as many copies as one wishes. (Lacasse 2006: 72)

I will simply add to this typology the existence of another multiple autographic object: the discs (and/or videos) of live performances distributed as such.

The musicological approach to this field is particularly interested in the object produced in the studio distributed in a medium, variable according to the time, the available technologies (vinyl, cassette, mp3) and the aesthetics of the genre. Currently, while different types of media coexist, studio work enables an almost infinite creativity to exist. Why insist on this phonographic character? For many musicologists specializing in popular music, the record is considered as the primary text, like the score in classical music. It is a question of considering the recording as the work, as a complete object resulting from a complex creative process and presented as a finished product.

> The work of art in rock music is a piece of work constructed in the studio. Tracks
> usually contain songs that can be played live. A cover version is a track intended
> to manifest (successfully) the same song as another. This ontology reflects the
> way the informed public talks about rock. It recognizes not only the centrality
> of recorded songs to tradition, but also the value placed on live performance
> techniques. It draws relevant distinctions between what happens in the studio
> and what ends up on the recording, as well as between what happens in the
> studio and what happens on stage – a very different relationship in rock and
> classical traditions. (Kania 2006: 412)

It should be noted that other types of approaches exist in this musical field, notably within performance studies, considering performance as the primary act (Cook 2001).

The musicological analysis of popular music thus takes into account a certain number of elements: the abstract parameters related to the musical composition (melody, harmony, rhythm), the performative parameters (timbre, accentuation) and the technological parameters (effects, spatialization) (Lacasse 2006).

The concert

Etymologically, the term concert refers to the tuning of an ensemble of voices and/or instruments. All styles taken together, it is defined by a unity of time, place and action (Nicolas 2000) which makes it unique and not perfectly reproducible.

It is also tied to an industrial system and responds to a certain form of collective ritual involving mediation and communication. In an expanded definition, I propose here to define the concert as a musical performance presenting one or more works in a defined spatio-temporal setting before an audience, including sociocultural and stylistic conventions. In the context of popular music, it would be relevant to add the style represented and to indicate that the content consists mainly of the work of the artists performing on stage. Previously (Mansion-Vaquié 2021), I indicated that the term interpretation was inappropriate for most popular music, as the musicians on stage offer an interpretation of their own creations, so I use the term 'intrapretation' instead.

Interpretation (or intrapretation) belongs to the more general concept of performance, of which the concert is a specific manifestation. This term 'performance', widely used in musicological and interdisciplinary research, brings together several aspects already mentioned (unity of place, time and action) as well as the presence of an audience, an aspect defended by David Shumway (1999). The audience plays an active role in communicating with the artists (through gestures, movements, shouting, singing, etc.) as Simon Frith (1996) stresses, and is included within the conventions governing concerts. These are linked to accepted sociocultural codes related to the musical genre. For example, in a rock concert, the wait for the beginning of the concert and the entrance of the musicians on stage is done with complete lighting of the stage on which the instruments are laid out, accompanied by background music.

Finally, the question of theatricality is important in the concert, whether it is a question of staging, gesture or audience reaction. The theatrical dimension may not be extraordinary or breathtaking, but still involve anything from the choice of stage clothes, even jeans and sneakers, to bursts of fire quite common in heavy metal performances for instance, or the use of video. Taking into account the dramatization of the musician's and/or singer's body implies a link to narrativity. In this context, Simon Frith develops an approach to the singer's persona in relation to recording, but which is also relevant to the stage:

> There is, first of all, the character presented as the protagonist of the song, its singer and narrator, the implied person controlling the plot, with an attitude and tone of voice; but there may also be a 'quoted' character, the person whom the song is about (and singers, like lecturers, have their own mannered ways of indicating quote marks). On top of this there is the character of the singer as star, what we know about them, or are led to believe about them through their packaging and publicity, and then, further, an understanding of the singer as a

person, what we like to imagine they are really like, what is revealed, in the end, by their voice. (Frith 1996: 198–9)

One can see here how not only the song, but also the interpretation of the song and the performance, can be related to writing, and therefore reading. Frith's perspective is echoed by Allan F. Moore (2005, 2012) and Philip Auslander (2004). The latter emphasizes that the persona can evolve and is shaped not only by the music (on record or on stage) but also by the media coverage linked to the industry (advertisements, album covers, interviews, photos, television appearances, etc.) which can all be considered, in different ways, as written objects.

Thus, performance, I would argue, is the implementation of all levels of expression (musical, theatrical, gestural, circumstantial) used, consciously or unconsciously, by a contemporary music artist or group in its creation and re-creation. Its analysis includes musical, theatrical, gestural and other viewpoints as well as elements relating to the presence of an audience.

The above definition of a concert does not, however, give any indication of the type of performance, in terms of venues, destinations and constraints. Yet these elements can have an impact on the musical and performative outcome of a work. A Prince concert in the O2 Arena in London or a Prince concert in a small Parisian club does not meet the same technical, musical or sociological needs. In the same way, going to see a band at a concert hall or a festival implies differences linked to format and audience. In one case, the audience comes to see a single group that it has chosen, in the other, several groups share the stage (or stages). In a tour, the study of the set-lists of a group shows similarities. If one considers the concerts, there will be differences in format according to the types of stages (small hall, a large building or a festival, for example), the duration of the performances but also the choice of the songs. Generally speaking, one tends to find short concerts covering a group's hits at festivals, and long and more experimental sets at dedicated concerts or even acoustic versions in small places like clubs or bars. Examining this typology enables us to inscribe rock in history. For example, one might think of James Brown's concert of 24 October 1962 at the Apollo Theater in New York, which led to a recording. This project, not supported by Syd Nathan (the head of King Records), was the result of the artist's own risk-taking and is considered a classic live album (Tellier 2017). Another example is Nirvana's acoustic concert for MTV, recorded in one take on 18 November 1993 (Mazullo 2000), which has become mythical in terms of both content and form.

As the notion of performance has shown, one of the characteristics of popular music is its link to spectacle and theatricality. In her work on Peter Gabriel, Ariane Bercier proposes the term 'rock-theatrical concert' to describe a concert that includes: 'scenographic components (sets, lighting, video projections as well as the use of shadow puppets) all serving to sculpt a fictional space on stage, dramatic (characters, fables and themes unifying the concert) and intentional' (Bercier 2016: 22): the whole space, especially the fictional aspect, is written. Eclectic artists such as Ghost (metal), Lady Gaga (pop), Radiohead (experimental rock) or U2 (rock) fall into this categorization. Although this idea is relevant, it is easy to find a theatrical dimension in any musical performance (Mansion-Vaquié 2014), which is why all the researchers on popular music indicate that it is important to take into account all the scenic aspects (from scenography to gestures; Valente 2008). On the other hand, as Bercier suggests, a concert is to be understood as an interartistic performance (drawing from theatre, visual arts or dance).

The concert can thus be understood as a varied performative medium found in various time-spaces. It can be categorized as a live concert, recorded concert, filmed concert, retransmitted concert, televised concert (live or recorded).

Authenticity

The notion of authenticity, omnipresent in discourse on rock, is as inescapable as it is problematic. Richard Middleton points out that the models supported by popular discourse are based on 'an opposition between "art" and "trash" or between "mainstream" and "underground" – in fact, between "pop" (commercial) and "rock" (authentic)' (Middleton 2004: 769). Thus, certain musical genres, such as folk music, for example, would in fact be more authentic than others, as Allan F. Moore (2002) indicates. The latter proposes a typology of the authenticities (2000) within musical performance articulating around the presence of a musician, of music allowing one to authenticate experience and belonging to a pre-existent musical tradition. His idea, shared by Auslander, is to consider authenticity as belonging to a cultural context (Auslander 1998) and resulting from a phenomenon of appropriation (Moore 2002; Butler 2003), which is consequently evolutionary (Hennion 1998).

The focus of authenticity lies in the performance in concert. For Philip Auslander:

The visual evidence of live performance, the fact that those sounds can be produced live by the appropriate musicians, serves to authenticate music as

legitimate rock and not synthetic pop in a way that cannot occur on the basis
of the recording alone; only live performance can resolve the tension between
rock's romantic ideology and the listener's knowledge that the music is produced
in the studio. (Auslander 1998: 13)

In other words, "'real" rock must justify itself to the public' (Chastagner 1998:
118). Thus, the concert plays a role of authentication of the music produced on
a disc; it shows that the musicians are able to play what is recorded but also to
adapt to the unforeseen. Moreover, Bertrand Ricard maintains that 'the concert
is an unavoidable rite of passage in an artist's career. It serves as an instance of
legitimization' (Ricard 2000: 98). David Pattie (2007) adds that a certain number
of extra-musical elements of a performance (gestures, images, tones) allow the
public to recognize an artist as authentic.

Analysing the concert

Mediated performance

Ian Inglis states: 'Although music is always "performative", in the sense that it
only truly exists when performed, the performance of much contemporary
popular music is routinely "mediatized", reaching its audiences through an
array of increasingly sophisticated audio-visual technologies, rather than live'
(Inglis 2006: XII). For Philip Auslander (2008: 187), mediated performance is
even the most common kind. Since the 2000s, certain paradigms have evolved.
Indeed, following the crisis of recorded music (Guibert 2020) and the advent
of streaming, the concert has become the main source of income for artists.
Moreover, the cultural industry has seized on this phenomenon, notably by
investing massively in festivals and large-capacity venues. Thus, the concert has
become a primordial stake in the existence of music (and musicians) and the
history of a genre.

However, in Inglis's book, many researchers from different fields (musicology,
performance studies, sociology) are interested in the concert of an artist. In
most cases, the form privileged by the authors is mediatized performances of a
concert (Otis Redding, David Bowie) or of a television appearance (the Beatles,
Elvis Presley, Patti Smith), performances which are taken to be more or less
representative of the career of the artists studied. The extreme of the form of
the mediatized concert is manifested in the films resulting from the concert

and shown at the cinema such as the 3D film of U2 resulting from the Vertigo tour. In this regard, Susan Fast (2013) conducts a comparative analysis between the live concert and the concert proposed in the cinema by questioning the musical content (set-list) but also the relationship to the physical presence of the spectators and the musicians. Despite technical efforts, this type of mediatized show moves away from the essence of a concert in its lack of physical and sound incarnation.

In these analyses, based mainly on description, many extra-musical elements are emphasized, and few truly musicological approaches are deployed. Thus, if we understand the contextual importance of a concert, its musical impact is only skimmed over.

Media without images

Having access to the images of a concert in filmed form can enable a detailed analysis of certain musical passages as well as the interactions between the musicians or their interpretative gestures. Beyond the context of the concert itself, its theatricalization, the impact of the image remains in the memory of the spectators. However, the recording of the concerts is almost always revised, remixed and reedited.

Tim Hughes's approach takes into account the search for a concert recording that is not subject to revision, often imposed in a commercial live album, by relying on a bootleg. This type of multiple object has several advantages, including that of hearing and/or seeing the performance without artifice and without editing. According to David Pattie (2007), the term 'bootleg' in the musical field has become interchangeable with the term 'pirate' disc. Yet the philosophy of bootlegs is quite different: as Tom Schultheiss states, they do not come 'from pre-existing recordings, but from unauthorized recordings of live performances or radio or television broadcasts, or from the use of stolen material' (1981: 396). Mark Neumann and Timothy A. Simpson (1997) have shown how the practice of 'bootlegging' is part of an alternative to representations of popular culture as a mere process of production and consumption. Indeed, if it is a question of capturing live concerts, they enable, in addition to the collection and the exchange, the keeping of an 'authentic' trace of the recorded concert. David Pattie indicates that there are mainly two types of bootleg: the one made by the spectator with variable technical means according to the time, and the one resulting from the mixing desk: 'Soundboard indicates a recording made from the mixing board or other source in-line with the PA system used at the concert. These can be the best possible recordings, as they are largely free from audience sound' (Pattie 2007: 244). Some artists, such as Bob Dylan or the Rolling Stones, changed their attitude towards these recordings, so that they eventually appeared in their own discographies (Farmer 2015). Some of these bootleg recordings are mythical, like the 'Live at the Apollo Theater in New York' by the band Korn. In a way, they write the history of the rock concert, or even of the genre itself.

Tim Hughes chooses to describe the songs in the order in which they appeared in concert, which allows him to discuss the sequences between the songs, to weave links between them and to analyse the construction of the set-list. If he mainly describes the musical and interpretative aspects that are remarkable in this concert, such as the guitar sounds, the drum patterns, the vocal interpretation or the tempo, he often does so by referring to the past or future phonographic version. For example, the song 'Breed' performed at a Nirvana concert has lyrics that differ from the phonographic recording that will later be produced on the album *Nevermind*. The result of this analysis allows us to highlight two characteristic aspects of Nirvana: the sound of the guitar and the treatment of the voice. They are developed around the notions of distortion, saturation, inarticulation and the production of chaos, whose origin is found in the constitutive fusion of grunge between metal and punk (Strong 2011).

Performance and gesture

Jane W. Davidson has conducted several analyses of musical performance in classical music and popular music. Her approach examines the non-verbal behaviours of performers based on the research of Ekman, Friesen and D'Argyle and involves the study of gestures, postures and facial expressions (Escal 1998). If music is a powerful means of communication, the body is the vector. Davidson relies on the analysis of filmed concerts. She highlights the links between music and gestures in a process of incarnation that we will link to the character and the persona according to Auslander. In her study of Robbie Williams (2016), she emphasizes the use of functions similar to discourse analysis (iconic, metaphoric, deictic and pragmatic). Ekman and Friesen's typology is applied to the study conducted on the Corrs (Kurosawa and Davidson 2005), showing the link between performative gestures related to playing an instrument and gestures from non-verbal behaviours impacting the relationship with the audience but also with the co-performers.

The study of these elements in relation to the musical and literary text can have several analytical and comprehension interests. With Amy Winehouse, for example, the gap between the character and the real person seems to be erased in her concert intrapretation of the song 'You Know I'm No Good' (Mansion-Vaquié 2014), where she goes so far as to modify the addressee of the song by changing the lyric 'I cried for you on the kitchen floor' to 'I cried for you 7614 my Blake' or 'I love you Blakey save me 7614', referring to her boyfriend – who was in prison at the time – and his prisoner number. In the light of this clue, the explicit gestures of the singer can also be read in another perspective.

An attempt to bring together several aspects of the concert is made by Stan Hawkins and Sarah Niblock (2011) in a study of Prince, particularly his concert at the O2 Arena (2007). By highlighting many extra-musical elements of this artist's concerts, such as the staging, the venue and the context of the concert, the media construction of the persona but also the study of his gestures, the authors only go a little way into musical analysis of the concert. Nevertheless, they show that Prince is aware of these different elements that he carefully orchestrates. Prince proposes new arrangements of his songs for his concerts: 'In any case, this means that his grooves are modified to suit the theme and the mood of a concert, which involves, say, tempi, changes from what we are used to in his recordings, new solo passages, modulations, extra verses, extended jam sessions and so on' (Hawkins and Niblock 2011: 164).

A concert is a multiple object that requires the consideration of various extra-musical elements, consciously or unconsciously constructed, having impacts on the music and the performance presented. If, without being the only one, Prince is an artist who modifies the musical arrangements of his works for the stage, how can we apprehend and measure this process as well as its impact on the work of an artist or even a musical genre?

Theatrical re-creation

The concert, as we have seen, is an essential component of popular music. The guarantee of authenticity and legitimization of the artists, it is also the place of direct communication, even of communion, with the public. The concert, beyond its spectacular side, is first of all the musical presentation of a production often written and recorded beforehand. The central question of the methodology presented here points to the idea that there is a difference between music listened to on record and music in concert.

Onstage re-creation

The notion of scenic re-creation (Mansion-Vaquié 2021) is articulated in a reflection of the concept of reprise in the specific case of the passage from a phonographic support to a scenic support. It designates a phenomenon that brings into play the processes of creation of a work in a new context without changing the essence of the original work.

To do this, a certain number of criteria are considered to determine the potential evolution of the musical elements or even their appearance or disappearance. These criteria depend on the type of piece studied, and generally include the following elements: instrumentation and orchestration, musical structure, text, musical motifs, solos and vocal performance. Thus, the integration of a guest or the reorchestration of a piece according to the number of musicians on stage is taken into account but also the changes or evolutions of musical motives.

The elaboration of degrees enabling one to classify the various criteria resulting from the analyses is carried out according to the phonographic version. The number of degrees depends on three selection categories. First, the criteria are identical to the phonographic version. Second, the criteria exist in the phonographic version but are varied on stage. This category measures the impact of the variation, which implies two subcategories: moderate variation and strong variation. Third, the criteria do not exist in the phonographic version; they are new; it is thus a question of modification. The result of this analysis allows us to establish six degrees of re-creation, the extremes of which are either playback (0) or another song (6).

Shaka Ponk is a French electro-rock band composed of seven members, including a virtual monkey named 'Goz'. The principle of this group is to propose interactions between the real world and the virtual world via music. The concert is essential for this group, and the video is omnipresent, both in terms of artistic proposal and in terms of images taken on the spot. The projected images are of several types: the video in which Goz is a musician (in 'Yell' he plays a mandolin), which implies a constraint of synchronization either with the broadcast recording or with the movements of the video if one of the singers interprets his part. The video uses a relationship to rhythm. There is also the interactive video in which the movements of the musicians are synchronized with the images, whose climax is the battle sequence between the drummer and a gorilla drummer (built in the studio by the drummer himself).

For example, in four different stage versions, the song 'Sex Ball' is always longer than the phonographic version, and all of them have a modified structure including an extended introduction, the addition of a musical part (B), the repetition of the choruses and part A, the modification of A and so on. Moreover, the structure always changes at the same place after the bridge, which consists of a video of band member Sam singing and dancing with her voice recorded. Thus, the song is constrained up to this structural part and allows more freedom afterwards.

If certain artists approve the existence of an accepted scenic re-creation, certain groups do not use the same strategies. In 'Karma Police' by Radiohead, the remarkable element of the passage from one medium to another is concentrated on the timbres. As of the second verse, it is possible to hear in the phonographic version a voice acting as a chorus treated with an effect of distortion supplemented by reverb and distributed in the panoramic space through left–right alternation. In all the stage versions studied, this voice is sung by the guitarist in a very particular posture: far from the microphone, his hands cupped to his mouth in the shape of a megaphone. This amplifies the idea present in the record that it is a distant voice, an effect augmented by the addition of reverb but not that of distortion.

Furthermore, the concert foregrounds the piano part, especially in the coda sections, while this is not heard much on the phonographic recording where a guitar delay effect (the vintage AMS DMX 15-80S) is used. We also note differences in instrumentation: in 1997, Jonny Greenwood uses his electronic keyboard (Rhodes Suitcase Piano Mark I 73), but for two later versions (2009

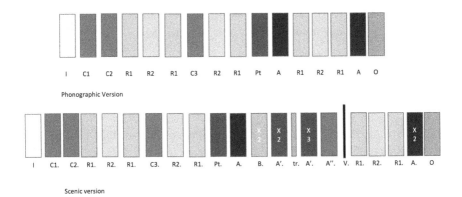

Figure 4.1 'Sex Ball': phonographic and scenic versions.

and 2017) he opts for an upright piano. Furthermore we note differences in what is played: in 1997, Greenwood finishes on a tone cluster, whereas in later versions he stops before the other musicians, leaving room for guitar effects. Finally, the effects used on O'Brien's guitar also evolve. In 1997, he uses the same delay as on the record, but in 2009 he plays instead on a phaser, and in 2017, he makes use of saturation coupled with delay. Thus, Radiohead's stage re-creation focuses not on the musical elements, which never change, but primarily on the sounds and use of technology. To study the onstage re-creation in all its complexity makes it possible to understand and evaluate the evolution of an artist.

Conclusion

The concert is a complex object requiring an interdisciplinary approach in which musicology can deepen understanding of the work, its evolution and its impact on other artists. Some of these artists have become new paradigms. Daft Punk revolutionized EDM concerts in Coachella in 2006 by proposing a grandiose and innovative scenography, remixing and rearranging several of their titles. Bob Dylan also created an upheaval in Newport in 1965 by electrifying his songs on stage, allowing the next generation to be unburdened. Musically, throughout his career, he took great liberties with arrangements and re-creations, moving from one style to another or making a song recognizable only by its lyrics (Mansion-Vaquié 2021).

While we often remember a concert by its media impact, an aspect supported by the industry, a concert actually conveys many other musical, emotional, and extra-musical elements. Thus, the concert, as one means of existence of the music, enables the history of popular music to be written.

References

Auslander, Philip (1998). 'Seeing is Believing: Live Performance and the Discourse of Authenticity in Rock Culture', *Literature and Psychology* 44(4), Research Library Galileo Edition: 1–26.

Auslander, Philip (2003). 'Good Old Rock and Roll: Performing the 1950s in the 1970s', *Journal of Popular Music Studies* 15(2): 166–95.

The Concert 61

Auslander, Philip (2004). 'Performance Analysis and Popular Music: A Manifesto', *Contemporary Theatre Reviews* 14(1): 1–13.

Auslander, Philip (2008). *Liveness. Performance in a Mediatized Culture*. 2nd edn. London: Routledge.

Bercier, Ariane (2016). 'Concert rock et théâtralité: Secret World Live de Peter Gabriel', Unpublished doctoral thesis. University of Ottowa.

Butler, Mark (2003). 'Taking It Seriously: Intertextuality and Authenticity in Two Covers by the Pet Shop Boys', *Popular Music* 22(1): 1–19. http://www.jstor.org/stable /853553 (accessed 24 January 2023).

Chastagner, Claude (1998). *La loi du rock*. Cahors: Climats.

Cook, Nicholas (2001). 'Between Process and Product: Music and/as Performance', *Music Theory Online*, 7–2. https://mtosmt.org/issues/mto.01.7.2/mto.01.7.2.cook .html (accessed 23 February 2023).

Davidson, Jane W. (2016). '"She's the One": Multiple Functions of Body Movement in a Stage Performance by Robbie Williams', in Elaine King (ed.), *Music & Gesture*, 208–25. London: Routledge.

Escal, Françoise (1998). 'Le corps rhétorique de l'interprète', in Luca Marconi, Gino Stefani, and Eero Tarasti (eds), *Musical Signification Beween Rhetoric and Pragmatics. Proceedings of the 5th international Congress on Musical Signification*, 213–22. Bologne: CLUEB.

Farmer, Steve (2015). 'Googling with the Stones: The Greatest Rock and Roll Corporation in the World and the Mainstreaming of Bootleg Recordings', *Rock Music Studies* 2(3): 239–56. doi:10.1080/19401159.2015.1093371 (accessed 20 February 2023).

Fast, Susan (2013). 'U2 3D: Concert Films and/as Live Performance', in Nicholas Cook and Richard Pettengil (eds), *Taking It to The Bridge: Music as Performance*, 20–36. Ann Arbor: University of Michigan Press.

Frith, Simon (1996). *Performing Rites: On the Value of Popular Music*. Cambridge, MA: Harvard University Press.

Genette, Gérard (1994). *L'œuvre de l'art: Immanence et transcendance*. Paris: Seuil.

Goodman, Nelson (1976). *Languages of Art*. Indianapolis: Hackett Publishing Compagny.

Gracyk, Theodore (1996). *Rhythm and Noise. An Aesthetics of Rock*. Durham: Duke University Press.

Guibert, Gérôme and Dominique Sagot-Duvauroux (2013). *Musiques actuelles: Ça part en live. Mutations économiques d'une filière culturelle*. Paris: Ministère de la Culture – DEPS.

Guibert, Gérôme and Dominique Sagot-Duvauroux (2020). 'Le tournant numérique du spectacle vivant. Le cas des festivals de musiques actuelles', *Hermès, La Revue* 86(1): 59–61.

Hawkins, Stan and Sarah Niblock (2011). *Prince: The Making of a Pop Music Phenomenon*. Farnham: Ashgate.

Hennion, Antoine (1998). 'D'une distribution fâcheuse: Analyse sociale pour les musiques populaires, analyse musicale pour les musiques savantes', in André Riotte (ed.), *Musurgia. Analyse et Pratique Musicales*, Vol. 5, no.°2, 9–20. Paris: éditions Eska.

Hughes, Tim (2006). 'Nirvana: University of Washington, Seattle, January 6, 1990', in Ian Inglis (ed.), *Performance and Popular Music. History, Place and Time*, 155–71. London: Routledge.

Kania, Andrew (2006). 'Making Tracks: The Ontology of Rock Music', *The Journal of Aesthetics and Art Criticism* 64(4): 401–14.

Keighley, Keir (2001). 'Reconsidering Rock', in Simon Frith, Will Straw, and John Street (eds), *The Cambridge Companion to Rock and Pop*, 109–42. Cambridge: Cambridge University Press.

Kurosawa, Kaori and Jane W. Davidson (2005). 'Nonverbal Behaviours in Popular Music Performance: A Case Study of the Corrs', *Musicae Scientiae* XIX(1): 111–36.

Lacasse, Serge (2006). 'Composition, performance, phonographie: Un malentendu ontologique en analyse musicale?', in Serge Lacasse and Patrick Roy (eds), *Groove: Enquête sur les phénomènes musicaux contemporains*, 65–78. Québec: Presses de l'Université Laval.

Mansion-Vaquié, Julie (2014). 'Théâtralisation du corps du chanteur dans la performance', in *Théâtralité de la musique et du concert des années 1980 à nos jours, Revue Musicorum* 15: 121–36.

Mansion-Vaquié, Julie (2021). 'Creation and Re-Creation in Dylan's Performances of "Blowin" in the "Wind" (1963–2016)', in Adrian Grafe, Andrew McKeown, and Claire Hélie (eds), *21st-Century Dylan: Late and Timely*, 99–120. New York: Bloomsbury Academic.

Mazullo, Mark (2000). 'The Man Whom the World Sold: Kurt Cobain, Rock's Progressive Aesthetic, and the Challenges of Authenticity', *The Musical Quarterly* 84(4): 713–49. JSTOR, http://www.jstor.org/stable/742606 (accessed 21 February 2023).

Middleton, Richard (2004). 'L'étude des musiques populaires', in Jean-Jacques Nattiez (ed.), *Musiques: Une encyclopédie pour le XXIe siècle. Les savoirs musicaux*, Vol. 2, 766–84. Arles: Actes sud Paris / Cité de la Musique.

Moore, Allan F. (2000). 'Constructing Authenticity in Rock', *E-PAI Journal*, Winter, Issue No. 001.

Moore, Allan F. (2002). 'Authenticity as authentification', in *Popular Music (2002) Volume 21/2*, 209–23. Cambridge: Cambridge University Press.

Moore, Allan F. (2005). 'The Persona – Environment Relation in Recorded Song', *MTO Journal of the Society for Music Theory* 11(4), https://www.mtosmt.org/issues/mto.05.11.4/mto.05.11.4.moore.html (accessed 21 February 2023).

Moore, Allan F. (2012). *Song Means: Analysing and Interpreting Recorded Popular Song*. London: Routledge.

Neumann, Mark and Timothy A. Simpson (1997). 'Smuggled Sound: Bootleg Recording and the Pursuit of Popular Memory', *Symbolic Interaction* 20(4): 319–41.

Nicolas, François (2000). 'L'analyse musicale du concert: Quelles catégories?', in Françoise Escal and François Nicolas (eds), *Le concert. Enjeux, fonctions, modalités*. Collection Logiques Sociales, 9–43. Paris: L'Harmattan.

Pattie, David (2007). *Rock Music in Performance*. London: Palgrave Macmillan.

Ricard, Bertrand (2000). *Rites, codes et culture rock. Un art de vivre communautaire*. Paris: L'Harmattan.

Schultheiss, Tom (1981). 'Everything You Always Wanted to Know About Bootlegs, but were Too Busy Collecting them to Ask: A Treatise on the Wages of Sinning for Sound', in Charles Reinhart (ed.), *You Can't Do That! Beatles Bootlegs and Novelty Records*, 395–411. Ann Arbor: Popular Music Ink.

Shumway, David R. (1999). 'Performance', in Bruce Horner and Thomas Swiss (eds), *Key Terms in Popular Music and Culture*, 188–98. Malden and Oxford: Blackwell.

Strong, Catherine (2011). *Grunge: Music and Memory*. London: Routledge.

Tellier, Albéric (2017). 'James Brown, *Live at the Apollo* (1963, King): Innovation et Initiative individuelle', in Albéric Tellier (ed.), *Bonnes vibrations: Quand les disques mythiques nous éclairent sur les défis de l'innovation*, 21–32. Caen: EMS Editions. https://doi.org/10.3917/ems.telli.2017.01.0021 (accessed 19 February 2023).

Valente, Heloísa de Araújo Duarte (2008). 'Le corps, les gestes et les mutations de performance (Quelques notes sur la mouvance du Fado)', in Dario Martinelli (ed.), *Music Senses Body: Proceedings from the 9th International Congress on Musical Signification*. Rome 19-23/09/2006, Acta Semiotica Fennica XXXII, 264–72. University of Rome Tor Vergata.

5

Class and race in popular music history

Jon Stratton

The majority of histories, in the broadest sense of the word, of popular music have focused on music produced and consumed in the United Kingdom and the United States of America. My interest here is on those where class and race have been given a privileged status. In this chapter, I shall concentrate on exemplary histories from these countries and how their different approaches have become characteristic of the ways popular music history is written.

America and the centrality of race

Reebee Garofalo (2008: 83) has written the most widely used American textbook history of popular music. In common with most American historians of rock and roll, his focus is primarily on race rather than class. However, as he writes, commenting on American preoccupations, 'in looking only at the dimension of race, ethnicity, and musical culture, issues of class and gender are conveniently ignored'. Garofalo (2008: 83) goes on to make the point which we will find is a constant refrain through classed narratives of popular music history: 'While rock 'n' roll certainly drew on a wide range of inputs, all of its immediate musical sources were firmly rooted in the tradition of working-class styles.' That is, rock and roll, and the many musical forms which derive from it, is working class in origin. Garofalo refers to the work of George Lipsitz who, as Garofalo (2008: 83) puts it, 'has located rock 'n' roll at the intersection of urbanization, multiculturalism, and class'. Nevertheless, Garofalo rarely mentions class in his book, being primarily preoccupied, in common with many American authors and those writing about the United States, with race. Garofalo (2008: 185) writes in the context of the Animals and the Rolling Stones, and more generally the rhythm and blues segment of the 1960s British Invasion, that in America where race was central to the organization of the social order the British Invasion 'touched off endless debate about white people singing the blues'.

The debate to which Garofalo alludes began with the African-American critic, LeRoi Jones. In *Black Music*, a 1968 collection of his essays, LeRoi Jones (1968: 143), later known as Amiri Baraka, was already concerned with the impact of the British Invasion. The collection includes a 1965 essay where he asked: 'Does anybody really think it's weird that all these English "pop" groups are making large doses of loot?' and went on to explain that it's because these groups 'take the style [. . .] of black blues, country or city, and combine it with the visual image of white American non-conformity'. A year later, Jones was much less forgiving. Name checking the Beatles and the Rolling Stones he wrote: 'They steals, minstrelizes. [. . .] Actually, the more intelligent the white, the more the realization he has to steal from niggers' (Jones 1968: 235). Jones's point is that the source of rock and roll, and therefore what drives developments in rock, is always Black music.

More recently this argument has been taken to its limit by Kevin Phinney. He introduces his book, published in 2005, by explaining that it 'asserts that African Americans are the unsung innovators of American music, while white artists tend to popularize and develop each trend to a creative and commercial end' (Phinney 2005: 18). The latter identifies such genres as gospel, R&B and rap and suggests they are 'combined with structural influences cribbed from European music traditions' (Phinney 2005: 18). Such a position can only be held by setting aside genres such as the ballad, the importance of the folk song tradition and the development of the musical.

Eldridge Cleaver in his collection of political essays, *Soul on Ice*, published in 1968, made a similar argument to Jones about appropriation by the groups of the British Invasion but with a different emphasis. Having been radicalized in prison, Cleaver joined the Black Panthers in 1967. In *Soul on Ice*, Cleaver emphasizes the importance of the body in the African-American experience. He praises jazz and claims rhythm and blues as the basis for rock and roll, describing it as the source for the 'gaudy, cacophonous hymns with which the Beatles of Liverpool drive their hordes of ultrafeminine fans into catatonia and hysteria' (Cleaver 1970: 235). The music has been appropriated but, Cleaver argues, what remains is its appeal to the body, and bodily expressiveness, as shown in the response of the Beatles' fans.

In her highly regarded 1994 book, *Black Noise: Rap Music and Black Culture in Contemporary America*, the title of which echoes the title of Jones's book,

Tricia Rose (1994: 5) makes a remarkably similar argument to Jones's if in more measured tones:

> Jazz, rock 'n' roll, soul, and R&B each have large devoted white audience members, many of whom share traits with Norman Mailer's 'white negroes', young white listeners trying to perfect a model of correct white hipness, coolness, and style by adopting the latest black style and image.

Rose suggests that in the passing of a generation little has changed in the racialized structure of American popular music. White artists can still succeed by taking on African-American music forms and marketing the music to white consumers.

Mailer's essay on 'The White Negro' was published in 1957. He argued that 'the source of Hip is the Negro' and that 'the presence of Hip as a working philosophy in the sub-worlds of American life is probably due to jazz, and its knife-like entrance into culture, its subtle but so penetrating influence on an avant-garde generation' (Mailer 1957). Mailer's reference point here is white culture, and the avant-garde to which he refers, those who are hip, are also white. For Jones (1968: 143), the white groups of the British Invasion were in part successful because 'these English boys are literally "hipper" than their white counterparts in the US'. Mailer's claim for the importance of jazz is echoed by both Jones, who had been a jazz critic, and Cleaver. Over twenty years later, Rose is making similar points but jazz has been replaced by hip hop.

In the UK, where in the early 1960s race was still subordinate to class as the primary organizer of the social order, there was little concern about white artists covering the work of African-American artists (Donnelly 2013). Indeed, the bigger debate was about the impact of American music generally on British culture. In the United States, as Garofalo indicates, by contrast, where the constructed racialized division between Black and white was the crucial feature, what the British groups were doing, playing music derived from African-American genres and sometimes covering African-American tracks without trying to sweeten the music for white, middle-class consumption, was quite shocking.

Nik Cohn's *Pop from the Beginning*

It is Nik Cohn's book, first published in 1969 as *Pop from the Beginning*, which is usually considered to be the first historical account of rock and roll. Cohn is the son of the esteemed British academic historian Norman Cohn and his wife, the Russian-born feminist Vera Broido. Cohn spent his early years in Derry where, in 1951, his father had been appointed professor of French at Magee College, a campus of Ulster University. Cohn didn't go to university. Rather, he became a journalist, at eighteen chronicling the London scene for *Queen*, where he had a regular column, and *The Observer*. He was twenty-two when he wrote *Pop from the Beginning*, better known by the title given to the book in 1970 when it was republished in paperback as *Awopbopaloobop Alopbamboom*.

Cohn's book is constructed around three binaries: the older generation who could neither identify with nor understand the new popular music and the younger generation, teenagers for whom rock and roll was the stuff of dreams and revolt against the crushing mundanity of everyday life; the music that came out of America and out of Britain; and a racial binary of Black and white which, Cohn claims, was amalgamated in the production of rock and roll. *Awopbopaloobop Alopbamboom*'s most important binary is left implicit: that between the rock and roll musicians and their first audience, both groups of whom Cohn identifies as working-class, while positioning himself as the middle-class voyeur. Cohn (1970: 16) dates rock and roll in Britain to the emergence of the well-paid working-class teenager in the 1950s. He is very clear about the racial input to rock and roll but for Cohn, in Britain, this is secondary to the importance of class. In the book's first paragraph, he writes: 'Modern pop began with rock 'n' roll in the middle fifties and, basically, it was a mixture of two traditions – Negro rhythm 'n' blues and white romantic crooning, coloured beat and white sentiment' (Cohn 1970: 3). This is not the place to discuss the accuracy or otherwise of Cohn's assertion. What he generates here is a foundational fusion which functions in the context of working-class experience.

Cohn's discussion of the popular music emanating from America and that from Britain is situated on the basis of the claim that all rock and roll is working class. Thus, he writes about Cliff Richard: 'His most lasting influence, however, hasn't been his singing, his conversion, even his white smile, but his speaking voice' (Cohn 1970: 65). Cohn argues that where previously pop singers sounded working class, Richard introduced a classless 'bland ramble' which became characteristic of British pop culture. Richard is Anglo-Indian and only moved to England with his parents when he was eight in 1948. His accent at the time Cohn was writing was a complex amalgam of English accents and Anglo-Indian with an acquired American inflection. Dominic Sandbrook (2005: 475) argues: 'Cliff Richard [. . .] sang his first hit, "Move It", in a strong American accent and continued to imitate

American intonation throughout his career.' The point to make here about Cohn's discussion is again not about its accuracy but that Cohn is making an argument about class. Cohn uses Richard to emphasize first that previous English pop singers had been working class and that, second, Richard marked an evolution in British popular music towards a new image of classlessness.

London's 'Swinging Sixties' were often characterized as classless. Sandbrook (2006: 258) writes about this in *White Heat: A History of Britain in the Swinging Sixties* where, for example, he quotes from an article in the *Weekend Telegraph* supplement in April 1965, in which the American writer John Crosby describes '"a sort of English renaissance", founded on youth, classlessness, fashion and sex'. Cohn disapproves of this new apparent classlessness, a pose which could morph into American imitation. Class as a social category runs through *Awopbopaloobop Alopbamboom*. Writing about the Beatles, Cohn (1970: 130) comments: 'At least, unlike any other British act ever, they didn't ape America but sounded what they were, working-class Liverpool, unfake, and that's what gave them their strength, that's what made Brian Epstein want to manage them.' For Cohn, here, there is an implicit argument about authenticity linked to an assertion of working-class origins, and their value in producing quality popular music. This claim will be discussed further later.

In *Awopbopaloobop Alopbamboom*, the most important aesthetic qualities of rock and roll are, as Mark Rozzo (2011) comments in an article in the *New York Times*, 'sex, noise, fun'. Cohn understands rock and roll as carrying opposing values to those of middle-class society. In his introduction to the 1999 republication of Cohn's book, Greil Marcus (1999) tells us that for Cohn: 'Pop music was about flash, glamor, excess, about self-invention and self-destruction.' Cohn writes about the change brought about by rock and roll, implying that pop's early years were the best. At that time, he writes: 'Anarchy moved in' suggesting that pretty much anybody could, as he puts it, 'clean up' (Cohn 1970: 25). Cohn opposes the restraint and phoniness and control of the middle class with a new opportunism.

In his 1996 preface to a republishing of *Awopbopaloobop Alopbamboom*, Cohn (1996: ix) tells a personal origin story. It involves his discovery, as a boy brought up in middle class, Protestant Derry, of a coffee bar in the Catholic slum of Bogside where he first heard Little Richard's 'Tutti Fruitti' on the jukebox and watched the local teddy boys jiving. There he felt: 'Glamour, yes, and wildness. But something else besides, which stirred me even deeper – the force of self-invention.' He explains: 'In every flash of fluorescent sock or velvet cuff, every leer

Class and Race in Popular Music History

and flaunt of their pompadours, they beggared the Fates. Made reality irrelevant.' We can begin by thinking about this self-invention. Cohn was a middle-class Jewish boy in Protestant Derry. He goes on to tell us: 'For an eleven-year-old weakling, class clown, mamma's boy and all-round loser, it offered nothing less than a second coming' (Cohn 1996: ix). In the transformation apparent in the working-class, teddy-boy youth culture, Cohn sees the possibility for making himself over into somebody who was acceptable and fitted into that youth culture. However, he doesn't become a teddy boy. Rather, he remains middle class and becomes an observer. Here we need to remember Cohn's background. His mother, the Jewish Russian feminist, was a woman with a 'liberated' past, who had lived in a ménage à trois, who had had photographs of her naked taken and exhibited by her lover, the former Dadaist, Raul Hausmann. If Cohn was a mama's boy, Vera was not your ordinary, middle-class 1950s housewife. Just as his mother's exotic premarital life would inevitably always escape him, Cohn sought excitement and self-worth in a working-class world to which he could only aspire.

Perhaps more importantly, Cohn's father, Norman Cohn, spent Nik's early life researching his highly regarded book on millenarianism, *The Pursuit of the Millennium*, which was published in 1957, the same year that Nik heard Little Richard and saw the teddy boys, with a revised version published in 1970, the year after *Pop from the Beginning* was published. In the new introduction, Norman Cohn (1970: 17) writes: 'again and again, in situations of mass disorientation and anxiety, traditional beliefs about a future golden age or messianic kingdom came to serve as vehicles for social aspirations and animosities'. Greil Marcus (2009: 93) has noted the link between father and son and writes that Nik Cohn 'disavowed all claims on meaning the form [of rock and roll] might make, affirming instead a pure sensual anarchy'. Marcus suggests a link between the glossolalia of Little Richard's 'Tutti Frutti', which provided the title for the paperback version of Cohn's book, and gnostic chants which became the prayers offered up by John of Leyden and the Brethren of the Free Spirit in the early sixteenth century about whom the older Cohn wrote in *The Pursuit of the Millennium* (1957, 1970). At the end of his book, Nik Cohn writes that the glossolalia AWOPBOPALOOBOP ALOPBAMBOOM (Cohn's capitals) sums up what pop was and is about. Marcus (2009: 94) interprets Cohn as meaning that 'Rock 'n' roll has nothing to say, only a divine noise to make'.

The link between the two Cohn books has deep resonances. Norman Cohn's book was about millenarianism. Nik Cohn describes his experience of the teddy

70   *Ink on the Tracks*

boys as a second coming. Norman Cohn (1970: 15) writes that millenarian sects think of salvation in terms of his five criteria: collective, terrestrial, imminent, total and miraculous. This is very much how Nik Cohn describes the experience of rock and roll. Cohn formulates his celebration of rock and roll, and working-class life, in the terms that his father used to characterize millenarian understandings of salvation. Noise without meaning, glossolalia, is not meaningless. *Awopbopaloobop Alopbamboom* is not only a class-based history of rock and roll, it is a secular millennial tract. It is no wonder that Ulf Lindberg et al. (2005: 128) comment that Cohn's 'idiosyncratic writings make him an outstanding figure [in rock history writing]'.

Simon Frith's *The Sociology of Rock*

The Sociology of Rock is divided into three parts: The Consumption of Rock, The Production of Rock, The Ideology of Rock. In his preface, Frith (1978: 7) remarks: 'I have tried to write a book which will make sense simultaneously to sociologists who know nothing about rock and to rock fans who know nothing about sociology; the result is bound to irritate both sorts of reader.' It is indeed the case that the book reads rather awkwardly. Frith leads his readers into rock by way of a discussion of youth, the title of the first chapter, already, at that time, a sociologically acceptable area of research. Commenting on a study by J. B. Mays in 1965 called *The Young Pretenders*, Frith (1978: 20) makes the following point: 'But if it was agreed that teenagers were working-class youngsters. [. . .] "Teenage" referred to consumption, to leisure, and this stress on leisure and pleasure has been retained in accounts of working-class youth ever since.' Rock gets contextualized as a youth leisure activity. Frith's account of youth and consumption is founded in the idea of class, and the pleasures of rock music were, in the first place, identified with the hedonism of working-class young people, teenagers. However, and this is where Frith's analysis begins to differ from that of Cohn, Frith (1978: 22) writes: 'Even before the Beatles the more astute observers of the teenage scene were remarking on the development of a culture that was specifically young but not specifically working class.' Frith (1978: 23) goes on to explain how the idea of the working-class teenager got absorbed into the more general concept of youth: 'Youth was an ideological concept, it reflected the observation that middle-class children were deliberately adopting lower-class values.' We might quibble over Frith's use of 'deliberate' here but, generally speaking, this is a good account of Cohn's personal taking-up of rock and roll, and the reasons why middle-class young people found rock and roll pleasurable.

Frith's turn to rock music in *The Sociology of Rock* comes by way of a study he conducted at a comprehensive school in Keighley, a town near Bradford in Yorkshire, Great Britain, in 1972. The specific analytical connection was made in a subsection titled 'The use of music'. In this time before Popular Music Studies, Frith led sociologists into a discussion of rock by constructing it as a form of leisure activity for youth. He did not try to legitimate this theoretically; rather, he used an empirical study to justify the connection. In this study, Frith found listening practices differed between the sixth-formers, who were more middle class, and the lower fifth who were of working-class background.

Frith was writing around the time that progressive rock evolved and that BBC Television, acknowledging that a split was developing in the popular music audience, had in 1971 started *The Old Grey Whistle Test*. The programme went to air at 10.00 on Tuesday evenings on BBC2. The acts broadcast during 1971 and 1972 included America, Alice Cooper, Stone the Crows and Buffy St Marie. Edward Macan (1997: 19) argues that 'Progressive rock could never have emerged from the working-class milieu that was responsible for the formation of genres such as heavy metal and later, punk rock; throughout the 1970s, progressive rock's audience consisted largely of a middle-class post-hippie extension of the counterculture.' Progressive rock groups started in public schools and universities. For example: 'Van der Graaf Generator formed at Manchester University; Henry Cow coalesced at Cambridge University; Pink Floyd was formed by a group of architectural students at Regent Street Polytechnic' (Macan 1997: 147). This was the music of Frith's sixth-formers and the preferred music of middle-class youth who listened to music rather than dancing to it. Cohn (1970: 229) liked Pink Floyd's early single 'Arnold Layne' but hated their more progressive rock instrumentals: 'twenty-five minute scream-ups, formless and tuneless and colourless, but always incredibly loud'. *Top of the Pops*, which broadcast chart music, had started on BBC1 in 1964. What Frith (1978: 41) found was, as he put it, that 'there were distinct rock cultures', that the sixth-formers watched *The Old Grey Whistle Test* while the lower fifth-formers watched *Top of the Pops*. The sixth-formers listened critically to the lyrics of the music they liked and bought albums while the lower fifth-formers simply enjoyed the music, often dancing to it, and bought singles.

The second part of *The Sociology of Rock* is a political economy of the music industry. The third part offers a discussion of popular music as an aspect of mass culture. In these two parts the class analysis developed in Part One has disappeared. The third part includes discussions of the ideas of F. R. Leavis, Theodor Adorno and Walter Benjamin. In the conclusion, Frith (1978: 203–4) returns cautiously to class: 'In general terms, the rock business is built on two great market discoveries: the discovery of the working-class teenage audience in the 1950s and the discovery of the middle-class youth audience in the 1960s.' Frith (1978: 206) argues that leisure is a necessary element in the social organization of capitalism and that rock music 'has a radical, rebellious edge: it carries a sense of possibility denied in the labour market'. He explains: 'The essence of rock, then, is fun' (Frith 1978: 206). In *Sound Effects*, the American, rewritten version of *The Sociology of Rock* published in 1981, Frith (272) ends by highlighting the importance of fun: 'Rock, for all the power of its individual dreams, is still confined by its mass cultural form. Its history, like the history of America itself, is a history of class struggle – the struggle for fun.'

Fun is a key trope in the understanding of popular culture, especially in America. LeRoy Ashby (2006: xxxv) describes his book, a history of popular culture in America, as 'an interpretive synthesis of almost two hundred years of American entertainment: the sale, and purchase, of fun'. In 1964, the Beach Boys had a number 5 hit in America with 'Fun, Fun, Fun'. Cohn saw rock and roll as fun, and by implication subverting middle-class respectability. Superpop, Cohn (1968: 251) wrote, 'has to be fast, funny, sexy, obsessive, a bit epic'. Frith understands rock as an element of mass culture and caught up in Marxian class struggle. In *Performing Rites*, he provided a class analysis of mass culture, arguing that one effect of mass culture was 'to "discipline" the nineteenth-century urban "unrespectable"; another, equally important, was to loosen up the nineteenth-century urban (or suburban) respectable' (Frith 1998: 34). Fun can be subversive. Frith is paving the way for a class politics of popular music located in the bodily experience of pleasure.

Popular culture, including popular music, has always been more highly valued in the United States, where it has been associated with democracy and egalitarianism, than in the UK, where it has been looked down upon as the outgrowth of working-class entertainment and compared unfavourably with the products of high culture such as classical music. It is not surprising then that both Cohn and Frith spent time in America. Cohn has remarked that, for him, London 'seemed dead' and going to America, 'it was just as if I'd been locked in a tight little box and suddenly somebody had given me the keys to the world' (Whitney 2016). Karl Whitney (2016) remarks that 'Cohn's writing instinctively tuned into the mythical dimensions of pop music, and the culture of pop.' Before writing *Pop from the Beginning*, Cohn had already written his first novel, *I Am Still the Greatest Says Johnny Angelo*, described in its blurb as 'Cohn's hymn to rock as myth, in all its crazed, absurd, and glorious excess.' In New York, working again as a journalist, in 1976 notoriously he wrote 'Tribal Rites of the New Saturday Night' which was published in *New York Magazine* as an observational piece of journalism. Its mythic quality led it to form the basis for the most important film based in disco, *Saturday Night Fever* (1977). By 1996, Cohn was admitting that much of the story was fiction. Cohn was a fabulist, and it was this quality which made *Pop from the Beginning* so successful.

Class in later British work on rock and roll

Towards the end of *Studying Popular Music*, in a chapter entitled '"Lost in Music"? Pleasure, value and ideology in popular music', Richard Middleton develops a class-based theorization of popular music such as Frith seemingly wants. Middleton's book, published in 1990, provides a theoretical system for the analysis of popular music founded in the Marxian work of the Italian political theorist Antonio Gramsci: 'If [my] position has any one predominant source, it is the "turn to Gramsci" so visible in British cultural studies ten years ago but now less prominent, in the babble of intellectual fashions' (Middleton 1990: v). Gramsci's importance for cultural studies lay in his inclusion of culture in his understanding of Marxian class theory. Middleton (1990: 8) explains that, 'while elements of culture are not directly, eternally or exclusively tied to specific economically determined factors such as class position, they are determined in the final instance by such factors'. Interestingly, the idea of economic determination in the final instance comes from Louis Althusser rather than Gramsci, but Althusser is only mentioned once, in a note, in Middleton's book. One of Middleton's (1990: 9) examples is Elvis Presley: 'Early Elvis Presley managed to link together elements connoting youth rebellion, working-class "earthiness" and ethnic "roots", each of which can evoke the others, all of which were articulated together, however, briefly, by a moment of popular self-assertion.' Middleton goes on to rework the claim to classlessness in 1960s England, in the context of hegemony. Middleton (1990: 9) argues that the idea of what he describes as 'man-in-the-street "classlessness"', an apparent classlessness that functioned to legitimate the established class structure built on the claim that the early Beatles, and by implication others identified as members of so-called swinging Britain were classless, was a strategy for enabling the meaning of the music to be interpreted by what he calls 'the dominant social interests', that is to say, the class having power in Britain at that time. These interests were those of the ruling class. Middleton's Gramscian approach, with its emphasis on culture, provides a significant degree of critical leverage.

In 2008, another Briton, Nathan Wiseman-Trowse, published another class-based analysis of popular music, *Performing Class in British Popular Music*. Wiseman-Trowse (2008: 173) concentrates primarily on British popular music, arguing: 'Articulations of class in British popular music work to connect popular music texts with a wider social and political environment.' He concludes that:

> As this work has shown, music that comes under the umbrella of rock discourse is capable of being understood in class terms. When it is, 'cleverness' becomes cast as a preoccupation of middle-class artfulness, pretension, introspection and feminization. (Wiseman-Trowse 2008: 169)

Wiseman-Trowse identifies a folk voice that runs through English folk music to rock and roll. He (2008: 88) argues that the folk voice is not 'a style of singing or even a particular style of music [. . .] but rather a strain that has run throughout popular music in Britain for the last 200 years'. It gives authenticity and legitimacy to music which expresses 'the concerns of the working man (and sometimes the working woman too) and acts as an authentic arena within which class preoccupations are often evident' (Wiseman-Trowse 2008: 88). The myth of the authenticity of the folk voice in British popular music goes back at least as far as the work of A. L. Lloyd in the 1950s. It was mentioned critically by Frith in *The Sociology of Rock*, and, along with the work of Cecil Sharp, critiqued by Middleton. In cultural studies its foundational moment lies in Richard Hoggart's romanticization of working-class life, *The Uses of Literacy* (1957). In his diary for 2014 published in the *London Review of Books* (2015), the playwright Alan Bennett, when told that late in life Hoggart remarked that he felt he should have been a novelist, comments that he could see how 'a book as romantic as *The Uses of Literacy* could lead onto literature'.

Hoggart's criticism of rock and roll as part of his portrayal of teddy boys is well known. Far from Cohn's revelatory moment, Hoggart (1957: 189) writes of milk bars that:

Class and Race in Popular Music History

Girls go to some, but most of the customers are boys aged between fifteen and twenty, with drape-suits, picture ties, and an American slouch. Most of them cannot afford a succession of milk-shakes, and make cups of tea serve for an hour or two whilst – and this is their main reason for coming – they put copper after copper into the mechanical record player.

Hoggart's mechanical record player, with his implicit criticism of the technological reproduction of music over direct performance, is a jukebox.

What is less well known is Hoggart's (1957: 115) celebration of communal, folk music:

Only a few months ago I heard a blind pianist, in a pub this time, in a West Riding mill-town. [. . .] He played songs which were sung seventy years ago and hit tunes from the latest American musical, and there was no sense of a break in manner. No doubt he enjoyed playing, but one did not think of him as an individualist, as an individual performer; he was, rather, a participant – a respected and important participant – in a group activity. Far back behind the whole scene one could just see the outlines of the generations of folk-singing and folk-musicians who had gone before.

Here we find the idea of community which pervades *The Uses of Literacy*, a vision of working-class community which Hoggart felt was being lost with the impact of Americanization and which was also a characteristic of the idea of folk music. Wiseman-Trowse appears to want to recapture Hoggart's valorization of the folk community in his idea of the folk voice for a legitimizing authenticity of certain popular music. Unlike for Hoggart, this includes rock and roll. It is this music, Wiseman-Trowse argues, which is working class, as against the more self-conscious popular music he identifies with the middle class, the music of Frith's sixth-formers, the music which, earlier, Cohn considered was destroying the pleasure, the fun, of rock and roll.

Conclusion

In this chapter I have suggested that class-based narratives of popular music history are more usually found in the UK than the United States where race has been a defining feature of histories of popular music. I have focused on key early texts by Cohn and by Frith and then two later texts which show the tradition of class-based popular music histories in Britain, those by Middleton, and Wiseman-Trowse. Middleton's and Wiseman-Trowse's books illustrate well the ways class continues to percolate through histories of popular music in the UK. When class-based analyses are theorized it tends to be using concepts drawn from Marxian work. In Britain, class has been a key issue in discussions of rock and roll and other popular music (see for other examples: Harker 1980; Gildart 2013; Simonelli 2013). However, change is taking place. With the emergence and establishment of vibrant and highly visible music scenes identified with constituencies of people of colour (such as hip hop), the concern with the class basis of rock and roll, and other popular music in Britain, is now more obviously deeply imbricated with histories of race than ever before (Stratton and Zuberi 2014).

References

Ashby, LeRoy (2006). *With Amusement for All: A History of American Popular Culture Since 1830*. Lexington: The University of Kentucky Press.

Bennett, Alan (2015). 'What I Did in 2014', *London Review of Books*. https://www.lrb.co .uk/the-paper/v37/n01/alan-bennett/diary.

Cleaver, Eldridge (1970). *Soul on Ice*. New York: Dell.

Cohn, Nik (1970). *Awopbopaloobop Alopbamboom: Pop from the Beginning*. London: Paladin Books.

Cohn, Nik (1996). *Awopbopaloobop Alopbamboom: The Golden Age of Rock*. New York: Da Capo.

Cohn, Norman (1970). *The Pursuit of the Millennium: Revolutionary Millenarians and Mystical Anarchists of the Middle Ages*. Oxford: Oxford University Press.

Donnelly, Mark (2013). *Sixties Britain: Culture, Society and Politics*. London: Routledge.

Frith, Simon (1978). *The Sociology of Rock*. London: Constable and Comp.

Frith, Simon (1981). *Sound Effects: Youth, Leisure and the Politics of Rock*. New York: Pantheon Books.

Frith, Simon (1998). *Performing Rites: On the Value of Popular Music*. Cambridge, MA: Harvard University Press.

Garofalo, Reebee (2008). *Rockin' Out: Popular Music in the USA*. 4th edn. Upper Saddle River: Prentice Hall.

Gildart, Keith (2013). *Images of England Through Popular Music: Class, Youth and Rock 'n' Roll, 1955–1976*. London: Palgrave Macmillan UK.

Harker, Dave (1980). *One for the Money: Politics and Popular Song*. London: Hutchison.

Hoggart, Richard (1957). *The Uses of Literacy: Aspects of Working Class Life*. London: Penguin.

Jones, LeRoi (1968). *Black Music*. New York: Morrow.

Lindberg, Ulf, Gestur Guðmundsson, Morten Michelsen, and Hans Weisethaunet (eds) (2005). *Rock Criticism from the Beginning: Amusers, Bruisers, and Cool-headed Cruisers*. New York: Peter Lang.

Macan, Edward (1997). *Rocking the Classics: English Progressive Rock and the Counterculture*. Oxford: Oxford University Press.

Mailer, Norman (1957). 'The White Negro', *Dissent*, Fall. https://www.dissentmagazine .org/online_articles/the-white-negro-fall-1957.

Marcus, Greil (1999). 'Introduction to Nik Cohn's *Awopbopaloobop Alopbamboom*', *Greilmarcus.net*, 30 January. https://greilmarcus.net/2019/01/30/introduction-to-nik -cohns-a-wop-bop-a-loo-bop-a-lop-bam-boom-1999/

Marcus, Greil (2009). *Lipstick Traces: A Secret History of the Twentieth Century*. 2nd edn. Cambridge, MA: Belknap Press.

Mays, John Barron (1965). *The Young Pretenders: A Study of Teenage Culture in Contemporary Society*. London: Michael Joseph.

Middleton, Richard (1990). *Studying Popular Music*. Milton Keynes: Open University Press.

Phinney, Kevin (2005). *Souled America: How Black Music Transformed White Culture*. New York: Billboard Books.

Rose, Tricia (1994). *Black Noise: Rap Music and Black Culture in Contemporary America*. Middletown: Wesleyan University Press.

Rozzo, Mark (2011). 'Nik Cohn's Fever Dream', *The New York Times Magazine*, 2 December. http://www.nytimes.com/2011/12/04/magazine/nik-cohn-fever-dream .html?_r=0 (accessed 5 April 2017).

Sandbrook, Dominic (2005). *Never Had It So Good: A History of Britain from Suez to the Beatles*. London: Little, Brown.

Sandbrook, Dominic (2006). *White Heat: A History of Britain in the Swinging Sixties*. London: Little, Brown.

Simonelli, David (2013). *Working Class Heroes: Rock Music and British Society in the 1960s and 1970s*. Lanham: Lexington Books.

Stratton, Jon and Nabil Zuberi (2014). *Black Popular Music in Britain since 1945*. Farnham: Ashgate.

Whitney, Karl (2016). 'Nik Cohn: "I was Right, the Stones, after the Age of 30, Didn't Create Anything Good"', *The Irish Times*, 21 January. https://www.irishtimes.com/ culture/books/nik-cohn-i-was-right-the-stones-after-the-age-of-30-didn-t-create -anything-good-1.2505387.

Wiseman-Trowse, Nathan (2008). *Performing Class in British Popular Music*. London: Palgrave Macmillan UK.

Part 2

Every Day I Write the Book

6

All the years combine

Digital media, the Grateful Dead archive and the wheel of time

M. Cooper Harriss

In his 'Letter from a Latter-Day Fan', Jacob A. Cohen describes the experience of downloading and listening to 'the only [Grateful] Dead show I ever went to':

> This is the first time, thirteen years later, that I've heard this music again. I don't know why, but something about it is just so incredibly meaningful for me – and it brings up so much sentiment for a band that, on a daily basis, does not always elicit that degree of emotion from me. . . . Jerry [Garcia] sings 'nothing's gonna bring him back' over and over again during a vocal jam at the end of 'He's Gone'. But he's wrong. Hearing 29 September 1994 again, a show that some dismiss as just another example of how the band was barely a sliver of its former glory by then, a show that most people would write off as any other '94 show, *has* brought him – them – back, and in a profound and deeply meaningful way. The music never stops. (Cohen 2012: 303)

While he does not specify, Cohen almost certainly downloaded this show from the *Internet Archive* database – an online repository that, alongside other collections, carries as its crown jewel nearly 17,000 different recordings of the roughly 2,300 concerts that the Grateful Dead performed during a touring career that spanned from 1965 to 1995. In keeping with the band's tolerance, and later sanction, of the recording and free distribution of their music on audiocassette and DAT, streams and (to a more limited extent) downloads of this music are available to anyone with an internet connection.[1] Still, the process of navigating this archive can prove tricky. One can execute and toggle rudimentary search

---

[1] There is some disagreement about how 'welcome' tapers were over the long haul of the Dead's career. Peter Richardson asserts that Jerry Garcia 'acknowledged his own affinity with the tapers' while

results, but with multiple recordings of every show, from a myriad of sources (including, in some cases, the band's own soundboard), the interface is not intuitive. Paired with the sheer mass of its contents, even the seasoned Deadhead or critic faces a learning curve.

In recent years a variety of digital tools have emerged that seek to systemize for listeners the Dead's massive archive. This chapter profiles three of them as varieties of 'writing' about rock and roll: the 'Grateful Dead of the Day' website and especially its Facebook group page, SiriusXM satellite radio's 'Today in Grateful Dead History' programme and the Deadsound iPhone application. It will discern the ways that these digital platforms organize and make sense of the archive and theorize these attempts as narratives of digital media. By 'archive' I refer to the *Internet Archive* collection of the Dead's recordings as a synecdoche for the broader excess of the band's recorded live production, which represents its metaphorical archive. Both uses denote a literal and/or metaphorical repository that these digital sources organize and narrate, using digital rhetoric to build a poetics of what one scholar calls the Dead's 'liveness' (Flory 2019). This liveness situates individual shows within a more manageable and meaningful temporal frame that enables fans, critics and other *Internet Archive* users like Jacob A. Cohen to experience the band, archivally, both now *and* then, bringing the Dead back 'in a profound and meaningful way'.

The Grateful Dead and their music are no strangers to digital media. The band were denizens of Silicon Valley before there ever was such a thing. Jerry Garcia was an early adapter of Musical Instrument Digital Interface technology, which he used to alter and synthesize the sound of his guitar in concert at least as early as 1989 (McNally 2007: 517). Bassist Phil Lesh, along with Garcia and drummer Mickey Hart, was a collaborator on Ned Lagin's electronic composition *Seastones*, which uses computers and synthesizers and was occasionally performed during Dead concerts in 1974 (McNally 2007: 474, 486–7). Lyricist (and official non-performing band member) John Perry Barlow was an important figure in the early days of the internet and pioneered advocacy of free speech for it that remains influential, for better and worse, to this day (Barlow 2018). Finally, the Usenet group rec.music.gdead provided a home for online Dead discussions and community exchange as early as the late 1980s, and Garcia's death in 1995 has been credited with inaugurating a new internet age of public mourning,

---

Peter Conners paints a less sanguine picture, noting that band members grudgingly went along with it until they officially sanctioned taping in 1984. See Richardson (2014: 221) and Conners (2017: 40).

deploying this then-nascent medium as a site of digital memorialization and catharsis.[2] In this way, though I focus on more recent iterations of the Grateful Dead's digital mediation, this is also an old, old story, an aspect of 'new-meets-old' that has become such a trope of Dead lore. The three digital sources profiled here all bear a similar function to one another, with key differences that depend both on their specific media and the audiences they serve. After profiling each one, I'll discuss them together, focusing especially on the digital narratives they create, how understanding their digital poetics generates these narratives as a mode of world-building and what all of this has to do with framing these experiences as a phenomenon of time, a digital mode that replicates a life both day by day, and as an ongoing cycle.

Three ways of listening to the Grateful Dead

'Grateful Dead of the Day' is a website that commemorates, daily, a year's worth of what it calls the 'best' available show performed on that very day. Its facilitators admit that their criteria are idiosyncratic, drawing on 'some combination of the most interesting, highest quality, [and] historically significant.'[3] The site's Facebook page delivers this daily dose, embedding from the *Internet Archive* a stream of the day's chosen show with an accompanying write-up. Significantly, the write-up itself assumes the rhetorical character of an anonymous Deadhead, serving as a digital guide who speaks in a hyperbolic set of phrases that confer a degree of splendidness upon choice sections of the day's best show. One might call this vernacular 'Dead-ese', a version of what Natalie Dollar (1999) calls the 'show talk' of Dead concerts. These concerts themselves represent a 'speech situation', according to Dollar. Consider this missive from 4 February 2023, referring to the concert performed exactly fifty-four years earlier:

> On this day back in 1969, the Dead played an off the hook show at the Music Box in Omaha as they made their way through the Midwest, churning through an eight-concerts-in-seven-days stretch. If anything, though, the hard traveling and long hours on stage seemed to have melded the Dead into even more of a seething, mind-melting, psychedelic steamroller of a band than

---

[2] For more on the rise of online connectivity of Dead groups and the use of such 'communications technology' for building community, see Adams (2000: 35–6). For online mourning of Garcia and the nascent Internet, see Adams (1998).

[3] http://gratefuldeadoftheday.com/about-grateful-dead-day

usual. And this show, with its classic Dark Star> Stephen> Eleven and massive, hallucinogenic Caution, to say nothing of the Schoolgirl and Other One Suite, is, quite arguably, the best of the tour. Listen to the whole show at Grateful Dead of the Day.

By virtue of its dissemination on social media, 'friends' of the site take the opportunity to weigh in: 'Completley [*sic*] Sacred Sound!! Good ole Grateful 69!!! NFA!!', writes one respondent, deploying a common phrase among the site's users, 'Sacred Sound', to identify a particularly moving performance (here 'NFA', or a cover of Buddy Holly's 'Not Fade Away'). Another respondent assesses individual performances while also situating himself in the world at the time of the concert: 'The Dark Star>St Stephen > The Eleven is amazing but it's the Death don't have no Mercy and the Other One that kill it . . . I was 12 when played.' Elsewhere respondents deploy other common phrases that pass as currency in the site's posts and replies alike. Concerning 10 January 1979 (posted on that day in 2023), one respondent writes: 'I was at this one . . . Face melter', which another respondent both affirms and doubles-down on: 'Absolute face melter'. Still others reply with the shorthand 'IWT' or 'I was there'. Users of the Facebook page experience a sense of 'being there', either through the listening experience, which can be mapped temporally onto the anniversary day, *and* through claims that locate their physical presence (singly and among a community of listeners/users) many years ago. Doing so enacts a kind of simultaneity in the act of listening, a link between then and now that is also consecutive, moving both horizontally (from day to day across the year) and vertically (through the years on a given day). We consider the workings of this temporal orientation more fully below.

A second example, 'Today in Grateful Dead History', broadcast on the Grateful Dead Channel on Sirius XM satellite radio, while bearing a similar premise to the Facebook page, differs in its deployment of a purely aural medium and in the way it values more diversity over time. The programme's host, official Grateful Dead archivist David Lemieux (the channel is affiliated with the band), frequently mentions his desire to cover as much different music as he can from year to year, jettisoning specific claims to something being the 'best', even if he frequently expresses deep appreciation for what he calls, like a classical music DJ, 'the piece of music' that he presents on a given day. On the rare dates the band never played (9 and 19 January, 29 February, 9 August and 25 December), Lemieux will select something from a proximate date or simply play something from a wholly different time, often from a summer or autumn date that has a surplus of available material.

In keeping with his job as the band's official archivist, Lemieux takes on a curatorial role. An individual episode usually clocks in at around 45 minutes in duration, though it can be shorter or longer, occasionally presenting an entire first set or even spotlighting the performance of one song (like 'Dark Star', which frequently clocks in at more than 30 minutes in length). More often, Lemieux presents an excerpt. Second set material will often dissolve into the beginning of 'Drums' (the extended percussion break at the centre of the second set that became standard later in the band's career) or emerges from the final notes of 'Space' (the extended free improvisation that flows from 'Drums'). Occasionally Lemieux will feature a deep dive into an entire concert over two or three days. Most trenchant to Lemieux's curation is the context that he offers. Affable, yet deeply knowledgeable and using a minimal amount of non-ironic Dead-ese, he presents each featured show as part of a larger legacy – part of a discrete tour or taking place near some important milestone for the band. He frequently spotlights a venue's character or the band's history in a certain city. An active Deadhead himself in the 1980s and 1990s, he draws on his own experiences as a taper and collector of recordings who often followed the band and, when not on tour, took part in the social networks for disseminating the music that Dead fans developed well before the ubiquity of the internet.

Lemieux and his show play important roles in the daily programming of the Grateful Dead channel on satellite radio. A typical hour on the station will feature (seemingly at random, though no doubt there is logic geared towards variability) a handful of live and studio versions of Dead performances from across the band's career, as well as work from solo projects and associated post-Garcia iterations of the band. Done this way, the effect can orient the listener to a broader sense of coherence. Even the full concerts broadcast three times every 24 hours bear little evident logic behind their selection and presentation and provide minimal listening guidance of the sort that 'Today in Grateful Dead History' provides.[4] In this way Lemieux offers an import tether of the band's music to a credible historical narrative.

---

[4] The full concerts do cycle through the three possible timeslots in a predictable order, but these repetitions come more than 50 hours apart and take place at off hours. The lack of contextual information offered about these shows may be for a good reason, seeking to replicate the experience of attending a show where one doesn't know what will be played and in what order – a hallmark of the Dead concert experience.

The Deadsound application for iPhone provides a searchable interface that one Substack author calls 'my Dead-specific interface of choice for searching and navigating Archive' (Connell 2023). Deadsound's search functions improve on the *Internet Archive*'s own, allowing a user to view and select from a comprehensive list of songs performed, by year, and even by which band members participate in a performance. In this way one who wants to find, for instance, concerts featuring Bruce Hornsby (a sometime member of the band between 1990 and 1992), can search the *Internet Archive* via the app, using his name as a preset filter.[5] Of greatest significance for our present purposes, a user's home screen on the application contains a section (not directly related to Lemieux's satellite radio programme of the same name) called 'Today in Grateful Dead History'. This feature allows one to swipe through a complete offering of concerts from that same date, taken from across the band's career. As I write on 2 March 2023, for instance, I am offered *Internet Archive* audio for concerts from 2 March in 1969, 1981, 1987 and 1992. The list also acknowledges shows from 2 March in 1966, 1968 and 1983 for which there are 'no tapes circulating on Archive.org'. Finally, the Deadsound application also includes curated sections such as a list of the 'top five' concerts from each year, sourced from DeadBase.com (with no additional criteria provided). DeadBase is a now defunct site whose final iteration from 2012 is presently mirrored on a different URL. Finally, Deadsound points a user to important concert milestones such as '1970s Original Song Debuts' and the like.

In many ways the Deadsound application represents a self-help tool. It makes navigating the *Internet Archive* less daunting. Its interface is both prescriptive (as with the suggested shows from the present day) and curatorial (as with the Deadsound Features lists), cultivating a user's potential experience while also leaving margins for search and discovery. Perhaps most importantly in this regard, the application provides a place, 'My Stash', where a listener can file and save concerts they enjoy or want to hear for the first time and may wish to listen to (again) at a later juncture – curating their own collection of meaningful shows. As a 'stash', this self-curated function deploys 'Dead-ese', with a wink to what a Deadhead may refer to as a 'stash' of drugs.

---

[5] A long-time friend of the band, Hornsby joined officially following the death of keyboardist Brent Mydland in 1990. Given that Hornsby's own solo career was ascendant at the time, he played with the Dead only sporadically between 1990 and 1992, bringing piano and accordion to supplement new keyboardist Vince Welnick's organ (McNally 2007: 584f).

Digital culture

Having described the nature and function of the three digital texts above, I now want to think about how they work, about purposes that they serve by writing, inscribing, a set of possible experiences made possible by their emerging media. What are the contours of their utility for ongoing engagement with the band, their music and the communities that embrace them? Here we'll situate our three examples in the context of digital media studies, aiming to provide a more sophisticated conceptual framework for thinking with these digital interfaces to the Dead and their archive. Digital media studies, while a more recent arrival in academic discourse, has grown quickly and cannot be dealt with here with any measure of fullness. For this reason, I focus on three aspects for organizing the present case: the category of 'archive', digital narrative and the digital poetics of this narrative that engage in modes of world creation. We'll begin with a brief discussion of these three categories before applying them to a reading of how they illuminate these representations of the Dead's digital footprint as important commentary on the narrative experiences of time.

Archives are notoriously recalcitrant. They give and they take away. They shout and remain silent. Their organization can be provisional, dependent on a variety of factors. Saidiya Hartman, for instance, writes of the 'limits [the archive] sets on what can be known, whose perspective matters, and who is endowed with the gravity and authority of historical actor' (Hartman 2019: xiii). Archives themselves, on this reading, are inherently narratival because they reflect the motives behind the very retention of what they contain as well as the curatorial impulses of those who oversee this retention. However unmanageable the Dead's *Internet Archive* section may seem, the fact that it exists and persists in this prodigious state endows it with a kind of authority and *gravitas* that few other bands possess.

Writing a couple of decades before Hartman, Lev Manovich stakes a different claim in his early landmark efforts to theorize nascent digital media – especially as he considers databases as digital archives. For Manovich, databases stand at odds with narrative. Indeed, the two are 'natural enemies'. As 'new media objects' they tell no stories; they lack a 'beginning' and 'end': '[I]n fact, they do not have any development, thematically, formally, or otherwise, that would organize their elements into a sequence. Instead, they are collections of individual items, with every item possessing the same significance as any other' (Manovich 2001: 218). Viewed in light of Hartman, Manovich seems short-sighted. Databases, after all, must be populated with information, and information is never neutral. At the same time, his claims may seem practically true for one who seeks to parse an undifferentiated archive like the Dead's. In this way, he gets at something like the vertiginous experience of confronting a mass of data and the need to make sense of it. For our purposes, we'll point to the seventeen thousand entries in the Dead's corner of the *Internet Archive*. They are labelled. We have a digital finding aid in the form of a rudimentary search function that includes dates, venues, set-lists and audio sources. Still, the task of differentiation remains. What is more, the task of making meaning out of this mass of information, which is the function of such differentiation, remains.

This mode of differentiation and the meaning that it generates model what Douglas Eyman calls digital 'invention', which offers a 'process of discovery' that locates extant digital materials for the purpose of creating 'new digital forms' (Eyman 2015: 66). Thus: 'Invention, as a function of digital rhetoric, includes the searching and negotiation of networks of information, seeking those materials best suited to creating persuasive works, as well as knowing which semiotic resources to address and draw upon (aural, visual, textual, hypertextual) and what technological tools are best suited to working with those resources' (66). This invention doesn't just interact, then, with archives but also with other users of these archives (67). In this way, our three digital media examples, profiled above, qualify as digital inventions and participate in that inventive process. They interact with the archive, negotiating its fullness to create persuasive narrative claims that may be mediated for and disseminated to other users. By focusing on music, they do so aurally, to be sure, but each medium also does so in the other ways that Eyman cites – through written accounts, images and hyperlinks to further information and related materials. While Lemieux's radio programme proves more limited in this regard, he still takes to Twitter and posts videos to Dead.net – the Grateful Dead's official website – to supplement this aural experience with links, images and texts.

With digital inventions charged with standing between the archive and other users, our examples take on a narrative function. Daniel Punday notes the historical proximity of the emergence of digital media and the rise of narratology as related modes of 'thinking about the nature of story and meaning' (Punday 2019: 9, see also 8 and 11). In other words, digital media don't just invent meaning and tell stories. They reflect on the meaning and technique of such narrative acts. Paul Frosh extends this point, noting that the story and meaning at the heart of digital media contribute creatively to their poetics: 'They perform poesis; they bring forth worlds into presence, producing and revealing them. . . . [They] do this not just through representing worlds, imaginary or otherwise, but by connecting us to worlds beyond our immediate physical perception' (Frosh 2019: 2). This duality of not only representing a world but of also connecting a user to another world surfaces in Jacob A. Cohen's sense not just of hearing his first show again, but also of being brought into the presence of Garcia and the band, across time, 'in a profound and deeply meaningful way'. Such poetics collapse time.

Time will tell

With these concepts well in mind, it makes sense to return to our examples detailed above. All three refer to and seek in some way to encode meaning on, and through, the Dead archive (as manifest in and represented by the *Internet Archive*). In this way they qualify as narrative. A follower of the 'Grateful Dead of the Day' on Facebook will, between 1 January and 31 December of any given year, encounter a narrative of the Dead's career organized according to the site's own criteria (and narrated in Dead-ese). Lemieux's anecdotes and deep dives also curate a daily narrative of the band and its fans that is sustained not over a single year, but over several years as Lemieux resists, but ultimately cannot escape, repetition. Deadsound, too, helps a user develop their own account of the *Internet Archive* by drawing on experience and preconceived predilections for the purpose of curating a 'stash'. All three do this through multimedia options that give shape to a kind of orderly narrative account. At the same time, by reflecting directly on these narratives, they enact poesis, they create worlds, by connecting users with archival material in meaningful and subjective ways that create immediacy within the prodigious accumulation of a thirty-year archive.

In this way, the problem of time becomes inextricable from the digital worlds that these three examples create in the poesis of the narratives that they inscribe. Each of them works through a chronological sense of time, one that is sequential, horizontal, as it moves from point to point, emplotting motion from past to future through a perpetual present tense of a given 'today' in the history of the band. At the same time this 'today' represents its own phenomenon consistently repeated in some fashion over the course of thirty years. It is, then, informed by the ongoing cyclical nature of chronological time. It is the phenomenology of this recursive moment that allows one to see this other aspect of Frosh's poetics, described above – the temporal verticality of years piled upon years that unites a contemporary moment with a set of other, related, horizontal moments.

In *Time and Narrative*, Paul Ricoeur takes up what he calls 'the *aporia* of time' – a problem organized around the question of whether time is time linear or cyclical (Ricoeur 1983: 7–16). He insists that time is both, that it flows from the past, through the present, into the future, *and* functions in terms of 'periodicity' – marked by the rhythms of ritual that matter in the way they repeat time and again like an anniversary or, for our purposes, a New Year's Eve show in the Bay Area or a Fall tour (Ricoeur 1990: 111). All three of our examples above exhibit something of this problem of time: they move from day to day (all of them mark specific days in horizontal progression) and yet they also derive meaning from a vertical sense of repetition. The Facebook group cycles the same set of shows every year. Lemieux wishes to avoid direct repetition but actively notes the recursive rhythms of the Dead's career. Deadsound takes a day and places this repetition, these anniversaries, literally side by side in the interface.

Ricoeur's solution to this problem of time posits both the linear and cyclical varieties not to work at cross purposes, but to function simultaneously. They are held together in what he calls a 'poetics of narrative', the world that is created through the common recourse to linear and cyclical time (Ricoeur 1990: 109). By extension we can understand our representative digital narratives, then, to emerge from a similar accounting of time, from the attempt to hold these different aspects together as a narrative that inscribes meaning and order on the vast undifferentiated archive. To use or participate in these digital narratives is to experience them both as they happen and as they relate to a sense of past and future.

This may be the last time (I don't know)

In closing, these three narratives of digital media qualify so thoroughly *as* narratives for the way they blend conceptions of time as Ricoeur sets them out. Days pass, we may mark the anniversaries of different shows moving day by day through the calendar. And yet – these concerts, in their repetition, as phenomena that the archive makes available for narration, do so much more. They invoke and enact a past event in the present tense. In navigating this phenomenon, fans may deploy Dead-ese to account for the 'face melting' experience of listening; they participate in following Lemieux around North America and Europe as a latter-day Deadhead; they search for and preserve important moments that transcend the timeline. With Joshua A. Cohen, 29 September 1994 (like 1 October 1977 or 31 December 1969, or like any other of the nearly 2,300 dates preserved through some 17,000 recordings) represents one in a sequence of thousands. And yet it does so much more. It bends and replicates time. It relates a narrative that resurrects and invokes the band's presence within an ongoing present even when long gone. This presence can be achieved as a solitary experience, but mediated digitally it can situate listeners more fully and phenomenologically in the broader social networks invoked by historical concert experiences made present.

The old Gullah song 'Turtle Dove' was performed five times by the Jerry Garcia Band, and only once by the Grateful Dead (according to Deadsound). All of the performances date to late 1987. In this song the singer claims that 'My name is written on David's line.' This line, an emplotment leading from King David and the Hebrew Bible through Jesus (the 'Son of David' (Matt. 1.1) of the 'House of David' (Luke 1.27)), yokes any present singer of the song in real time to a grand lineage of the faithful. The lyric is also cyclical, repeated twice again before it resolves with a rhyme. The third instance goes like this: 'My name is written on David's line / I'm going home on the wheel of time.' This pairing of time as both linear and cyclical, a genealogy and a wheel, consistently renews the past as it mediates an archive of meaningful data. In this way it marks both the singer (and all who sing along) as both descendants of and ongoing participants in the world created by the song's poesis. This is what Jacob A. Cohen describes in the experience of hearing again the audio of 29 September 1994 – his only Dead show. He understands it as one of many in a long line of concerts available to him in a vast archive. At the same time the experience of listening to this one, and our three examples cultivate this experience more broadly across the archive, throughout the year, places him on the wheel of time. The band is present, resurrected, even if only for a moment, written as it were in the ones and zeros that encode this artefact.

References

Adams, Rebecca G. (1998). 'Inciting Sociological Thought by Studying the Deadhead Community: Engaging Publics in Dialogue', *Social Forces* 77(1): 1–25.

Adams, Rebecca G. (2000). '"What Goes Around, Comes Around": Collaborative Research and Learning', in Rebecca G. Adams and Robert Sardiello (eds), *Deadhead*

Social Science: You Ain't Gonna Learn What You Don't Want to Know, New York: Altamira.

Barlow, John Perry and Robert Greenfield (2018). *Mother American Night: My Life in Crazy Times*. New York: Crown Archetype.

Cohen, Jacob A. (2012). 'Tapes and Memories: A Letter from a Latter-Day Fan', in Nicholas G. Meriwether (ed.), *Reading the Grateful Dead: A Critical Survey*, Lanham: Scarecrow Press.

Connell, Dave (2023). 'Right Outside the Lazy Gate', *The Die Must Fall* (Substack Email of 19 February).

Conners, Peter (2017). *Cornell '77: The Music, the Myth, and the Magnificence of the Grateful Dead's Concert at Barton Hall*. Ithaca: Cornell University Press.

Dollar, Natalie (1999). 'Understanding "Show" as a Deadhead Speech Situation', in Robert G. Weiner (ed.), *Perspectives on the Grateful Dead: Critical Writings*, Westport: Greenwood Press.

Eyman, Douglas (2015). *Digital Rhetoric: Theory, Method, Practice*. Ann Arbor: University of Michigan Press.

Flory, Andrew (2019). 'Liveness and the Grateful Dead', *American Music* 37(2): 123–45.

Frosh, Paul (2019). *The Poetics of Digital Media*. Medford: Polity.

Hartman, Saidiya (2019). *Wayward Lives, Beautiful Experiments: Intimate Histories of Riotous Black Girls, Troublesome Women, and Queer Radicals*. New York: Norton.

Manovich, Lev (2001). *The Language of New Media*. Cambridge, MA: MIT Press.

McNally, Dennis (2007). *Long Strange Trip: The Inside History of the Grateful Dead*. New York: Crown.

Punday, Daniel (2019). *Playing at Narratology: Digital Media as Narrative Theory*. Columbus: Ohio State University Press.

Richardson, Peter (2014). *No Simple Highway: A Cultural History of the Grateful Dead*. New York: St. Martins.

Ricoeur, Paul (1983) *Time and Narrative*. Vol. 1. Trans. Kathleen McLaughlin and David Pellauer. Chicago: University of Chicago Press (1984).

Ricoeur, Paul (1985). *Time and Narrative*. Vol. 3. Trans. Kathleen Blamey and David Pellauer. Chicago: University of Chicago Press (1988).

Ricoeur, Paul (1990). *Soi-même comme un autre*. Paris: Seuil.

7

'I obliterate myself in song'

Music, selfhood and discovery in YA fiction

Ben Screech

In *Nick and Norah's Infinite Playlist* (2006), the titular character Nick discusses his desire to 'obliterate myself in song' (Cohn and Levithan 2006: 23). Characters' experiences with music in literature for (and about) young people are also, however, as much about *finding* oneself – locating a sense of identity and belonging in a phase of life fraught with change and transition – as about Nick's identified need to *escape* selfhood. With this in mind, through exploring a range of contemporary texts, this chapter aims to consider the representation of rock and pop music in YA fiction, as it exists in relation to emerging notions of selfhood, identity and belonging.

There is a long-standing interdisciplinary connection between literature and music. 'All art aspires towards the condition of music' (Pater 2010: 129), Walter Pater believed. Throughout the centuries, artists and writers have attested to the potent impact of music on their work, as an art form that can touch on the most visceral aspects of the human experience. YA fiction specifically has a long history of engagement with music. An early example of this can be seen in S. E. Hinton's *The Outsiders* (1967), generally considered to be a 'touchstone' text in the establishment of the YA genre. The book centres on two teenage 'outsider' subcultures named the 'Socs' and 'Greasers' (Hinton 1967: 3). Their mutual love of Mustang cars, gang fights and drive-in movies is only surpassed by their devotion to rock and roll music. For the Socs, the group of choice is the Beatles, whereas the Greasers favour Elvis Presley. This demonstrates the ubiquity of musical preference to 'ingroup' belonging, something that the texts explored in this chapter habitually make reference to.

A diverse variety of YA novels have since been published in both the UK and the United States in the contemporary period that demonstrate the role of music as a formative element in adolescent characters' lives. These include works such as Rachel Cohn and David Levithan's *Nick and Norah's Infinite Playlist* (2006), Stephen Chbosky's *The Perks of Being a Wallflower* (1999), Hayley Long's *Fire and Water* (2004), Melvyn Burgess's *Kill All Enemies* (2011) and Frank Portman's *King Dork* (2006), to name just a few. These primary texts portray characters making musical discoveries, relating specific songs to an emerging and evolving sense of self and using music as a means by which to foster communication and engagement with others, for example, through playing in bands and the giving and receiving of mixtapes.

'Sex and drugs and rock and roll', Ian Dury proclaimed in his 1977 single, 'are all my brain and body need' (Dury 1977). These three interrelated components are integral to YA fiction focusing on characters' musical experiences, to the degree that the lyric could almost be interpreted as a mantra for such texts. Perhaps because literature is primarily interested in the representation of formative human experiences (and arguably YA literature is particularly concerned with this), it is little surprise that such 'limit experiences', to use Michel Foucault's phraseology (Foucault 2002: 248), play such a key role in YA narratives of adolescence.

For example, while Hinton's *The Outsiders* demonstrates the ever-present alliance between popular music and adolescence, originally forged in mid-twentieth-century America, more recent books such as Melvin Burgess's controversial Carnegie Medal-winning novel *Junk* (1998) explore the drug use prevalent in the 1980s UK punk scene. Sub-genres of music are notable here because it is often through these that, as suggested previously, teenage characters are depicted locating what the sociologist Henri Tajfel terms 'ingroup' (Tajfel 2010: 338) belonging. This, for example, is explored particularly effectively in Philana Bole's novel *Glitz* (2011), about an African-American teenager's search for 'her people' in her hometown's underground hip-hop community. It is also a crucial aspect of *Nick and Norah's Infinite Playlist*, in which Nick realizes that participation in a musical scene through dancing, listening to and playing music, results in becoming what he terms: 'this one flailing paramecium mass, fever connected' (Cohn and Levithan 2006: 23). The cultural historian Magdalena Waligorska also attests to the way that 'purchasing, listening to and dancing to music implies a profound sense of belonging to and participation in the creation of a scene, subculture, culture, or imagined community' (Waligorska

2013: 6). This is the situation we see occurring consistently in this chapter's primary texts.

Stephen Chbosky's *The Perks of Being a Wallflower*, written and set in the late 1990s, is a good place to start considering the role of music in YA fiction. Music arises regularly in this novel and plays a key role in the character development of its protagonist, Charlie. An epistolary text, the narrative is comprised of a series of letters written to an unknown recipient. In these, Charlie recounts his freshman year of high school and in particular, his initial feelings of being an outsider in this setting. He eventually befriends Sam and Patrick who are similarly marginalized, but have learnt to revel in their otherness, scornfully defining themselves against the more popular high-school cliques – predictably, the athletes.

In addition to joyriding in cars on the freeway and smoking marijuana, Charlie, Sam and Patrick's favourite activity is listening to and sharing music. Charlie's favourite song is *Asleep* (1986) by the Smiths. The track itself is noteworthy because of its lyrics focusing on discovery and escape ('there is another world / there is a better world' (Marr and Morrissey 1986)), themselves central concerns in this book. However, as the novel progresses, Charlie's friends also introduce him to other bands, such as Nirvana and Smashing Pumpkins, as well as singer-songwriters like Suzanne Vega whose records often speak for the dispossessed, in addition to the insular, melancholic Nick Drake. At one point in the novel, Charlie decides to create a mixtape for his friend Patrick's Christmas present. He begins by describing its contents:

> The present is going to be a mixtape. I just know that it should. I already have the songs picked. It has *Smells Like Teen Spirit* by Nirvana, *Asleep* by the Smiths, *Vapour Trail* by Ride, *Scarborough Fair* by Simon and Garfunkel, *A Whiter Shade of Pale* by Procol Harum, *Time of No Reply* by Nick Drake, *Dear Prudence* by the Beatles, *Gypsy* by Suzanne Vega, *Landslide* by Fleetwood Mac, and finally . . . *Asleep* by the Smiths (again!) I hope it's the kind Patrick can listen to whenever he drives alone and feel like he belongs to something when he's sad. (Chbosky 2010: 61)

Subsequently, Charlie explains what the process of making the mixtape has taught him about music itself:

> I had an amazing feeling when I finally held the tape in my hand. I just thought to myself that in the palm of my hand, there was this one tape that had all of these memories and feelings and great joy and sadness. Right there in the palm

of my hand. And I thought about how many people have loved those songs. And how many people got through a lot of bad times because of those songs. (Chbosky 2010: 62)

Music, as Charlie observes, is strongly associated with one's emotional state. It is an accompaniment on life's journey and also functions in the novel to underscore the '*bildungsroman*' or 'coming-of-age' nature of his narrative. Music is also, as Charlie indicates in the first extract, associated with 'belonging' and an erasure of otherness.

However, we might ask, is this character simply falling victim to music's attractively visceral, escapist virtues? With this in mind, it is perhaps notable that the criticisms that have been made of both YA fiction and popular genres of music are similar. They centre on the argument that both are inherently frivolous, disposable or escapist forms, in contrast to 'weightier' more established forms of music, such as that stemming from the classical tradition, or what is ambiguously defined, from the perspective of children's literature studies, as the 'adult novel' (Hill 2014: 15).

Proponents of both art forms argue contrary to this, however. For example, Radiohead frontman Thom Yorke explains his conviction that: 'I've never believed pop music is escapist trash' (qtd. in Uitti 2022). I suggest that the same could be said for YA, a genre which is far too frequently 'written off' by the literary establishment for similar reasons as mentioned before, but which nevertheless produces some of the most consistently challenging and 'dark' works in the contemporary literary canon. These include early examples of the genre, such as the early example of YA, *Catcher in the Rye* (1951), to more recent texts such as Kevin Brooks's award-winning *The Bunker Diary* (2013) which harrowingly portrays a teenager's abduction and subsequent incarceration by his captor. This point is also attested to each year through the presentation of major literary awards (such as the Carnegie Medal in the UK and Printz prize in the United States) for the year's most mature and compelling examples of writing for young people.

Despite being set in the previous decade (the 1980s), Rainbow Rowell's *Eleanor and Park* (2012) shares common ground with *The Perks of Being a Wallflower*. Both novels focus on misfits and their attempt to navigate the rocky terrain of high school. Both texts also examine burgeoning romantic relationships. In *The Perks of Being a Wallflower* this plays out between the secondary characters, notably in terms of a calamitous gay relationship between Patrick and closeted athlete, Brad. In the eponymously titled *Eleanor and Park* it is the central characters who discover their romantic attraction early in the novel, and its development is chronicled throughout the text.

The narration shifts between both Eleanor and Park's perspectives, and their courtship is mostly conducted with headphones on, because as Eleanor explains 'where there was a Walkman, there was the possibility of music' (Rowell 2012: 13). Ultimately, Rowell depicts music as being, not just a shared interest, but a crucial means of relationship enablement between Eleanor and Park. Like Charlie in *The Perks of Being a Wallflower*, Park makes Eleanor a mixtape. The chapter in the novel in which she is described receiving and listening to the tape is noteworthy because of the way Rowell explores the notion of music as not only existing as an auditory experience, but a physical one too:

> She had Park's songs in her head – and in her chest, somehow. There was something about the music on that tape. It felt different. Like, it set her lungs and her stomach on edge. There was something exciting about it, and something nervous. It made Eleanor feel like everything, like the world, wasn't what she'd thought it was. (Rowell 2012: 57)

In addition, as Park comments later, music, if it is about anything, is about connection; about 'feeling something'. Often, as Eleanor discovers, such a 'connection' with a song is reliant on sustained and repeated listening.

> She felt like someone was hooking her insides out through her chest. 'It was awesome. I didn't want to stop listening. That one song – is it *"Love Will Tear Us Apart"*?' 'Yeah, Joy Division.' 'Oh my God, that's the best beginning to a song ever. I just want to listen to those three seconds over and over.' (Rowell 2014: 103)

Wishing to reciprocate, Eleanor finds herself struggling with what tracks to choose to make as significant an impact on Park, as his tape has had on her:

> She flipped through the records matter-of-factly, on a mission. Looking for *Rubber Soul* and *Revolver*. It seemed as if she would never be able to give Park anything like what he'd given her. It was like he dumped all this treasure on her without even thinking about it, without any sense of what it was worth. She couldn't repay him. She couldn't even appropriately thank him. How can you thank someone for the Cure? Or the X-Men? Sometimes it felt like she'd always be in his debt. And then she realized that Park didn't know about the Beatles. (Rowell 2014: 181)

For Eleanor here then, music becomes a kind of currency, in which extraordinary tracks or bands the recipient has not yet discovered are particularly valuable. It becomes what the literary theorist Paul Hernadi terms a 'cultural transaction' (2019: 46).

Notably too, such a 'transaction' may even take on an extra-textual dimension, for example, when it is innovatively extended to the recipients of the authors' acknowledgements in *Nick and Norah's Infinite Playlist*. Here, Rachel Cohn and David Levithan attribute a personally chosen track to each of the sixteen individuals who inspired and supported the creation of this novel (2006: 191).

British YA author Hayley Long prefaces her novel *Fire and Water* (2004) with an affectionate nod to a setting also indicative of music's 'transactional' nature, the record shop. The book is dedicated to an Aberystwyth record store called 'Music Warehouse' which she frequented as an adolescent and which, she laments, 'intrigued her for over a decade but is sadly now boarded up' (Long 2004: v). Such was the unfortunate fate of many independent record shops after the internet/digital boom, when music became more freely available online. Nevertheless, record shops still hold pride of place in many people's nostalgic reflections of teenage musical discovery, and this is certainly the case in *Fire and Water*. In the novel, twenty-something Ally attempts to pass the time during a long train journey, while reflecting on her decision to collect vinyl albums as a teenager. She describes the first record shop she ever enters as being 'like her own Pandora's box' (Long 2004: 35) in terms of the atmosphere of mystery and opportunity it exuded.

However, it is initially the radio that has the most direct influence on Ally's choice of listening material. Specifically, she describes the selections the BBC Radio 1 DJ Annie Nightingale plays on her Sunday Request Show:

> I sat and listened and listened and then I began to make some lists in a notebook. The Undertones. The Doors. Lloyd Cole. The Damned. I soon had a whole book filled with information like:
>
> '*Stories of Johnny*', Marc Almond – released 1985 – played by Annie at 8:17 on 8th March 1987.
> '*She's not there*', The Zombies – released 1964 – first track played by Annie on 26th April 1987.
> '*Fire and Water*' by Free (a very very good record!) – taken from the 1970 album of the same name, never released as a single (tragically) – played by Annie at 8:42, 3rd May 1987. (Long 2004: 5)

BBC Radio 1, the teenage radio station *writ large* has consistently influenced teenage musical taste in the UK, its DJs playing a selection of mostly contemporary rock and pop music, which historically, along with the so-called pirate radio stations such as Radio Caroline and Luxembourg that preceded it, was renowned for its rebellious, edgy and somehow slightly illicit mood. Radio 1 is also notable for being one of the few non-commercial stations to continue playing vinyl records even when other musical mediums (such as the cassette tape and compact disc) rendered them obsolete. In this way, the station has contributed to the ideal of vinyl as the original, best and certainly *coolest* way of listening to and experiencing music. This has been particularly evident in recent times, with the BBC reporting in 2017 that vinyl sales were the highest they had been for twenty-five years (Sillito 2017). Indeed, as Ally comments in *Fire and Water*, 'when CDs came along, everybody said that vinyl was dead. They were so wrong' (Long 2004: 5).

In addition to being a YA author, Hayley Long is also a music collector and DJ. I was lucky enough to interview her for *VOYA Magazine* to discuss the role of music in her life and writing:

> Ben: The discovery of music, and its influence on teenagers plays a considerable role in your fiction. What is it about the influence of music that continues to interest and excite you as both a writer (and human being), and what impact did music have on you as a teenager?
>
> Hayley: I can hear a tune on the radio and often date it correctly because it takes me back to a specific flat-share or city or wherever I was at that time. Music is a really powerful thing. Some songs even remind me of smells! I think my record-hoarding love-affair has something to do with my own adolescence. I wasn't actually very good at being a teenager. I was small (still am), had a crippling lack of confidence. As a result, I wasn't massively popular and spent hours in my bedroom taping the Top 40 off Radio 1 or listening to pirate radio stations. Music gave me confidence. As a teenager, I discovered the Doors and – for a while anyway – that defined who I was. Then I saw people like Tanya Donelly (Throwing Muses/Belly/The Breeders) playing guitar on TV and I thought, 'THAT'S who I want to be,' – even though I had no skills any band could ever use. But I suppose it was just about finding my own identity. Or finding someone to identify *with* anyway. I still have a very strong emotional connection to a lot of pop music and I hope I always do have that. And that's why I write about it. (Screech 2019: 21)

Hayley Long neatly articulates the way in which music can function as an antidote to the emotional puzzlement of adolescence, through her suggestion of it existing as a way of 'defining identity'. Moreover, as Long suggests, music's sensory aspect locates our lives within its temporal sphere of influence, while reminding us of the different forms of connection and inclusion it fosters. Such experiences are specifically allied to analogue experiences of music in Long's book, which the author reflects on with a record collector's zeal.

Fire and Water begins with Ally documenting her various 'collections', from erasers that smell of different foodstuffs, to trivia facts and her notebook full of the dates and times that Annie Nightingale plays her tracks on the *Sunday Request Show*. She then discusses her 'greatest and most dearly loved collection – vinyl' (Long 2004: 5). Her reflections on the medium and its visceral nature mirror Aden Evans's suggestions in *Sound Ideas* (2005), that 'the digital misses whatever falls between its articulations' (Evans 2005: 69). This sense of what the listener may miss in terms of analogue music's crackles, blips and other forms of sound-based fallout, all of which are picked up when the record player's needle slips into its groove and is regrettably 'cleaned up' in digitized recordings, is a crucial aspect of Long's experience of listening to music. Like the sound of the name of the Welsh town (Aberystwyth) where Ally's record-collecting youth begins, listening to vinyl records offers her a 'vibrant and varied carnival across the eardrums' (Long 2004: 5). This is explored similarly in Nick Hornby's novel *High Fidelity* (1995) – also a celebration of record collecting which, while not technically a YA novel, does nevertheless focus on a group of adults who inhabit an almost adolescent-like state of arrested development, and in whose eyes music and records take on an almost fetishistic obsession. At one point in the book, Rob, the protagonist wonders:

> Is it so wrong, wanting to be at home with your record collection? It's not like collecting records is like collecting stamps, or beermats or antique thimbles. There's a whole world in here, a nicer, dirtier, more violent, more peaceful, more colourful, sleazier, more dangerous, more loving world than the world I live in; there is history, and geography, and poetry, and countless other things I should have studied in school. (Hornby 1995: 65)

What music can offer that school cannot is a central concern in Melvyn Burgess's 2011 novel *Kill All Enemies*. Less focused on listening to music, this text is interested instead in the role of musical performance as both 'limit experience' (Foucault 2002: 248) and solution to characters' feelings of outsiderness. The novel is told through the different perspectives of three teenagers who have been excluded from school and placed in a pupil referral unit (PRU) for a variety of misdemeanours. The story's primary protagonist is Billie, a teenage girl who has seemingly been 'written off' by her family and school, but in whom her care worker identifies a spark of something unique. Burgess's novel charts the teenagers' experience of life in the PRU, and the final section centres on Billie's attempt to start a band with her friends Rob and Chris. This results in the formation of the eponymously named 'Kill All Enemies' that plays Metallica-inspired rock music.

The children's literature critic Michele Gill considers how the band legitimates the characters' arguably 'dysfunctional' relationships. 'Friendships which may appear anti-social to those outside, can still have a positive effect on the young people involved' (Gill 2013: 56). For these perennial outsiders then, the band represents belonging and the music with its 'deathgrowl' (Burgess 2011: 293) cadence seemingly acts as a cathartic influence. Music is shown to be an empowering vehicle for these teenagers. It restores some of the self-confidence and self-belief lost in the processes of exclusion and abandonment they have previously been victims of: 'New mates, new life' Chris reflects; 'I have the band. Things are definitely looking up' (Burgess 2011: 306).

The primal otherness of the band's output (which, in addition to a 'deathgrowl', is also described as a 'screaming gibber' (Burgess 2011: 244)) is a liberatory sound that might be compared to the famous 'yawp' in Walt Whitman's poem 'Song of Myself': 'I too am not a bit tamed, I too am untranslatable, / I sound my barbaric yawp over the roofs of the world' (Whitman 1986: 85). Here, the speaker's voice with its primal energy and 'untameability' is unleashed upon the 'world'. The 'yawp' in its 'barbaric' inarticulacy bypasses the limits of conventional language. The music that 'Kill All Enemies' play has a similar function. The 'untranslatable' aspects of the teenagers' 'limit-experiences' are voiced, not through words, but rather 'growls' and 'gibbers' (Burgess 2011: 244).

As the philosopher Joachim Oberst asserts in his exploration of language and the human condition: 'language does not just consist of the communication of the communicable. [. . .] The non-communicable resides [there] and seeks new forms of expression' (Oberst 2011: N.P.A). In this novel, such 'new forms of expression' are the means by which agency is restored to these three individuals, previously rendered voiceless by virtue of their outcast status, through being expelled from school and having instead to attend the PRU. In this way, music becomes Billie, Rob and Chris's sanctuary. The band encourages them to exalt in their otherness, results in them finding their voice and ultimately allows them to transcend the obstacles that abandonment by school and, in Billie's case, family, has imposed on them.

Rob, in particular, believes irreducibly in music's transformative powers, describing early on in the novel his belief that it 'solves problems'. As a result, he asserts: 'You don't have to be angry [. . .] You don't have to be scared, you don't have to worry' (Burgess 2011: 28). Rob's role in the band is a source of considerable pride to him, due to his prior outcast status: 'Can you believe it? Yesterday I was nothing and today, look at me! I am in a band!' (Burgess 2011: 248).

In school, Rob is a figure of ridicule due to his size and penchant for alternative clothes, and has seemingly learnt to accept that 'a kid like me gets beatings' (Burgess 2011: 75). He is rejected by his peers, abandoned for failing to adhere to their brand of cultural normativity: 'It's like the style police, if you're not like them. [. . .] Kids get beaten up for listening to the wrong music or wearing the wrong clothes' (Burgess 2011: 27). This can be viewed as an almost Foucauldian example of normativity being 'policed' by individuals who, in the context given, have the power to exclude those who display 'perversions' (Burgess 2011: 27) of behaviour, such as the wearing of clothes not mandated as 'cool' (Burgess 2011: 29). When Rob boldly decides to wear his new Metallica T-shirt (arguably, itself a form of rock and roll writing) to school he is, predictably, 'beat up' [sic] (Burgess 2011: 122). The school authorities promptly exclude him to the PRU, assuming that, due to his size and strength, he instigated the fight.

Billie comments on the absurdity of this situation, defending Rob to her form teacher: 'Rob doesn't bully – he gets bullied. [. . .] So what really happened is he gets beaten up for wearing the wrong clothes and then he gets excluded by you lot for wearing the wrong clothes. You're no better than the kids' (Burgess 2011: 84). Here, Billie comments tellingly on the divisive nature of this decision. The school, she maintains, in its exclusion of Rob, is simply mirroring the behaviour of its pupils. Schools, Foucault attests in *Discipline and Punish* (1975), are inherently exclusory institutions, surveilling and punishing pupils for inconsequential misdemeanours. In this way, as Billie suggests, they operate in a comparable manner to the 'bullies' that occupy their playgrounds, continually seeking ways to expose differences and disenfranchise those deemed to be in some way other.

Music similarly operates as a form of rebellion from the disenfranchising aspects of education in Frank Portman's debut YA novel *King Dork* (2006). The book's first-person narrator, Tom Henderson, a self-confessed 'skinny, awkward, nervous' (Portman 2006: 5) kid, uses music to both elevate and distance himself from his frequently bewildering journey through his sophomore year of high

'I obliterate myself in song'   103

school. Struggling to deal with the standard adolescent fare of bullies, crushes and difficult teachers, Tom moots the idea of starting a band with his friend Sam. Despite a slow start in which the boys obsess over the design of their future album covers without actually writing any songs, the band gradually takes shape when they steal a set of amplifiers from their school and subsequently perform at their school's Battle of the Bands.

Although their debut 'wasn't a triumph [. . .] it totally sucked' (Portman 2006: 252), (to quote Tom's review), the band does nevertheless manage to make something of a cult impression, prompting their classmates to discuss the performance 'for the rest of the day and well into the following week' (Portman 2006: 258). Tom and the rest of the band's social status in school is suddenly transformed and he becomes a 'quasi-celebrity' (Portman 2006: 261). His experience in this regard is in alignment with musicologist Johan Fornäs's exploration of garage band subcultures in *Garageland* (2014), wherein he considers how the wannabe musician's perception of being 'hip' and 'cool' (Fornäs 2014: 80) perhaps inevitably factors into the myriad reasons young people may choose to form a band.

Fornäs also suggests a further element of motivation in this regard, that is: that 'as a musician, one "rates" in girls' eyes' (Fornäs 2014: 80), and this, it would seem, is also part of music's appeal for Tom. In fact, post-gig, he is handed a note from his crush Deanna, saying: 'Thanks for rocking my world. I'm totally callable Mon/Thurs from 6 to 10 if you're into it' (Portman 2006: 258). This appears to work as evidence for Tom's belief that 'if you're in a band, even a sucky one, girls will mess around with you' (Portman 2006: 306). Fornäs goes on to consider the ubiquity of drug use in garage band subcultures and *King Dork* interestingly examines the alignment between musical genre preference, social group and soft drugs:

> They all do various mild drugs continually and are pretty much always stoned to some degree. The stoners wear heavy metal t-shirts while doing it. They tend to be nicer to be around than full on normal people, though, because their ideology includes a self-perceived admiration for social misfits. (Portman 2006: 154)

It is notable that, for Tom, this 'ingroup' to which he finds himself wanting to belong (and ultimately gains admittance, as a result of his band's performance and his demonstrably 'encyclopaedic knowledge of rock and roll history' (Portman 2006: 155)) is itself an 'outgroup' in the school, a sanctuary for 'social misfits'. Here, then music appears to function as what Kathryn Lum and Paul

Harvey term a form of 'social lubricant' that has the ability to 'ease differences' (Lum and Harvey 2018: 257).

This, I suggest, is the case more generally in terms of the primary texts this chapter has considered. I have shown how music facilitates different forms of community and belonging, and provides sanctuary to those who, at different times in their lives and in different ways, may feel lost or other. Our discussion has engaged with issues of identity construction and its role in typical settings representative of the adolescent experience, that is: from school life to friendship groups. Through readings of Foucault, it has also been shown how music functions as a form of 'limit experience', in which language's role as a homogenizing influence is challenged and, at times, disrupted, and where sound fills the gaps where words fall short. We have also considered music's ability to transport us back to key people, situations and places in our lives. Indeed, for many of us, the most pertinent and poignant 'site' to which music can transport us remains adolescence. Ultimately, this is because, as Hornby puts it in *High Fidelity*, our teenage years are when 'the really important stuff, the stuff that really defines us, goes on' (Hornby 1995: 18).

References

Boles, Philana (2011). *Glitz*. London: Penguin.

Burgess, Melvyn (2011). *Kill All Enemies*. London: Penguin.

Chbosky, Stephen (2010). *The Perks of Being a Wallflower*. New York: MTV Books (1999).

Cohn, Rachel and David Levithan (2006). *Nick and Norah's Infinite Playlist*. New York: Alfred Knopf.

Dury, Ian (1977). *Sex and Drugs and Rock and Roll*. London: Stiff Records.

Evans, Aden (2005). *Sound Ideas: Music, Machines and Experience*. Minneapolis: University of Minnesota Press.

Fornäs, Johan et al. (2014). *In Garageland: Rock, Youth and Modernity*. London: Taylor and Francis.

Foucault, Michel (1975). *Discipline and Punish: The Birth of the Prison*. Trans. Alan Sheridan. London: Vintage (1979).

Foucault, Michel (1969). *The Archaeology of Knowledge*. Trans. A. M. Sheridan Smith. London: Routledge (2002).

Gill, Michele (2013). 'Boyhood in *Doing It* and *Kill All Enemies*', in Alison Waller (ed.), *New Casebooks: Melvin Burgess*, 41–59. London: Palgrave Macmillan.

Hernadi, Paul (2019). *Cultural Transactions: Nature, Self, Society*. Ithaca: Cornell University Press.

Hill, Crag (2014). *The Critical Merits of Young Adult Literature*. London: Taylor and Francis.

Hinton, S.E (1967). *The Outsiders*. London: Penguin (2006).

Long, Hayley (2004). *Fire and Water*. Cardigan: Parthian.

Lum, Kathryn and Paul Harvey (2018). *The Oxford Handbook of Religion and Race in American History*. Oxford: Oxford University Press.

Marr, Johnny and Steven Morrissey (1986). *Asleep*. London: Rough Trade Records.

Oberst, Joachim (2011). *Heidegger on Language and Death: The Intrinsic Connection in Human Existence*. London: A&C Black.

Pater, Walter (1873). *The Renaissance: Studies of Art and Poetry*. Floating Press (2010).

Portman, Frank (2006). *King Dork*. London: Penguin.

Rowell, Rainbow (2012). *Eleanor and Park*. London: Orion.

Screech, Ben (2019). 'An Interview with Hayley Long', *Voice of Youth Advocates* 42(3): 20–4.

Sillito, David (2017). 'Vinyl Sales at All Time High', *BBC*. https://www.bbc.co.uk/news/av/entertainment-arts-38503500 (accessed 28 November 2022).

Tajfel, Henri (1982). *Social Identity and Intergroup Relations*. Cambridge: Cambridge University Press (2010).

Uitti, Jacob (2022) 'The 20 Best Thom Yorke Quotes', *American Songwriter*. https://americansongwriter.com/the-20-best-thom-yorke-quotes/ (accessed 28 November 2022).

Waligorska, Magdalena (2013). *Music, Longing and Belonging: Articulations of the Self and the Other in the Musical Realm*. Newcastle Upon Tyne: Cambridge Scholars.

Whitman, Walt (1855). *Leaves of Grass*. London: Penguin (1986).

8

Rock music and the contingencies of history

Dawnie Walton's *The Final Revival of Opal & Nev*

Adrian Grafe

Introduction

Dawnie Walton's first novel, *The Final Revival of Opal & Nev*, blends polyphony, collage, journalism, fiction, autofiction and docufiction. It is grounded in the present day and the social and technological complexity of the digital age, but it also goes back to the 1960s and 1970s and the rock industry at that time. At the same time, it stands as a social, cultural and political history of Black consciousness in America over the past fifty years. The novel owes its strength to the tension between these two things since the eponymous artists are forced, despite themselves, to confront political and social forces. It is mainly, but not solely, an examination of the creative and personal life of Opal Jewel, an African-American female rock musician reminiscent of Grace Jones and Tina Turner, battling against racism and sexism.

The narrative is presented as *reportage*, an oral history – in part – of rock duo Opal Jewel and Nev Charles through interviews with them and the people around them, mixing the characters in the novel with allusions to bands like U2 and White Stripes, as well as what is possibly a veiled nod to the Rolling Stones' concert at Altamont at which a Black man was killed by white Hell's Angels. The interviews are transcribed in the now-familiar fashion with the non-verbal aspects included in italics and square brackets, such as [*Shrugs*], [*Long pause*] and [*Laughs*]. It is also a reflection of relatively recent colloquial language tics, such as the a-grammatical word 'like', used as though the speaker was pausing for thought: 'And I just wonder, like, why wasn't her music ever at the top of, like, the urban charts?' (Walton 2021: 335).[1]

---

[1] Further references to the novel will be to page numbers alone of the cited edition.

The novel thus aims for maximum verisimilitude. Tightly plotted and tightly constructed, the novel is formally original to the extent that it is made up largely but not solely of interviews. Hence, it is an oral history of two artists whose art is in itself oral (because they are both singers). This is a way of giving priority to orality, including singing, over the written word. The heart of the plot is concerned with racism, and actions that lead to the death of Jimmy Curtis, the Black drummer who plays with Opal and Nev. At the same time, the novel reflects the history of Black women artists who have struggled to achieve success and make their voices heard in the face of resistance from white business interests, and more broadly the social reality faced by Black people. As Opal's friend Virgil Lafleur points out to Sunny Shelton, the 'editor' of the interviews which largely make up the novel, Opal's personal story must be set against the perception of her, a perception held by young Black people in particular, of someone who stands up for the 'marginalized, bullied, discriminated against' (265). Sunny, the journalist who conducts the interviews, is herself Black, and her own story is bound up with Opal Jewel's life as well as Nev Charles's, the Brummie musician with whom Opal pairs up. Although Maureen Mahon's *Black Diamond Queens: African American Women and Rock and Roll* (2020) came out just as *Opal & Nev* was going to press, Walton has mentioned it in interviews as being relevant to her novel in terms of the portraits of Black American women struggling for artistic recognition on their own terms, especially in relation to the image of the '"strong" Black woman' (Shaw 2021).

This chapter, then, sets out to examine the structure of the novel, its formal features and its assessment of racism at the heart of the popular music industry in America, and how these things fit together, especially with reference to the social and cultural context. It is arguable that, through the characterization of Opal in particular, but also Nev, rock music is depicted by Walton as something more than mere 'commodity culture' (Babaee and Siva 2014: 191).

'Gimme shelter'

The temporal beginning of the narrative – but not the novel – is the Opal and Nev concert at which drummer Jimmy Curtis, Sunny's father, is killed. In this respect, the novel can be understood as a critique not necessarily of the rock concert as a type of event, but of the Dionysiac energies unleashed at certain rock concerts which contain within them a potential for destruction. This concert takes place in 'fall 1971' (153) at a theatre in New York City, the Smythe, a name possibly based on the Smythe Jack theatre in that city. The concert is billed the 'Rivington Showcase', aimed as its name suggests at showcasing acts who record for the Rivington label, including Opal and Nev. Some forty-five years later, the 'revival' of Opal and Nev takes place at what seems to be an annual rock music festival, called Derringdo, in 'summer 2016' (6). The Rivington Showcase is tragic; both of these concerts are catastrophic. The narrative links these catastrophes to racism and therefore critiques American society, whether it be the hippy philosophy of the 1960s or the ongoing prejudice against Black people to which the Black Lives Matter movement has drawn attention. The latter is specifically, if not ironically, mentioned in the novel, for example 'the Black Lives Matter booth' outside the auditorium at the Derringdo concert (334).

Although Dawnie Walton has stated in an interview that she at least partly based Opal and Nev on Grace Jones and David Bowie, the novel does not mention Jones although it does mention Bowie (if only once). Within the text, the parallel is closer to Mick Jagger and Merry Clayton, the Black female singer on the Rolling Stones' original studio recording of 'Gimme Shelter'. Merry Clayton is an explicit template for Opal. The founder of Rivington Records is Howie Kelly, who is described by his receptionist, Rosemary Salducci, as being able to 'bully his way into whatever he wanted' (50), like Bucky Wunderlick's agent in Don DeLillo's novel *Great Jones Street* who says: 'Mogul is written all over me. How did I get there? Aggressiveness got me there. [. . .] Loudmouthedness' (DeLillo 1999: 235). Kelly wants Nev to team up with 'a Black chick with a giant voice' (60) in order to boost Nev's record sales. He wants to 'imitate' the Jagger-Clayton pairing on 'Gimme Shelter':

> At the time, 'Gimme Shelter' was the biggest hit out there, and it featured Merry Clayton just wailing away about God knows what. What was that chorus. . . . About murder, about *rape*? Who ever heard of such a thing in a song? But she was raw, and she had grit, and she was a real soul sister with lots of attitude – *you* know what I'm saying. Her whole vibe just married with that guitar, and she's going back and forth with Mick in a way that knocked everybody out. (59)

Whether by accident or by design on Walton's part, a couple of the statements made by Kelly are not quite accurate: if by design, it would mean that she was cocking a snook at the record company executive for his ignorance of his own product. First, 'Gimme Shelter' (1969) was never, strictly speaking, a 'hit' in the way Kelly describes it, if what he means is that it went to number one in the singles chart, since it was never released as a single. Second, when he says that a song about rape or especially murder had never been heard of before, that is not correct. The Beatles' lyric to 'Getting Better' (1967) involves woman-beating and emotional abuse, while Dylan's 'Ballad of Hollis Brown' (1964) ends with a multiple murder. And when Kelly says that Clayton 'goes back and forth with Mick' this is not quite accurate: it is Jagger who goes 'back and forth' with Clayton, when she breaks free of the backing-singer role and suddenly steps up to take the lead vocal – to become the foreground vocalist in fact. Maureen Mahon eloquently describes what Clayton does on, and to, the song:

> In the song, Clayton starts in traditional background mode, entering after Jagger has sung the first verse. She doubles his voice on the chorus, instantly increasing the song's volume, tension, and sense of foreboding. But, departing from standard practice, she takes a solo, singing the phrase, 'Rape! Murder! It's just a kiss away'; her bracing timbre bursts into the foreground of the song. Jagger's voice supports her as he echoes her 'kiss away' phrases. Beautifully conceived, the song places one of rock's consummate lead singers in the uncharacteristic position of being a background vocalist, if only for a few measures. (Mahon 2020: 119–20)

Greil Marcus wrote of Clayton on this song: 'She can stand up to Mick and match him, and in fact, she steals the song' (Mahon 2020: 120). Although Clayton does indeed steal the song, it could not be described as a collaboration of equals. It is easy to see why Walton responded so warmly to Mahon's study. It chimes with many of Walton's preoccupations in *Opal & Nev*, not least the fact that, according to Mahon, a 'white male/black female rock collaboration' had never existed before Tina Turner began working with white musicians and producers (Mahon 2020: 135). It is surprising, perhaps, that Walton does not mention Turner in the novel, either because she was a too obvious a template for Opal, or for reasons of chronology, since she only began collaborating with white artists from 1984 on, according to Mahon.

When Walton has spoken about Clayton in interviews, she has not foregrounded Clayton's contribution to 'Gimme Shelter', preferring to comment on what she sees as Clayton's ambiguous attitude towards the Confederate flag, which plays an important part in her novel. This, plus the words she puts in Kelly's mouth, confirms the idea that Clayton is one model for Opal.

Embedded structure

The text proves to be more sophisticated than it initially appears, given that its topic is entertainment and that its focus, as its title indicates, is on character. When Sunny Curtis writes about the *Polychrome* album by Opal and Nev on which each of the songs 'told a vivid story about an offbeat character' (95), this is in itself an embedded structure, since Walton makes the two main characters, and the vast majority of the characters, 'offbeat'. In fact the novel as a whole is an embedded structure, by which the text that the reader of the novel reads is actually being written to be published within the diegesis itself: the journalist S. Sunny Shelton, the fictive editor-redactor of the whole of the text, is researching and writing the story of Opal and Nev for publication by the magazine she works for, *Aural*, a music and popular cultural journal in the style of *Rolling Stone*. She presents herself from the outset as the editor of the text that follows, by beginning the text with the words 'EDITOR'S NOTE' (1). This is a sleight of hand, since the reader is unsure whether the 'editor' is fictitious or, rather, Walton's own editor: this sort of ambiguity and semi-illusiveness runs, in various forms, throughout the novel and is one of its chief pleasures. Shelton acts as a sort of pseudo-stand-in for Walton (the two surnames are both bi-syllabic and end in '–lton'), who was for many years herself a journalist. The chapters of the novel comprise transcripts of interviews with the leading players in the story, as well as some peripheral figures and fans. The text of each chapter is preceded by an introduction in italics in which Shelton writes in propria persona and contextualizes the various interviews that follow, often given in snippets to suit the editor's – that is, Shelton's – purposes; Shelton also interrupts the series of interview extracts at times in order to recount her own personal and professional trajectory. The latter in certain respects mirrors Opal's. For example, Shelton 'ponders' what she calls 'the frightening decline of my own career' (328) just at the time when Opal is making poor albums, her final one dating from 1988 filled with 'the tired feminist schtick that wore out two albums ago' according to one reviewer, and 'terrible' films (327). This mirror effect helps create the novel's emotional complexity. This is due in great part to the fact that Shelton is the daughter of Opal and Nev's drummer Jimmy Curtis, with whom Opal had an affair at the time Opal's mother was pregnant with Opal, and it was while that affair was ongoing that Curtis was killed at the Rivington Showcase concert. In the same way as Shelton never knew her father, the reader learns that Opal lives in a certain 'loneliness' and 'confusion' because of her 'never knowing [her]

Rock Music and the Contingencies of History 111

daddy' (249). It is almost as though the respective identities of the journalist-editor of the text one is reading, and of the artiste, overlap if not blend. The novel in a sense hangs on the rapport between Opal as Jimmy's lover and Sunny Shelton as the daughter of a father she never knew. Because of this intimate tie, Opal cannot treat Shelton as she would an ordinary journalist. This relationship is further complicated by the fact that when she achieves financial success as an artist, Opal starts sending cheques to Opal's mother Corinne: she was 'investing' in Sunny's upbringing, and Sunny's successful career as a journalist can be put down in part to the financial help her mother received from Opal for Sunny's education (247). The novel is really the story of Sunny's quest to find out exactly how and why her father was killed at that concert, a fact that has never been elucidated before she sets out to write a book about it. In this respect, the history of the rock act *Opal & Nev* is incidental to Shelton's quest; but on the other hand, Opal's relationship with Jimmy Curtis, and the fact that he was killed while playing onstage with Opal and Nev, makes them intrinsic to how Jimmy came to be killed – as indeed they are. Some of Shelton's interviewees are fictional, others are real. The photographer Marion Jacobie, 'famous' for the photograph she took of Opal and Nev fleeing the scene at the Rivington Showcase concert once it had turned into a riot during their set, and who shoots photos for *Vanity Fair* and *Vogue*, is fictitious (168). Real-life American guitarist Tom Morello, another interviewee, is quoted as discovering Opal and Nev when he was 'seven years old and up past my bedtime watching Opal & Nev perform on TV' (246). Perhaps Walton's technique in this respect corresponds to the idea that the rock star's life is a blend of illusion and reality in which the pressures of fame and fandom make it hard for the artist to distinguish the two things, hence the idea of blending them.

A case in point regarding ambiguity and illusiveness is the footnotes. When asked about the literary influences on her novel, Walton referred to *The Brief Wondrous Life of Oscar Wao* (2007) by Junot Diaz: 'the usage of footnotes in there to bring in history that made me be like, "Okay, that's been done before, so maybe it's not so crazy for me to do it"' (Hart 2021). But in fact Walton does do it in *Opal & Nev*. Although Walton's footnotes do not amplify the narrative to the extent that Diaz's do, hers still fill in either personal detail regarding the characters or historical background. These footnotes are explicitly those of an 'I' persona, that of editor Sunny Shelton; given that much of the main text is interview transcript, the footnotes sometimes offer information that is not given by the interviewees themselves. This has the effect of, in part, creating a shadow narrative to the one that the interviews give, once pieced together and interpreted by the reader. Some footnotes are one-sentence summaries of sometimes major historical events, such as the Watergate crisis of 1974, providing the story of Opal and Nev with context while highlighting the corruption of the white governing class. Others, such as the footnote about Altamont (227), offer analogies with what happens in the main narrative as well as historical or cultural background. For example, an allusion to activist Bree Newsome triggers a footnote with a very brief history of how, days after the massacre in Charleston, South Carolina, of nine Black Americans by a white supremacist in a church to which he had been invited by the worshippers themselves, Breesome climbed a pole outside the South Carolina State House and took down the Confederate flag. Press coverage of the incident included allusions to Opal's destruction of the Confederate flag at the Rivington Showcase concert. Opal is not only an artist or musician but a composite character (cf. below) one part of which corresponds to an activist like Newsome. Typical of Walton's method in relation to the interweaving of fiction with fact, in the footnotes in particular, is the note about Artis Purdie, a roadie with Opal and Nev. The whole note is worth citing: 'After his time on the road with Opal & Nev, Artis Purdie moved to Oakland, California, to help support Black Panther Party official Elaine Brown's city council run in 1973. He still lives in Oakland today, and manages a community center offering after-school tutoring and activities for teenagers' (263). Through such statements, Walton is constructing a history of recent Black militancy in America while relating the story of a rock act. It would not be quite correct, though, to call such history a subtext, since Opal herself talks in a TV interview about the 'work to do in this revolution' (254). Brown was, in a way, the reverse mirror image of Opal: a politician who was also an occasional singer. Despite Purdie's – fictional – help, Brown failed to get elected as mayor of Oakland. This is in fact more than background to the main narrative, since it involves a character (Purdie) within it, rather than merely telling the history of Brown. The latter was one of the first woman members of the Black Panthers, and did lead the party from 1974 to 1977. The height of her political career coincides more or less with Opal's (and Nev's) musical one. Thus, although Purdie only has a bit part in the novel, Walton uses such mini-biographies as the one in the note about Purdie in order to further one of the ideological dimensions – if not agendas – of the novel. And, as will be developed below, the novel is an embedded structure because the whole text purports to be a book written by Sunny Curtis.

Rock Music and the Contingencies of History 113

Orality, polyphony, voice, lyrics

Walton has cited the *Live from New York* volume, edited by James Andrew Miller and Tom Shales, as the major literary influence on the novel (Hart 2021). The Acknowledgements page of *Live from New York* begins: 'Participation is the life-blood of an oral history' (Miller and Shales 2015: xi). Walton stays remarkably close to the form of Miller and Shales's book. In both works, each chapter title is followed by an introductory text by the editor or editors, in italics. This in turn is followed by a series of snippets from interviews. Each snippet is preceded by the name of the speaker (and a colon) in bold type. *Opal & Nev* also imitates *Live from New York* in generally not reproducing the questions asked by the interviewer, and the reader cannot know whether the extracts are from one or more interviews. As in *Opal & Nev*, in some chapters the interview snippets are interrupted by explanatory editorial passages. Given the similarity of the formal and typographical features of *Opal & Nev* to *Live from New York*, as well as keeping the oral style of the direct speech, with liberal use of the f-word for example, one might argue that Walton is consciously attempting to do what the first book does: show the collaborative nature of the entertainment being produced, since both works are polyphonic and 'participative' ('Participation is the life-blood . . . '), while applying the *Live from New York* method to material which is not straightforwardly fictional. In other words, the crossover from the *Live from New York* method (extracts from interviews, tightly edited to form a coherent story, with heavy editorial presence) reinforces the impression that what one is reading (in Walton's novel) really happened. The plot thus develops out of each speaker's oral testimony, which naturally has to be corroborated by the others, and can be contradicted. Hence, the technique of polyphony multiplies the perspectives, and in fact some characters in the novel know more than others, so that the novel gradually becomes rich in dramatic irony. One might apply the word 'composite', used by Walton (107), to this method of writing narrative, which is thus a collective, cooperative creation. In this way, although Opal and Nev are rock stars, the text itself has a levelling effect on their interview contributions, since their voices are only two among many others. Thus, Walton's textual method arguably calls into question the star system. True, Opal and Nev appear – catastrophically as it turns out – in the Rivington Showcase (the full title of which is the Rivington All-Star Showcase), but they are never referred to directly as stars. The word itself is used sparingly in the novel, and it cannot be accidental that the artist (nick–)named Estella 'Star'

Arcadia has a 'heroin addiction [which] finally claim[s] her life' (345). The fact that Opal and Nev are not explicitly called stars is contrastable with the first-person narrator of Don DeLillo's novel *Great Jones Street*, Bucky Wunderlick, who is described in a newspaper as an 'American rock star' (DeLillo 1999: 96). Wunderlick's girlfriend is called Opel, and one wonders whether Walton's Opal is not a possible if unconscious echo of this, although he himself says he 'was a hero of rock 'n' roll' (DeLillo 1999: 1) which is not the same thing as a rock and roll star.

Hence, it is not merely Walton's real-world references which heighten that aspect of her novel, but its very method, and the novelist's explicitly revealing her methodological source in interviews of her own. One major factor that makes the novel more than the story of one Black female artist's struggle for success and recognition is the fact that it is mingled with Nev's. Nev can be argued to represent sheer artistry in the novel since, unlike Opal, he is neither Black, nor a woman, nor American, and therefore – at least in relation to the way Opal is depicted – has no axe to grind. As said above, the novel cannot be reduced to polyphony, because of the framing device of the editor. Nev is conceived as a Bowie doppelganger, although unlike Bowie Neville 'Nev' Charles is not a Londoner but a – less glamorous – Brummie (Opal is from Detroit, perhaps as a nod to Motown: 'I'm a Negro from Detroit, U.S.A.' [101]). When it comes to accents, Walton's ventriloquism of British English is perfect: when Nev was a teenager he and his mother would 'still listen to the radio, yeah, but watching television is what really sticks: It was *Top of the Pops* on Thursday nights, *Juke Box Jury* on Saturdays' (34). Apart from the cultural references, Nev peppers his sentences with the typically British, slightly rising-intoned 'yeah'. But Nev's voice can also be heard through his lyrics, occasionally quoted in the course of the novel. One might then examine the case of one song in the novel, which also demonstrates Walton's narrative technique: 'Black Coffee' – clearly titled by Walton after the Stones' 'Brown Sugar' – written by Nev for Opal to sing. This is Walton ventriloquizing Nev ventriloquizing a young Black single mother with a low-paid factory job, whom he intended to be ventriloquized by Opal:

Drop of milk for the baby, black coffee for me
Or I'll be collapsed by the time it hits three.

[...]
Alone once again, I settle for sleep
And pray for the baby, and my soul to keep

Rock Music and the Contingencies of History 115

> I dream of the day we'll get what we're due
> But for now there's that kettle, screaming on cue. (108)

This lyric is admittedly not outstanding, especially because of the hackneyed rhymes, that of the fifth line in particular, which justifies its presence by virtue of its rhyme preparing for the sixth. The latter, with its screaming kettle echoing the baby, is the finest of the six. However, it does show Nev trying to empathize with a person and a situation foreign to him, even though both are stereotyped. As Barry Shank argues: 'The racial meaning of a song can never be discussed in the abstract, but must always be considered in terms of the musical and lyrical traditions out of which it comes, as well as the social uses to which it is put' (Shank 269). Both Opal and Jimmy Curtis dislike the song intensely: to Opal, Nev's song is the product of a 'white liberal' who does not understand Black culture. In addition, the song is out of step with the zeitgeist: as Opal explains, the key Black song of the time was James Brown's 'Say it Loud – I'm Black and I'm Proud' (108), which represents the opposite of the 'morose' song. The 'lyrical tradition' mentioned by Shank would be the English ballad form with its tetrameter quatrains. Record producer Bob Hize says of the song that it risked alienating the Black audience 'by being tone-deaf to the times' (109). Nev's well-meaning effort shows he both misunderstands the culture and Opal's own combativeness as a woman and an artist.

Opal & Nev as 'rock history'

When Opal and Nev are about to make their *Polychrome* album, Opal is required to learn the songs that Nev has written in his notebook, both their lyrics and musical notations. She cannot read music and gets by in this respect by taking some 'hazy lessons' just before the recording sessions begin (92). In order to compensate for the lack of technical musical knowledge, helped by her fashion designer friend Virgil, who also has definite opinions about what she does musically, Opal undergoes a physical transformation, using make-up, clothes designed by Virgil and by shaving her head and leaving it visible, rather than hiding her alopecia. Walton makes Opal bald, a condition or attribute more commonly associated with men than with women, perhaps to suggest androgyny or to emphasize the idea that Opal is marked by difference; Opal ends up capitalizing on this trait. The reader is left to interpret the symbolic significance of this attribute of Opal's, the cause of which is merely explained

116   *Ink on the Tracks*

medically. It may hint at the idea that Opal stands outside traditional canons of female beauty (be they white or Black) and will have to work harder to become a successful artist; references to her baldness recur in the novel. Opal's shaving her head is an allusion to Grace Jones, who did shave hers in the 1970s, although unlike Opal she was not bald. This transformation, with a pun on the adjective 'colorful' in reference to her clothes, 'is one of the most colorful stories in rock history' (92).

Conclusion: *Opal & Nev* as both 'rock history' and 'African American history and culture'

The LCSH categories for *The Final Revival of Opal & Nev* are as follows: 'Women *Rock* musicians – Fiction; *Rock* musicians – Fiction; *Rock* groups – Fiction' (the word 'Rock' is in bold type). However, Sunny Curtis's own description of the work inflects this reading, and our own. This means that the novel and Sunny's text work together or, rather, against each other, as narrative and counternarrative. Sunny Curtis confirms in a footnote towards the end of her book – to her it is a book of interview extracts edited by her with her comments, while to the reader that book is the novel by Dawnie Walton they have in their hands (or on their screen) – that it is ideologically driven. For much of the timespan covered by the novel, Sunny Curtis works first as a journalist at the magazine *Aural* and then as *Aural's* editor-in-chief. Aural Media initially agrees to publish the book Sunny sets out to write about Opal and Nev, but in the wake of bad publicity after she gatecrashes the funeral of Opal and Nev's record producer, Bob Hize, Aural Media drops her. Opal and Nev reunite in 2016 for the Derringdo festival – their 'final revival' as it turns out, since they had been intending to tour, but their performance, as at the Rivington Showcase, goes wrong. This creates scandal and outrage, which prompts Aural to renew their interest in Sunny's book. In the footnote (357), Sunny states that Aural make her a 'flattering' bid. She tells the reader this to prove her integrity, since she rejects this offer in favour of another one, by definition lower, from Sojourner Books, an imprint dedicated to stories of African-American history and culture. True to the verisimilitude Walton aims at, Sunny thanks Sojourner 'for believing in this project and embracing the risks'. This implies, first, that African-American culture does not have the same prestige or financial profitability as white culture. Second, it means that

Rock Music and the Contingencies of History   117

Sunny Curtis sees her own text, unlike the LCSH, as not primarily about rock music and rock artists but about African-American history and culture, thus shifting the entire focus of the text from Opal and Nev to Opal alone. It makes Nev incidental to Opal's story, and a case could be made in this respect. Nev is, however, crucial to the plot of the novel. One must also take into account the fact that, rather than American, Nev is British, so that Opal and Nev as an entertainment duo cannot be considered as a piece of Americana unlike, for example, Bruce Springsteen and Clarence Clemons as they appeared on the *Born to Run* album cover (1975). One arguable facet of the African-American emphasis in the novel is the fact that Opal does not write the duo's material, especially the lyrics. What she does is perform, and she brings to their performances her voice, body, outlandish costumes and stage presence. The duo thus combines white logocentric culture (Nev's: he is depicted as writing stories and songs in notebooks from childhood onwards, and as an adult he is constantly seen making up snippets of songs as the mood takes him) with the 'deep structure' in Black culture that is music (Nelson quoting Stuart Hall). Left to her own devices, Opal will not write. She 'improvises' and 'composes' but does not write; she scat-sings a nondescript group of words as a vehicle for her voice. To take an example of her foregrounding of her body, she plays a concert in a small record shop in Paris during a several-month layoff from work in America. During this concert, she has a set-list 'with a couple Opal & Nev songs, a couple of pop covers', and tells amusing stories about her family and friends (284). As if to prove this point, Opal writes some 'flowery poems' (288) in the Luxembourg Gardens and sets them to music, but the audience thinks she is singing 'nursery rhymes' and is 'confused' (289), and Opal quickly decides these songs are 'terrible' (288). What prompts Opal to write, in Paris, is her reading of James Baldwin, Maya Angelou, Toni Morrison and Toni Cade Bambara. But, given the failure of her own writing, these namechecks seem more like a way for Walton to set up a literary tradition in which to inscribe her novel.

The Rivington Showcase and the Derringdo 'Final Revival' concert show how contingent events contribute to the history of rock and, here, African-American history. The text of the novel is thus, in Sunny's words, both a page of 'rock history' (92) and one of 'African American history' (357). This novel is more than a performance of polyphonic writing. It is the ways in which rock history overlaps with African-American history and culture – and vice versa – which most properly characterize it.

References

Babaee, Ruzbeh and Shivani Siva (2014). 'The Function of Pop Music in Don DeLillo's "Great Jones Street"', UPM Book Series on Music Research, UPM Press. No. 6, 191–8.

DeLillo, Don (1999). *Great Jones Street*. London: Picador (1973).

Hart, Michelle (2021). 'Dawnie Walton Shares the Influences Behind Her Debut Novel', *The Final Revival of Opal & Nev*, interview with Michelle Hart, 2 April. https://www .oprahdaily.com/entertainment/books/a35875052/dawnie-walton-interview-final -revival-of-opal-and-nev/ (accessed 7 June 2023).

Mahon, Maureen (2020). *Black Diamond Queens: African American Women and Rock and Roll*. Durham and London: Duke University Press.

Miller, James Andrew and Tom Shales (2015). *Live from New York: The Complete, Uncensored History of Saturday Night Live, as Told by its Stars, Writers, and Guests*. New York, Boston, and London: Back Bay Books/Little, Brown and Company (2002; 2014).

Nelson, Angela (2009). 'The Repertoire of Black Popular Culture', *Americana: The Journal of American Popular Culture (1990-present)* 8(1). Https://americanpopularcu lture.come/journal/articles/spring_2009/nelson.htm (accessed 7 June 2023).

Shank, Barry (2001). 'From Rice to Ice: The Face of Race in Rock and Pop', in Simon Frith, Will Straw, and John Street (eds), *The Cambridge Companion to Pop and Rock*, Cambridge: Cambridge University Press.

Shaw, Matthew (2021). 'The Music that Made Opal & Nev', interview with Dawnie Walton by Matthew Shaw. https://wjct.org/jme/2021/06/the-music-that-made-opal -nev/ (accessed 7 June 2023).

Walton, Dawnie (2021). *The Final Revival of Opal & Nev*. London: Quercus.

9

Writing into the canon

Women and music memoir

Lucy O'Brien

The last decade has marked the steady rise of women's music memoir as a thriving literary genre. I would define memoir as a life-writing journey, where history, memory and personal knowledge collide to create an artful document of life experience. Pre-internet a degree of fame and status as an artist determined the life stories worthy of publication, and in a music business skewed in favour of male musicians, women's work was often overlooked.

This bias was (and still is) compounded by 'Best Of' lists in the music press that prioritize male work in the popular music canon. The canon tells a single authoritative account of a popular music past where artists are positioned in order of importance and innovation. Von Appen and Doehring's (2006) study of 'Best Of' lists in the music press showed how the white male guitar bands and artists (from the Beatles to Bob Dylan, Nirvana and Radiohead) were enshrined as the pinnacle of achievement, reinforcing male canon narratives, while silencing women through omission. This, plus the lack of memoirs or music autobiographies written by women, meant that the lives of many female musicians went undocumented. Approaches from feminist history (Morgan 2006), which, for instance, analyse patriarchal structures and relations between men and women, provide a way of discovering a hidden female canon, decentring the male subject.

The male canon traditionally footnoted women, conveying the idea that women's stories were less interesting than their male peers. Singer Tracey Thorn began her career in all-girl indie-punk band the Marine Girls, before achieving global success in the 1980s and 1990s with Everything But the Girl. Despite eleven best-selling albums and a thirty-year career in the music industry, in

2013 she felt nervous about publishing her memoir *Bedsit Disco Queen*. 'The career I've had has been one that's existed mostly on the margins, outside of the genre-specific accounts of the period', she writes in her introduction, 'I haven't always fitted in' (Thorn 2013: Author's note). But as she read her manuscript, she realized 'it was a good story and deserved to be told' (Thorn 2013: Postscript). In her book, she recounts the inspired creative moments involved in writing huge hit songs like 1994s 'Missing', or 'Protection', her collaboration with Massive Attack. But Thorn also unpicks the awkwardness she feels in the pop star role. In 2009, she watches Lady Gaga performing on X Factor and afterwards the star is asked if she has any tips for contestants. 'Be yourself', Gaga says breezily. This prompts Thorn to reflect on what that might mean for her as a female vocalist, someone who loved composing and singing in the studio but who felt uneasy with live touring and the whole self-promotion process:

> I wrestled constantly with the problem of how to be myself, and whether or not that self would be good enough; whether it could ever compete in a world of bigger and brasher selves. Since the days of singing from inside the wardrobe I had never learned to enjoy being looked at. Being listened to was OK, but the public gaze, so empowering and enriching to the natural extrovert, to me was kryptonite. (Thorn 2013: 232)

Bedsit Disco Queen made an impact when it was first published in 2013, and in the UK her book became one of the first female music memoirs to provide a necessary counterpoint to a male-defined view of what constitutes talent and success in popular music (Thorn 2013). Thorn's determination to tell her story as she experienced it, without feeling the need to valorize it, is in keeping with the way she has always approached her career as a feminist singer-songwriter and musician. Music memoir is now less about celebrity biographies and grand narratives, more about the 'other stories', the stories less covered.

The internet has been a democratizing force, particularly for writing and making music. With the proliferation of blogging and social media, female artists are bypassing industry gatekeepers to engage directly with their fans and their audience. This has opened up new avenues in music book publishing, enabling the growth of female music memoir as a flourishing genre. Since the publication of Patti Smith's 2010 memoir *Just Kids*, there have been key titles such as Viv Albertine's *Clothes Music Boys* (2014), Kim Gordon's *Girl in a Band* (2015), Carrie Brownstein's *Hunger Makes Me a Modern Girl* (2015), Alicia Keys's *More Myself: A Journey* (2020), Vashti Bunyan's *Wayward: Just Another*

Life to Live (2022), Miki Berenyi's *Fingers Crossed* (2022) and PP Arnold's *Soul Survivor* (2022).

In this outpouring of women's testimony, there are detailed accounts of their lived experience, creating a huge historical resource and a radical development in the popular music field. In this chapter, I will look at how this kind of rock and roll writing uncovers women's buried history and documents their experience.

Hip kitties

Memoir can also be defined as a story written from personal experience, often capturing a particular period in someone's life, rather than their whole life, while biography is an account of a life written by someone else, and autobiography is an account of someone's life written by the subject. The latter is sometimes executed with a more formal approach, like Diana Ross's *Secrets of A Sparrow* (1993), emphasizing deeds and achievements in a way that reads like a glorified press release.

In co-writing two memoirs – *It Takes Blood and Guts*, with Skin, frontwoman of rock band Skunk Anansie (Skin 2020), and *The Liverbirds*, with Mary McGlory and Sylvia Saunders, surviving members of the 1960s all-girl beat band (McGlory and Saunders 2024) – I see a collapsing of boundaries between these forms. It is more helpful to use the term 'life writing', which encompasses overlapping elements of history, collaboration and self-reflection. Ann Oakley argues that biography at its most powerful is a liminal form existing at a crossroads of literature, history and poetry (Oakley 2010). Many current female music memoirs are driven by that fluid 'life-writing' approach.

For her memoir, Skin drew on a wide variety of data – gig flyers, notebooks full of lyrics, old family photos, tour schedules and her diaries – data that not only enabled us to check dates and events but also the vernacular and energy of the time. Words and phrases she used at thirteen were different to her words and thought patterns at fifty-three. Life experience modifies and sometimes eradicates a past self, and such data aids in retrieving valuable memories. In her book, she reflects, for example, on how early 1990s Seattle grunge changed her world:

> Cock rock was dead, and out of the ashes flowered this beautiful wilted thorny rose called Nirvana. . . . I'd finally found the music that suited my nightly visions.

Nirvana to me weren't about groupies and tight, bulging pants; they were honest and real and they looked like us. We recognised the same dark lyrical landscape, the same shy, painful outsider life. . . . We definitely weren't Britpop. (Skin 2020: 106)

Miki Berenyi, too, plundered her teenage journals to present a vivid picture of an ardent fan on the 1980s post-punk scene who later drew on that experience to form her own band Lush with Emma Anderson.

In 1983, I go to ninety gigs; in 1984, 150 – big gigs, small gigs, student gigs, political rallies, free London festivals, the lot. In later years when Lush was up and running, the music papers claimed we would 'attend the opening of an envelope', based on our frequent appearances at shows. But we'd been at it for years. . . . Emma and I were muckers together, selling the fanzine, dancing down the front, getting into scrapes and having each other's backs. (Berenyi 2022: 144)

Skin and Berenyi go on to chart their development as musicians, weaving these formative influences into their songs to create their unique sound. This painstaking analysis is a feature of many female life writers – Viv Albertine, for instance, provides a fascinating account of how she arrived at the Slits' scrawling, resonant guitar riffs:

I decide I want a thin buzzsaw-ish/mosquito type of sound. . . . I keep thinking, 'What would I sound like if I was a guitar sound?' It's so abstract. . . . I find I like the sound of a string open, ringing away whilst I play on the string next to it. . . . I like hypnotic repetition. . . . Slowly I start shaping a guitar style, twisting strands together. (Albertine 2014: 104)

Memoir and life writing become a co-construction of self, work done between the former self and current self. It offers a way to reflect on experience and on one's practice – and that is exactly what the female life writers are doing. By reflecting on their practice they gain and claim authorship for their work. Artists like Skin, Berenyi or Albertine 'work out' what their original contribution is to the popular music field, and in so doing the canon becomes more inclusive. They make themselves visible and heard – I am here, I am an artist, this is my practice, this is what I have discovered and this is how I have moved the genre forward. Their books are a reframing of recent popular music history, a process not so much of re-writing, but a 'writing in'. They are writing themselves into that history, providing evidence for a place in the canon.

This is a comparatively recent trend. Long after the emergence of rock and roll in the 1950s, female musicians were written about through the filter of the 'official' music press (often by male journalists and authors), but a few texts stood out for their frank insider perspective. Billie Holiday's *Lady Sings the Blues* (1956), for instance, is fascinating for its detail on the jazz scene and Holiday's conversational idioms. She was a sharp dresser, describing herself in her young days as a 'hip kitty'. Her verbal language was idiosyncratic, a private code that she spoke with Lester Young, the seminal jazz saxophonist and one of her closest friends. They called a white man a 'grey boy', an attractive girl a 'pound cake' and 'just play vanilla, man' meant delivering the music unembellished and unembroidered. Holiday's vocabulary was forceful, mocking and vulgar; she would, according to her friend Maya Angelou, use common words casually in new arrangements – in the same way she reframed popular song. Her autobiography reflects this world, where she comes across like the streetwise star of her own drama.

Certain books have been trailblazers for the female memoir – interestingly, though much of the 2010s writing has been located in genres like punk, riot grrrl and rock, in the 1980s and early 1990s groundbreaking testimonies came from soul and R&B pop: notably Tina Turner's *I, Tina* (1986), Mary Wilson's *Dreamgirl: My Life as a Supreme* (1986) and Ronnie Spector's book *Be My Baby* (1990). These books exposed the everyday reality of these women's experiences with the music industry, their producers and the men who controlled them. They also revealed the crushing impact of racism on their career and life opportunities.

Tina Turner (with writer Kurt Loder) speaks about her escape from husband Ike Turner's domestic violence, and how she gradually built up her strength and discovered her power as a solo artist. Ronnie Spector, too, describes being incarcerated by her husband, the producer Phil Spector, and how after breaking free from his abuse she regained a sense of agency and independence, going on to record four solo albums. She captures the exhilaration of hard-won artistic freedom in this passage:

> I'd just spent more than five years living like a millionaire in a twenty-three-room mansion, and I felt helpless the whole time. Now, here I was standing at the corner of Sunset and Doheny, barefoot and without a penny to my name, and I'd never felt stronger in my life. (Spector 1990: 199)

In *Dreamgirl: My Life as a Supreme*, Mary Wilson explores the battle of wills between bandmates Diana Ross and Florence Ballard, observing the gradual disintegration of the group as Motown pushed Diana to be the Supremes' main star. Her book offers insight into the mechanics of the girl group in the 1960s era, and the commercial pressures that tore apart their friendship.

Literature scholar Tomasz Sawczuk argues that the language and the narrative of female music memoirs are divergent from those of male music memoirs, displaying high levels of self-awareness and authorial self-creation (Sawczuk 2016). The main theme of female memoirs is their route to empowerment, a liberation that is self-questioned and continuously formulating. Sawczuk quotes Couser saying that our selves are always in the process of being constructed, that identity is a performance and that writing a life narrative produces a new subject (Sawczuk 2016: 74).

Sawczuk talks about how in memoir-writing the author reaches a critical point, a state of intensified creativity, which 'entails moving from one frame of mind to an entirely different one' (Sawczuk 2016: 76). There is a reassessment of the past. In *Hunger Makes Me a Modern Girl*, Sleater Kinney guitarist Carrie Brownstein reimagines her childhood from the standpoint of her artistic self.

> My mother and I started to fight all the time. She was retreating from the world, a slow-motion magic trick. Meanwhile, I was getting louder, angrier, wilder. I experimented with early forms of my own amplification – of self, of voice, of fury – while my mother's volume was turned down lower and lower, only ever audible when she broadcast searing feedback and static; broken, tuneless sounds. (Brownstein 2015: 41)

The book title points to the impact on her life of her mother's anorexia and how her Riot Grrrl band offered Sleater Kinney a way to express that experience. Within their sound can be heard Brownstein's anger, questing and experimentation, striving to find a new way of existing in the world.

The Brownstein's pet dog is symbolic of family dysfunction. Brownstein remembers that during her childhood the dog had a glossy coat and bags of enthusiasm, but as her mother's anorexia worsens and puts a strain on her parents' marriage, the dog is neglected and half-starved, dragging itself around with a matted coat and sad eyes. This thread is picked up later when Brownstein writes about how Sleater Kinney went on hiatus in 2007 and she was lost without the band. She becomes careless with her pets and one day comes home to find that her dog killed one of her cats.

Her memoir shows the struggle a female musician goes through, on both a personal and public level, to be acknowledged as an artist in her own right.

She is aware that a space has already been taken, saying 'the archetypes, the stage moves, the representations of rebellion and debauchery were all male' (Brownstein 2015: 127).

As a woman in a rock band, she was always seen as Other, made to feel like she was an interloper or imposter. She pulls apart a question she was continually asked during interviews: What does it feel like to be a woman in a band? She realizes that this question – that talking about the experience – had become part of the experience itself.

> More than anything, I feel that this meta-discourse, talking about the talk, is part of how it feels to be a 'woman in music' (or a 'woman in anything', for that matter – politics, business, comedy, power). . . . There is the music itself, and then there is the ongoing dialogue about how it feels. . . . I doubt in the history of rock journalism and writing any man has been asked, 'Why are you in an all-male band?' (Brownstein 2015: 128)

Kim Gordon, too, captures the conflicting power of being a woman in the band. 'For high end music labels, the music matters, but a lot comes down to how the girl looks. The girl anchors the stage, sucks in the male gaze, and throws her own gaze back out into the audience' (Gordon 2015: 4). She brings coolly devastating observation into her analysis of Sonic Youth's last show:

> Thurston double-slapped our bass guitarist Mark on the shoulder and loped across the stage, followed by Lee, our guitarist, and then Steve Shelley, our drummer. I found that gesture so phony, so childish, such a fantasy. He's never been the shoulder-slapping type. It was a gesture that called out, *I'm back. I'm free. I'm solo.* (Gordon 2015: 1)

Gordon feels excluded from the band dynamics, ousted from her place at the centre of the stage. Partly about the dissolution of her marriage to Thurston Moore, Gordon's memoir forms one slow letter of revenge as she demarcates, chapter by chapter, her contribution to this seminal post-punk band.

Contact zones

Robert Lloyd's discussion of horror writer Shirley Jackson's memoirs is useful for looking at the way the life writer determines the feminist 'self' in their work. There is identity creation, a construction of the self that often involves stepping out of or reframing social and cultural expectations. He considers life writing 'as a figuration of femininity, which also reveals the ways femininity is discursively invigilated and regulated' (Lloyd 2020: 817). In her book *More Myself*, Alicia Keys, for instance, recounts a chilling example of having her sense of agency taken away during a photo shoot in which she is pressured to go topless and objectify herself for marketing purposes. 'My spirit is screaming that something is wrong, that this feels sleazy. But my protests, lodged in the back of my throat, can't make their way out. . . . *If I say no, what doors will be closed to me?*' (Keys 2020: 3). This is written about as a pivotal point in her early career, when she learns with tough realization that the sense of agency she needs will be continually contested, something that she continually has to fight for. When she later sees that image on the cover of a magazine, Keys has a visceral response.

> I almost throw up. I want to buy every copy around the world, just so no one will see me in a photo that does not represent who I am. I swear that I'll never again let someone rob me of my power. It's a promise I still work to keep. (Keys 2020: 4)

In her memoir *Wayward*, Vashti Bunyan recalls recording a song in 1966 for Andrew Loog Oldham's Immediate label. The singer-songwriter created a demo with guitarist Mike Crowther, and for the studio session she wanted to keep the song's pared-down arrangements. Instead Oldham asked conductor Art Greenslade to arrange it for a huge orchestra, with an operatic diva singing a note in the middle. Bunyan could feel her confidence ebbing away, but at one point during the session she spoke up. 'Just once I found the courage to say I thought the guitar parts Mike and I had written for "Winter Is Blue" needed to be played a bit softer. They weren't – and I don't think I said another word' (Bunyan 2022: 40).

Finding it hard to muster support for her music and her vision, Bunyan drifted into obscurity. But when her 1970 album *Just Another Diamond Day* was re-released in 2000, she reached a new generation of folk fans, and by the 2010s, she was recording, to great acclaim, the music that she heard in her head, not a producer's idea of that music. Her book concludes with the emergence of this mature self, enjoying the success with a sound that people want in its original form. Her 2015 album *Some Things Just Stick in Your Mind* includes two versions of 'Winter Is Blue', and the demo is the one listeners seek out. In July 2023, for instance, the orchestral Immediate version had 579,495 plays, while the simple, more personal demo had plays of 2.5 million. Bunyan also recounts gleefully

Writing into the Canon 127

how in 2006 she accepted a request for her song 'Diamond Day' to be used in a T-Mobile phone advert.

> I upset a lot of people by saying yes though, from those who loved the song for its seemingly anti-commercial stance. My response was to say that I had always been told in my young days that my songs were 'uncommercial, dear', and so this was a kind of validation, a deeply, darkly, wonderfully unexpected thing to happen – and I loved it. (Bunyan 2022: 208–9)

In detailing stories like this, Bunyan's book becomes a quietly reflective vindication of her art.

Lloyd argues that life writing involves a degree of difficulty and struggle 'both in grasping the self and communicating it' (Lloyd 2020: 3–4). A kind of creative non-fiction that constructs space for 'alternative voices and alternative ways of remembering' (Edgar, Mann and Pleasance 2019: 3), women's life-writing narratives are often fluctuating and fragmentary, capturing emotion and a critical self-reflection. In that reflexivity, there is an element of autoethnography, with artists illuminating through their experiences the gendered cultural practice in popular music. Miki Berenyi is honest about the divisiveness that is created in Lush when the press focus on her as a marketable lead singer, and how she is constantly wrestling with her own self-image versus the public presentation of the band.

> There's an inevitable focus on the lead singer in bands, even more so when that singer is a woman and has bright red hair. But Lush had been born out of a defiantly indie scene – anti-star, anti-contrivance – and I had no desire myself to be singled out as frontwoman, carrying the full weight of the band's public image. It smacked of the whole 'Blondie is a band' struggle and I was no Debbie Harry. (Berenyi 2022: 223)

When I was working with Skin on her memoir she recalled moments when she was propelled from one self, one state of being, to another – like when as a shy woman in her early twenties she turned around to her stalker, a man who had sexually assaulted her, and screamed in his face, thus finding the deep, wild voice that has become such a dynamic force in her rock performance. Ana Garcia refers to 'storytelling practices [. . .] as the construction of an activist self still in the making' (Garcia 2019: 212), and the writing of *It Takes Blood and Guts* allowed Skin to explore an emotional and political journey, from the young girl in Brixton who felt powerless, to later finding strength as the lead singer of a high profile band. Coining the term 'Clit Rock' as an antidote to 'Cock Rock', she then applied it in campaigning, travelling to Ivory Coast in the late 1990s to lead a conference against Female Genital Mutilation (FGM), and working for anti-FGM charity FORWARD. She also considered how racism marginalized her experience as a Black woman singing rock music, providing an alternative narrative to a 1990s Britpop scene dominated by white male guitar bands like Suede, Blur and Oasis (Skin 2020).

Juliane Egerer considers the importance of life writing for marginalized groups – 'listening to and understanding those whose voices are in danger of being silenced by dominant cultures' (Egerer 2023: 2). Narratives become contact zones for exploring identity and belonging. In writing about what inspired songs for Skunk Anansie's 1994 debut album *Paranoid and Sunburnt*, Skin recalled that even though she was born in the UK people kept asking, 'Where are you from?' Yet when she visited her family in Jamaica, she realized she didn't belong there either: 'In the country markets of Jamaica I couldn't understand a word anyone said to me' (Skin 2020: 125). The 1990s music scene for her represented a crucial moment of belonging: 'when my black British generation developed our own culture, which came out so strongly in the music and the hybrid collisions of soul, rock and rap' (Skin 2020: 126).

Soul singer PP Arnold, too, graphically describes that sense of constructing a new existence for herself, leaving behind the harsh conditions of poverty and racial segregation in 1950s and 1960s America to find acceptance and freedom hanging out with the Rolling Stones on the London rock scene and living in leafy Epsom. 'I was learning so much from Mick (Jagger) about British culture and about this new rock 'n' roll lifestyle. No woman in my family had ventured this far from our roots and I was grateful for this opportunity' (Arnold 2022: 152). After a while, she noticed covert racism on the UK scene, as in the three-way affair she had with Jagger and Marianne Faithfull. 'I didn't yet understand the power I had as a black chick from the States. The relationship started to feel uncomfortable; there was a plantation feel about it, like I was a plaything, only there to entertain the two of them' (Arnold 2022: 180).

By the end of her book, Arnold comes to understand the power of her heritage and how much she has contributed to the soul scene in the UK, from working with Steve Marriot and the Small Faces in the 1960s, through to her solo records and her collaboration in the 1990s and 2000s with groups like the KLF, Ocean Colour Scene and Primal Scream, and this heals some of the old hurts. Egerer pinpoints the fluidity of identity in life writing, how trauma can be processed and healed in the act of writing, opening up lines of 'transcultural identity construction', an act that is ongoing (Egerer 2023: 1).

Authentic voice

My work with bass player Mary McGlory and drummer Sylvia Saunders from the Liverbirds shows how consideration of class opens up a new contact zone. Both came from poor, working-class backgrounds in Liverpool and left school at fifteen in the early 1960s, when women had very restricted career opportunities. Music was their way out. Seeing the Beatles at the Cavern inspired them to form a girl band, and when John Lennon once said to them backstage: 'Girls don't play guitars' that hardened their resolve to become successful. They travelled to Hamburg and landed a regular slot at the Star Club, where the Beatles first started. Within a year they were recording their first album and had become stars in Europe and Japan, touring extensively and honing their craft. Sylvia reflects on how being in a band transformed her life. 'Being in the band and travelling through different countries gave me the confidence to start a business in Spain. It was nothing for (my husband) John and I to say, "Let's go and do it"' (McGlory and Saunders 2024: 330).

In writing their memoir, she and Mary reframed the experience of their mothers and grandmothers, and how much that propelled them to seek a life that transcended barriers of class and gender. Mary notes in one of her concluding paragraphs:

> Writing this book has made me re-evaluate my family and my life. I realise what a hardworking woman my grandma was, and how hard it must have been for my mother and she still got it all together, settling down with my father and having all those children. We were young girls having the courage to make a go of something; it's an easygoing story that wasn't easy to do. (McGlory and Saunders 2024: 335)

Because they didn't score chart hits in the UK or America, the significance of the Liverbirds as one of the first all-girl beat groups has been missed, and only now, uncovering their story fifty years later, has their contribution been recognized.

Memoirs often involve collaboration with a writing partner or ghostwriter, as in my work with Mary and Sylvia. There was constant data triangulation, not just in our conversations about past events, but also with interviewing friends and peers, beat musicians who knew them in Hamburg and Liverpool, like Lee Curtis, Beryl Marsden and Roy Dyke from beat band the Remo Four. These interviews were important for fleshing out the wider context and building on their memories of particular events or eras. There was also the work to remember and document the experience of deceased members, lead singer Pam Birch and guitarist Valerie Gell, both vibrant personalities in the evolution of the Liverbirds.

Working in this collaborative way inevitably raises potential problems as to the nature of the autobiographical voice. As Garcia notes (2019) in her study of the life-writing texts of Malala Yousafzai, the Pakistani schoolgirl who was shot by the Taliban because of her advocacy for girl's education, there are problematics surrounding complex notions of a self that is co-constructed. Through *New York Times* documentaries, a celebrity blog, magazine articles and Twitter account, there was always someone else involved in the process of writing Malala's story – whether it was an editor, journalist, manager or translator. But in that collaborative process, there is a co-creation of knowledge and a growing awareness of the 'self' within a broader cultural context. Malala 'emerges as an empowered individual that no longer requires someone to speak for her. Her "I" is a powerful agent, drawing from traditions of human rights, testimonial writing and ethics' (Garcia 2019: 204).

Capturing the 'voice' in life writing is a challenging process. With the Liverbirds, for instance, it was important to convey the spontaneity of working-class girls who refused to be marketed as a novelty or dolly bird musicians, fusing their sparky dialogue with a wider historical narrative about the revolutionary pull of the 1960s. And Skin, writing her memoir during lockdown and the Black Lives Matter demonstrations across America, was adamant about the diverse audience she wanted to reach. That meant, for instance, not translating any phrases she had written in Jamaican patois or over-explaining the mechanics of the London dancehall and pirate radio scene. In a popular music landscape where their efforts have been overlooked, misrepresented or misunderstood, female memoirists work hard to keep their authorial voice clear and authentic.

An important outcome in the growth of female music memoir is the way it ensures that women's experience is not lost. As Sanjek has noted, there were dozens of feisty female rockabilly singers in the 1950s, but they weren't taken seriously by major labels and very few of those voices were committed to vinyl, or, like Barbara Pittman on Sun Records, they cut a number of singles that weren't promoted and were then dropped (Sanjek 1997). There is intense poignancy to the fact that because their stories weren't considered important, as that generation passes away, their lives and their music disappear from the public record. The life writing of female musicians, therefore, forms an imperative and evolving part of feminist history.

References

Albertine, Viv (2014). *Clothes, Music, Boys*. London: Faber.

Arnold, 'PP' (2022). *Soul Survivor: The Autobiography*. London: Nine Eight.

Berenyi, Miki (2022). *Fingers Crossed: How Music Saved Me from Success*. London: Nine Eight.

Brownstein, Carrie ([2015] 2016). *Hunger Makes Me a Modern Girl: A Memoir*. London: Virago.

Bunyan, Vashti (2022). *Wayward: Just Another Life to Live*. London: White Rabbit.

Edgar, Robert, Fraser Mann, and Helen Pleasance (2019). *Music, Memory and Memoir*. New York: Bloomsbury Academic Press.

Egerer, Juliane (2023). 'Afro-Swedish and Ojibwe-Canadian Trauma Life Writings: Storms from Paradise, Reasons for Walking, and the Opening of Planetary Circles of Conversation', *Scandinavian-Canadian Studies* 30: 1–35.

Gordon, Kim (2015). *Girl in a Band*. London: Faber.

Holiday, Billie with William Dufty. ([1956] 2018). *Lady Sings the Blues*. London: Penguin Classics.

Keys, Alicia (2020). *More Myself: A Journey*. New York: Flatiron Books.

Lloyd, Robert (2020). 'What's Haunting Shirley Jackson? The Spectral Condition of Life Writing', *Women's Studies* 49(8): 809–34.

Martinez Garcia, Ana Belén (2019). 'Construction and Collaboration in Life-Writing Projects: Malala Yousafzai's Activist "I"', *Journal of Writing in Creative Practice* 12(1&2): 201–17.

McGlory, Mary and Sylvia Saunders (2024). *The Liverbirds*. London: Faber.

Morgan, Sue (ed.) (2006). *The Feminist History Reader*. Oxon and New York: Routledge.

Oakley, A. (2010). 'The Social Science of Biographical Life-Writing: Some Methodological and Ethical Issues', *International Journal of Social Research Methodology* 13(5): 425–39.

Ross, Diana (1993). *Secrets of A Sparrow*. New York: Villard Books.

Sanjek, David (1997). 'Can a Fujiyama Mama be the Female Elvis? The Wild, Wild Women of Rockabilly', in Sheila Whiteley (ed.), *Sexing the Groove: Popular Music and Gender*, 137–67. London and New York: Routledge.

Sawczuk, Tomasz (2016). '"I've been Crawling up So Long on Your Stairway to Heaven": The Rise of the Female Rock Memoir', *Crossroads. A Journal of English Studies* 15: 71–81.

Skin with Lucy O'Brien (2020). *It Takes Blood and Guts*. London: Simon & Schuster.

Smith, Patti (2010). *Just Kids*. London: Bloomsbury.

Spector, Ronnie ([1990] 2022). *Be My Baby*. London: Pan Macmillan.

Thorn, Tracey (2013). *Bedsit Disco Queen*. London: Virago.

Turner, Tina with Kurt Loder ([1986] 2010). *I, Tina*. New York: Dey Street.

Von Appen, Ralf and André Doehring (2006). 'Nevermind the Beatles, Here's Exile 61 and Nico: "The Top 100 Records of All Time" – A Canon of Pop and Rock Albums from a Sociological and an Aesthetic Perspective', *Popular Music* 25(1): 21–39.

Wilson, Mary ([1986] 2000). *Dreamgirl: My Life as a Supreme.* Lanham: Cooper Square.

10

Rock obits

Patti Smith and the deceased

Janneke Van Der Leest

For good reason we may call Patti Smith an 'elegist'. The elegy is the age-old poetic genre in which the topic is the traumatic experience of loss of a loved person. Many of Smith's songs are meant to remember dead friends and musicians. Elegies are regulated by strong conventions, focusing on lament and praise for the dead beloved and progressing from grief to consolation for the mourning poet. Although modern poets abandon and even resist the strict norms of the genre, this means that they still maintain a strong bond with it.[1] Elegies on deceased poets (Shelley's famous elegy on the death of Keats, 'Adonaïs', for example) form a specific subgroup within the elegiac genre. I consider Smith's elegies for rock musicians as a variant within this group. In this chapter, I follow the elegiac path of tributes to early deceased rock stars throughout Smith's career so far. The deaths of her heroes turn out to play a decisive role in her (artistic) life, and she transforms these sad turning points into literary and musical expression.

Brian Jones

As in Smith's personal life in which she lost many loved ones, many of her *heroes* died early too – including Brian Jones. She frames his death within a personal story. It was July 1969, together with her sister Linda she was staying in Paris for a few months where she wrote poetry, drew and tried to sell her work to galleries. Prompted by her impressions of Jean-Luc Godard's movie *One Plus*

---

[1] For a discussion of modern versions of the elegy, see Ramazani (1994).

One[2] together with the news in an English rock magazine that said that Jones might leave the Stones, she started to develop nightmarish visions in which she saw that 'Brian Jones was in danger, that Brian Jones was hurt, that Brian Jones was about to sink beneath the surface' (Thompson 2001: 41). To reduce the pain and fever caused by an accident with boiling water on her leg, Smith used medicine that intensified the hallucinatory dreams. Several nights she dreamt of Jones, and there was always water involved in the disturbing dreams. A few days later she saw in the French newspapers the picture of Brian Jones accompanied by the words 'Est Mort, 27 Ans'. He had drowned in his swimming pool. She remembers: 'I laid my drawing pencils aside and began a cycle of poems to Brian Jones, for the first time expressing my love for rock and roll within my work' (Smith 2012: 83).

Indeed, after the Smith sisters returned to America, writing became the core business for Patti. 'I had gone to Paris to find myself as an artist, [. . .] but I came back to New York filled with words and rhythms' (Thompson 2001: 46). Jones's death not only led her to writing but also triggered her to utter her love for *rock and roll* – from then on, a recurring theme in her work. His death effected a creative rebirth for Smith.

Not long after her return from Paris, Smith moved together with Robert Mapplethorpe to the smallest room in the Hotel Chelsea. There, Bobby Neuwirth took her under his wing. When they first met, she was working on her requiem for Jones. And according to her, Neuwirth 'didn't really understand the whole Brian Jones thing, [. . .] but the thing was, he recognized something within the pieces, something that I didn't see. I didn't know what I was doing. I wasn't trying to create art or change the world, I was trying to rid myself of my guilt, my mania about it, my obsession' (March 2021: 45).

The spoken word poem 'Brian Jones' is a result of the Jones poems Smith worked on in this period. On a later recording (on 7″ vinyl, 1973), Lenny Kaye supports the poem with a distorted and atonal guitar sound. We hear the thrill of Smith's Paris nightmarish prophecies and the repeating rhythm of sorrow, of sobbing. The text consists of much repetition. Smith calls it her 'own mantra', and she chants 'Brian Brian / I'm not crying / I'm trying / to reach you' (Smith 1973). It stems from a blending of personal memories – the one of the nightmares in Paris as well as that of the only time Smith met Jones in real life at

---

[2] During her stay in France, Smith repeatedly watched this movie in which the recording of the Stones' song 'Sympathy for the Devil' alternates with avant-garde monologues and dialogues.

Rock Obits

an overcrowded, chaotic Stones concert in 1966. In an article for the magazine *Creem*, she recounts how the audience pushed her forward, right on to the stage: 'a million girls busting my spleen. oh beaudelaire. I grabbed Brian's ankle and held on like a drowning child. it seemed like hours. (...) Bill Wyman cracked up. Brian grinned' (Smith 1973).

Jim Morrison

Smith had discovered poetry to be her artistic discipline, and Jones's death 'added more kindling to the fire under her rock poetry' (Katz 2021: 34). This resulted in *Seventh Heaven* (1972), Smith's first published collection of poems, which included a poem for both Brian Jones and Jim Morrison, 'Death by Water'. Smith took Morrison as an example to shape her image as a rebel poet, based on their mutual 'hero', the enfant terrible of French nineteenth-century poetry: Arthur Rimbaud. But Morrison's performance as the Doors' singer inspired her to become a singer too.

At the time around his death, Smith saw a billboard in Los Angeles for the Doors' new album *L.A. Woman* and at the same time heard the strains of their new single coming over the radio. At that moment she felt remorse that she had almost forgotten what an important influence Morrison had been on her: 'He had led me on the path of merging poetry into rock and roll, and I resolved to buy the album and write a worthy piece on his behalf' (Smith 2012: 187). By the time she was back in New York, the news reached her of his passing. He died in a bathtub in a Paris apartment on 3 July , two years to the day after Jones. In Smith's poem 'Death by Water', the two deaths are literally mentioned: 'brian jones drowned [. . .] in a child's pool of water' and 'jim Morrison [. . .] died in a bathtub' (Smith 1972: 40).

In the poem, Smith enters into dialogue with T. S. Eliot. The title is derived from the part of his epic poem *The Waste Land*, which is titled 'Death by Water'. In that section, Phlebas the Phoenician drowns. He is a personification of the dying and rising fertility god, and his 'successor': Christ. By death he can become the redeemer. The promise of the first line of Smith's 'Death by Water' ('How long was man promised?') might refer to 'the "promise" that Christ's sacrifice would put an end to *all* sacrifice. With Jones's death this promise appears to have been betrayed' (Shaw 2008: 53). Christ's sacrifice was not for eternity as it turned out when *modern culture* replaced Christianity – and

136   *Ink on the Tracks*

therefore Phlebas and his sacrifice replaced Christ. And now that in its turn *popular culture* replaces the modernist culture of the early twentieth century, new offerings have to be made and Phlebas is replaced by Jones and Morrison. Christ and Morrison seem to merge in the figure of 'our leather lamb'. Christ is born from the Immaculate Conception of Christ's mother, but Morrison is called '*truly* immaculate'. He is also suggested to be 'a marked man' with prophetic gifts. Smith imagines Morrison's last words are 'but you promised', referring to the opening line – and therewith a possible complaint against Christ's Father.

Smith does not honour Morrison solely with poetry. For example, on 13 July 1973, she gave a reading in memory of him. And in October of the same year, she travelled to France on a pilgrimage to both the grave of Rimbaud and Morrison. In 'jukebox cruci-fix' (1975), an article she wrote for *Creem*, Smith recalls how she sat at Morrison's grave for a couple of hours, covered with rain and mud, afraid to move, and how then, suddenly:

> racing thru my skull were new plans new dreams voyages symphonies colors. I just wanted to get the hell outa there and go home and do my own work. to focus my floodlight on the rhythm within. I straightened my skirt and said good-bye to him. an old woman in black spoke to me in broken english. look at this grave how sad! why do you americans not honor your poets? [. . .] I brushed the feathers off my raincoat and answered: because we don't look back. (Smith 1975)

Morrison inspired her while he was alive, but now that he is dead and she has made her pilgrimage, she felt he offered her a precious insight. The pilgrimage convinced her that she no longer needed to look back to her idols and predecessors for approval. She had to look ahead, to her own future.

In 'jukebox cruci-fix', Smith also evokes the vision she had of a Morrison-like angel during the grave visit: 'I remembered this dream I had. I came in a clearing and saw a man on a marble slab. it was Morrison and he was human. but his wings were merging with the marble. he was struggling to get free but like Prometheus freedom was beyond him. [. . .] I finished the dream. the stone dissolved and he flew away' (Smith 1975). This vision was the basis for the song 'Break It Up', on *Horses* (1975), which Smith wrote with Tom Verlaine. The words 'break it up' refer not just to the dreamt Morrison who eventually tears away from the marble, but also to the step Smith took herself thanks to 'this artistic calling' (Whiteley 2006: 90) at the grave. Her debut album *Horses* is proof of this step. It proves she can perfectly well stand on her own two feet as a unique artist.

The suggested parallel with the immortal Prometheus is not so much that Morrison was doomed to be bound to stone. The parallel lies in *bringing fire*, in this case to the creative and assertive mind of Patti Smith. In the song, she first wants to imitate the boy, that is the winged Morrison of her vision: when the boy broke out of his skin, the I-person crawled in. Whereas later she tore off her clothes and, next, she also ripped her skin open. The song is not only about Smith mourning Morrison who broke with life to which he was chained as an alcoholic pop star. The urge to 'break it up' is also about release: freeing Prometheus/Morrison and freeing herself from her bondage to him.

The narrator in the song first does not understand: 'He cried break it up, oh, I don't understand' (Smith 2015: 45). Also after a struggle, she does not immediately comprehend: 'Break it up, I can't comprehend'. This struggle with 'the angel' is a reference to Jacob's struggle with the angel (Gen. 32.22-32). Jacob knew only afterwards that he had a fight with God. Likewise, in the song, the I-person gradually started to understand, until she herself 'broke through' and could cry 'Break it up, oh, now I understand' (Smith 2015: 46). The boy stands not just for Morrison, echoing Prometheus, but can also be identified as the angel, since he 'flew away'. If this is all the same person, does Smith then equate Morrison here with God? Is this a description of her fight with her god? It seems so.

Jimi Hendrix

Next to 'Break It Up' two other songs on *Horses*, 'Land' and 'Elegie', honour deceased rock stars. During the last recording session of the singing part of 'Land', Smith had the following experience:

> it was obvious that I was being told what I wanted to know about Hendrix's death. The song is like 8 or 9 minutes long, so it's obvious I'm gonna lose control sometime – but I felt like it was *The Exorcist*, or somebody else talking through my voice. I said 'How did I die . . . I-I-I tried to walk thru' light' . . . and it ended up with 'in the sheets, there was a man' – it really frightened me. (Shaw 2008: 130)

In the song we have 'wild-boy imagery fused with the stages of Hendrix's death' (Smith 2012: 249). Although Hendrix serves as Smith's main reference in the song, Morrison and Joplin and their deaths also play a part. In an interview, she specifies that Morrison is 'intimately linked' to Johnny, the main character of 'Land' (Shaw 2008: 127). The title and the transitional section to the second part of the song – 'horses, horses, horses, horses' – refer to the word 'horse' as slang for heroin, the drug which Morrison, Joplin and Hendrix used.

Nevertheless, the album is drenched in Jimi Hendrix. It is recorded at the Electric Lady Studios, founded by him. Smith's description of entering the studio for the recording of *Horses* is full of memories of Jimi, such as: 'I opened the doors of Electric Lady studio. As I descended the stairs, I could not help but recall the time Jimi Hendrix stopped for a moment to talk to a shy young girl' (Smith 2012: 248; Smith refers here to her encounter with Hendrix in 1970 (Smith 2012: 169; Edmonds 2021: 225–6)). Also, the first single Patti Smith recorded at a studio, together with Lenny Kaye, Richard Sohl and Tom Verlaine, was recorded at Electric Lady in 1974. The A side, 'Hey Joe (Version)', was a tribute to Hendrix. When she started the recording Smith whispered 'Hi, Jimi' into the microphone (Smith 2012: 241). In the wake of that single's release, a show by Smith and her band members was videoed. There, the close of an early version of 'Land' was followed by 'Hey Joe (Version)'. In between those songs Smith gives

> a roll call of the great and the good: a mythical killer shoots down Baudelaire and Rimbaud, they fall down on one knee; the sequence shifts to the United States: Jan and Dean, Chuck Jackson, James Brown, Marvin Gaye, the Rolling Stones, Arthur Lee, all fall down on one knee, heralding the arrival of the 'black angel' Jimi Hendrix, whose set at the Monterey Pop Festival in 1967 climaxed with the rock legend going down on *both* knees to set his guitar alight. (Shaw 2008: 90)

Hendrix is – through Smith's imagination – honoured by great poets and famous musicians. Above all, she suggests that from the ashes of his legacy new songs and new styles arise. She honours not the dead Hendrix, but the inspiration he ignites for something new.

Horses is full of references to those who paved the way before Smith and are gone now. In this sense the last song on the album, 'Elegie', is the crowning achievement. The song, written with Allen Öyster, was recorded on the fifth anniversary of Hendrix's death. It was initially written for him and was originally named 'Elegy for Jimi Hendrix' (Shapiro 2021: 28). But the song was also meant to pay homage to Jones, Morrison and Joplin (Aston 2015: 80). Smith even dares to extend it to everyone 'we had lost, were losing, and would ultimately lose' (Smith 2012: 249). Note how strange it is to write an elegy for those who are not yet gone.

Frequently, she concludes concerts with 'Elegie' together with a list of names she calls out of musicians and friends who have passed away. Because of the growing list, it becomes on the one hand 'increasingly harder' and 'difficult' for her to sing the song, but on the other hand it is 'liberating', for 'we're celebrating these people, it's not all sad. It keeps their energy and life force around' (Aston 2015: 80). Here we witness Smith practising her motto: 'the living are meant to remember the dead. That's how the dead [are] remembered, by the living' (Holland 2021: 387).

'Elegie' speaks of the 'richness of death, of how loss can be transformed into profit; of how a singer can feed on the legacy of the dead (Morrison, Hendrix, Rimbaud), and of how declarations of self-reliance and autonomy ("moving on my own" and "I have the will") are haunted and undermined by attendant feelings of guilt and sorrow' (Shaw 2008: 137). In this observation, there resonates, on the one hand, the power that Smith experienced at Morrison's grave that she can do it on her own; on the other, the painful matter of guilt because she lives off her dead heroes to legitimize her own artistry. The words of grief she utters at the end of the song illustrate this literally. These are namely quotations from Hendrix's '1983 . . . (A Merman I Should Turn to Be)': 'But I think it's sad, it's much too bad / That all our friends can't be with us today' (Smith 2015: 53). Smith practices what she regrets. But the poet reaping profit commemorating the deceased colleague is an unavoidable feature of elegies on poets: Ramazani (1994: 6–8, 53 and 343) speaks of 'the economic problem of (poetic) mourning'.

So indeed, Smith can be labelled an 'elegist', as Aidan Levy states (Levy 2021: 380) in an introduction to the printed radio interview from 2012 by Eric Holland, who noticed that it is one of the defining characteristics of Smith's career that she takes loss and channels it into art. Her reaction is that indeed her very first poem ever published was about loss, an elegy to Charlie Parker. 'Bird is free', as it was called, was published in the school paper. 'So I've been consistent. You know, *Horses* has an elegy to Jimi Hendrix and an elegy to Jim Morrison. And, you know, I'm consistent', as she herself concludes (Holland 2021: 387).

Kurt Cobain

While Smith grows older, she gets confronted with losses in the circle of family and friends. The 1996 album *Gone Again* is about these losses. In five years, she lost her close friend Robert Mapplethorpe; the keyboardist of the Patti Smith

Group, Richard Sohl; and in 1994 within weeks both her husband, Fred 'Sonic' Smith, and her brother and road manager, Todd. But even then, Smith devotes a song, 'About a Boy', on her death-inspired record to a deceased rock star: Kurt Cobain, who shot himself. The song title is an allusion to Nirvana's song 'About a Girl'.

Smith wrote it for two reasons: 'to wish Cobain well as his soul continued its journey' and 'to chastise him for leaving the world to get along without him' (Thompson 2001: 207). In an interview, she tells that as a parent she was 'deeply disturbed to see this young boy take his own life. The waste, and the emotional debris he left for others to clean up' (Edmonds 2021: 224). She was concerned about how the suicide of Nirvana's front man would affect young people who looked up to him and was of the opinion that Cobain had a responsibility as a star to himself, his family and the younger generation. Smith looks down at his act like an indignant, disappointed, sad 'parent'. For her, 'the godmother of punk', Cobain was 'just a boy' (Smith 2015: 151). She was about twenty years older and had been in the business for two decades when Cobain took his life.

The chorus – the repeated line 'About a boy beyond it all' (Smith 2015: 150) – evokes diverse connotations. Smith says that one way of looking at the chorus is

> that he's beyond this particular plane of existence. But it's also a wry statement, a frustrated refrain. It relates to my sorrow for the various boys we have lost. Whether it be Jim Morrison or Brian Jones; any of these young, gifted, driven people who *do* feel they're beyond it all, that they can completely ravage and ruin their bodies or have no sense of responsibility to their position and their gifts. (Edmonds 2021: 225)

Then nature images follow that evoke the idyll of the pastoral elegy, and in the third couplet, Smith describes a move from chaos to 'another kind of peace', and 'toward the great emptiness' (Smith 2015: 150).

Next comes a more obscure part. Is the 'I' Smith or Cobain? There is something to be said for the idea that it is herself who stands among her dead beloved ones and then switches to the voice of God, although it can also be Cobain's voice. In a live version of 2000 it is clear (23 June 2000 at the Mural Amphitheatre in Seattle, WA: https://www.youtube.com/watch?v=1pi8_qu8Wyo). Smith first brings in her own voice and changes it into a dialogue in which we hear both Cobain and God through the I-person. Smith speaks of the world of corruption and cynicism, of the 'seekers of celebrity' with whom Cobain had to deal. He could not take it anymore and asks 'If I cannot be pure, take me Lord'. The

Lord answers 'Walk through with your sour stomach'. But he could not and 'he put a gun in his mouth and blew his fucking head off'. Smith then encourages everyone to face the future and not to give up. With this, she reprimands the dangerous temptation that Cobain provokes in many young fans.

The boy who committed suicide is eventually embraced and welcomed by God. At the end of the song, there is again an image of nature, of the winter season, the season of death: 'He was just a boy whirling in the snow / Just a little boy who would never grow' (Smith 2015: 151). Cobain will forever be remembered as a promising young man who took his own life at the age of twenty-seven.

Amy Winehouse

Smith generally mentions Bob Dylan, Jimi Hendrix and Jim Morrison as her predominant rock heroes, sometimes supplemented with Keith Richards, Brian Jones and Janis Joplin. The four deceased rock heroes from this list belong to the so-called 27 Club. In 2011, Amy Winehouse completed the member list of the 27 Club, at least for now. And since Smith is very consistent, as she herself claimed, she wrote a song for the deceased Winehouse: 'This is the Girl' on the album *Banga* (2012).

The mature artist Smith referred to Kurt as 'a boy' and now calls Amy 'the girl'. She speaks of Winehouse and her death from the perspective of both a 'mother' and a 'fan':

> I felt badly for two reasons. One, because I greatly admired her voice. [. . .] But also, you know, as a mother, she's the same age as my kids, and you know, I was concerned as a fan and a human being, that her lifestyle was going to, you know, destroy her voice, be so bad for her health, and so of course, the worst of scenarios happened, and I wrote her a little poem. (Holland 2021: 388–9)

In this song Smith first gives a sketch of Winehouse, 'the girl who was having a ball' (Smith 2015: 258). Her eyes were masked with 'a dark smear'. Through her mask, her deeper inner self is 'spirited away', which also refers to Winehouse's alcohol abuse that led to the cause of her death.

In the next couplet, Smith becomes more severe. She says Winehouse 'crossed the line'. She condemns her lifestyle, like she condemned Cobain's last act. She plays with Winehouse's family name: 'the smothering vine, twisted a laurel to crown her head'. Winehouse (or her root) forms her own funeral wreath as she is found dead on her bed. Her name, her addiction, her body, her symbol – it all falls together in these lines.

The opening line of the third couplet, 'The blood that turned into wine', refers to the last supper when Jesus took a cup of wine and said: 'This is my blood of the covenant, which is poured out for many for forgiveness of sins' (Matt. 26.28). Here, the wine is a symbol for Christ's blood and thus for redemption. In the song, it goes the other way round – blood turns into wine – which implies an opposite result: no forgiveness of sins. Then Smith again refers to elements of Winehouse's biography. Winehouse sang like a bird, but this bird was 'smouldering', while the world witnessed her self-destructive fire. Smith keeps mingling tenderness and rigidness.

Smith's age and experience makes her freer. The early Brian Jones ode consisted of much repetition, including repeating his name. The experience at Morrison's grave made her find her own voice. We see the creative explosion on *Horses* with its complicated, artfully elaborate texts ('Break It Up' and 'Land') and timeless piece of sadness ('Elegie'). In the later odes to deceased pop stars, Smith responds as an older admirer of the young stars, and this permits her also to judge, with a sterner voice and room for a joke.

Smith the elegist, celebrating life

When Patti Smith is labelled an elegist, a long tradition of an old genre resonates. In modern times, poets may break out of the strict conventions of the elegy, but on the other hand, their wrestling with the psychological dimension of the genre increases. The traditional elegy follows the trajectory of *healthy mourning*: a process that leads via diverse emotional states from grief to consolation. In Freudian terms, the process implies that the mourner loses a love-object and in the course of time the ego points itself to a new love-object. The ego is free and uninhibited again, the mourning poet lets the love-object go. Further, the act of writing the poem itself has a therapeutic function: 'redirecting [. . .] affection from the lost friend to the brilliant artifact that is in some measure a replacement for the man it mourns' (Ramazani 1994: 3). Modern elegies, on the contrary, typically follow the path of *unhealthy mourning*, or melancholia, which causes a split within the ego: a part of the mourner's ego continues to identify with the lost object (for the application of the Freudian concepts *mourning* and *melancholia* in the analysis of the elegy, see, for instance, Hühn (2016) and Ramazani (1994)). Melancholic mourners attack the dead and themselves; melancholic elegists attack tradition and their poems. They do not accept comforting images and consolatory endings in their work. In the modern elegy, there is no 'transcendence or redemption of loss but immersion in it' (Ramazani 1994: 4). The consoling goal of the genre becomes the major target of change for the elegist. That is why Ramazani (1994: 10 and 16) speaks of the 'melancholic turn' in the modern elegy.

Patti Smith is not fanatically bound to her dead idols, certainly not in the sense of a melancholic. It is interesting to see how much she – the one who is 'consistent' in remembering dead artists – loves life:

> I love life, and I love being on Earth. I love being an Earthling. I don't revel in the death of these people. I don't love Jimi Hendrix because he died. I loved what he did when he was most alive, you know, and consulting the gods on stage. That's what I loved. I don't have any interest in him consulting the gods to the death. (Burroughs 2021: 156)

Aidan Levy summarizes it well after he summed up many dear friends and heroes Smith had lost: 'We don't come to Patti Smith [. . .] to experience what it's like to suffer through grief; we come to her to experience what it's like to survive it' (Levy 2021: 167). She survives grief through her writings (in particular elegies) and rituals (such as pilgrimages). These acts of commemoration free her ego from the dead. She can let them go. The vision at Morrison's grave even pushes her to do so: after that experience she can still identify with him, but without him and the grief for his loss possessing part of her ego. She imagines Hendrix as 'black angel', Morrison angel-winged and Cobain welcomed by God. These transcendent images are signs that she let her deceased heroes go, and remind us of classical elegies. Beside these imageries, Smith does not use the genre's traditional themes, rhetoric or form. Nevertheless, her psychological approach does follow the path of the traditional elegy. She laments and praises deceased musicians without fighting, ignoring or delaying the goodbye. She does not linger melancholically in mourning, but finds consolation in practising elegiac activities.

Smith's attention to lost geniuses is led by historic sensibility and gratitude for reaping the harvest of her predecessors. She chooses her heroes carefully. Yet there is another possible consequence of the elegy on poets. As Peter Hühn notices, an important difference between mourning the loss of a beloved person and mourning the loss of a fellow-poet is the private and public dimension. A poet lamenting another poet's death always takes into account the status of the poet in society, the function and power of poetry and the exemplary function of the deceased one. This last point indicates that for the elegist, on the one hand,

> the death of his *alter ego* deeply affects him emotionally, somehow prefiguring his own death and the future fate of his own poetry; on the other hand, sharing the fellow-poet's artistic pursuit may create a latently competitive constellation of the two poets, which is liable to induce the elegist to attempt to emulate or possibly surpass the deceased model. (Hühn 2016: 193)

The dead poet thus becomes more or less a competitor. Patti Smith takes her deceased heroes as examples and wants to be associated with them. They guide her, but she is also in the lead: she lets them play their roles at important moments in her life, she lets them construct her life, her rock and roll autobiography and image. Jones's death makes her switch from visual arts to writing and makes her express her love for rock and roll for the first time. When she records her first single in a studio and next an album, she feels the support of and connection with the deceased Hendrix. Mourning for Morrison gives her the insight she can do it herself. Later, Smith does not 'need' Cobain and Winehouse in order to construct her image and life story, like she needed the dead when she was young. But she uses those younger artists, to remind the new generation to honour life. All those fellow-artists for whom she wrote elegies certainly are her exemplars and inspirers, but *she* as the survivor takes up the task of remembering them.

References

Aston, Martin (2015). 'I Think We Accomplished Our Mission', *MOJO* October: 79–84.

Bennett, Andrew (2004). *Romantic Poets and the Culture of Posterity*. Cambridge: Cambridge University Press.

Burroughs, William S. (2021). 'When Patti Rocked', in Aidan Levy (ed.), *Patti Smith on Patti Smith: Interviews and Encounters*, 147–58. Chicago: Chicago Review Press.

Edmonds, Ben (2021). 'The Rebel: Patti Smith', in Aidan Levy (ed.), *Patti Smith on Patti Smith: Interviews and Encounters*, 223–38. Chicago: Chicago Review Press.

Holland, Eric (2021). 'Patti Smith Discusses *Banga* on *Words and Music*', in Aidan Levy (ed.), *Patti Smith on Patti Smith: Interviews and Encounters*, 380–94. Chicago: Chicago Review Press.

Hühn, Peter (2016). *Facing Loss and Death. Narrative and Eventfulness in Lyric Poetry.* Berlin and Boston: De Gruyter.

Kane, Daniel (2012). '"Nor Did I Socialize with Their People": Patti Smith, Rock Heroics and the Poetics of Sociability', *Popular Music* 31(1): 105–23.

Katz, Robin (2021). 'Patti Smith: Poetry in Motion', in Aidan Levy (ed.), *Patti Smith on Patti Smith: Interviews and Encounters*, 30–7. Chicago: Chicago Review Press.

Levy, Aidan (ed.) (2021). *Patti Smith on Patti Smith: Interviews and Encounters.* Chicago: Chicago Review Press.

Marsh, Dave (2021). 'Patti Smith: Her Horses Got Wings, They Can Fly', in Aidan Levy (ed.), *Patti Smith on Patti Smith: Interviews and Encounters*, 38–52. Chicago: Chicago Review Press.

Ramazani, Jahan (1994). *Poetry of Mourning. The Modern Elegy from Hardy to Heaney.* Chicago and London: The University of Chicago Press.

Shapiro, Susin (2021). 'Patti Smith: Somewhere, Over the Rimbaud', in Aidan Levy (ed.), *Patti Smith on Patti Smith: Interviews and Encounters*, 23–9. Chicago: Chicago Review Press.

Shaw, Philip (2008). *Horses.* New York and London: Bloomsbury.

Smith, Patti (1972). *Seventh Heaven.* Boston: Dynamic Learning.

Smith, Patti (1973). 'Jag-arr of the Jungle', *Creem*, January. http://www.oceanstar.com/patti/poetry/jagarr.htm.

Smith, Patti (1975). 'Jukebox Cruci-fix', *Creem*, June. http://www.oceanstar.com/patti/poetry/jukebox.htm

Smith, Patti (2012). *Just Kids.* London: Bloomsbury.

Smith, Patti (2015). *Collected Lyrics 1970–2015.* London: Bloomsbury.

Thompson, Dave (2001). *Dancing Barefoot: The Patti Smith Story.* Chicago: Chicago Review Press.

Whiteley, Sheila (2006). 'Patti Smith: The Old Grey Whistle Test, BBC2, May 11, 1976', in Ian Inglis (ed.), *Performance and Popular Music. History, Place and Time*, 81–91. Aldershot: Ashgate.

11

'The magic runes are writ in gold'

Writing mythology, transcendence and faith in rock

Simon McAslan

Rock and roll is much more than the music; it is a lifestyle, a worldview, lending itself well to mythology and mythologizing. Indeed, it has not only its own royalty but also its pantheon of rock gods. Even those who would overthrow these monarchs and renounce these deities become ensnared in rock mythology themselves, the punks punked. Rock makes otherworldly the ordinary, mystic the mundane. Despite rock's supernatural essence, some writing around it seems to miss this aspect, becoming mere chronicling or sycophancy, drawn into a spider's web of pretentious pondering and pandering. However, other rock writing engages with its subject in kind and navigates the ethos of rock's mystical side.

Some texts informed by rock both celebrate that mystic element or lovingly mock it. *The Rock Bible: Unholy Scripture for Fans and Bands*, a book 'assembled, organized, edited and manifested by Henry H. Owings' from a shared concept by Brian Teasley (Owings 2008: copyright page), satirizes the doctrines of rock culture; Greg Simmons's *Rock and Roll Hotels: Sex. Drugs. Fluffy Pillows*, a witty guide to hotels frequented by rocks stars, is in part a glorification of those sites as shrines for fans on pilgrimage, particularly those seeking the chambers of death or destruction; Joan Jett and Greg Kihn's short story 'Bad Reputation' chronicles the supernatural power of rock and roll to destroy evil forces; and Erik Davis's book on Led Zeppelin's fourth album appraises the ultimate mystical record by that ultimate mystical band. These texts all characterize rock as being more than the music, more than the concerts, more than mere mortality: rock is faith.

No band is as mythologized – by themselves and others – as Led Zeppelin. From their first studio album released in January 1969 to their last released in

August 1979, Led Zeppelin epitomizes the 1970s like no other rock band, having bludgeoned that decade into submission. Often considered the greatest rock band ever, they are excessive, frustrating, bombastic, derivative, pilfering, vulgar, sexist and pretentious, while at the same time innovative, challenging, exciting, resplendent, sensitive and transcendent. Too large to be contained by mere words, Led Zeppelin resists being subsumed by encapsulation or definition. Led Zeppelin is sound, but also strut and swagger, forever teetering between the brilliant and the bathetic, the innovative and the imitative, and, of course, the ethereal and the earthly. Led Zeppelin are defined by not just their music but their active myth-making and mystic-making of the band itself.

Much of this mythification is manifested in the sacramental album covers, with the iconography of the Hindenburg zeppelin on the covers of the first two albums giving way in the later albums to an inscribing of enigmatic and evocative symbolic gestures of the mystical and the mysterious, as the name of the band and its members become effaced. Led Zeppelin albums embody not only the sacred and the profane but also the secret and the profane.

The most esoteric of their albums is the fourth. Often erroneously referred to as being untitled, the album does in fact have a name, albeit one defying pronunciation, since it is composed of cryptic sigils suggestive of some sort of otherworldly power. In the packaging and presentation, especially of the original vinyl release, this album – titled in images rather than words – effaces the band name and reinscribes the members' names, the four symbols being signifiers functioning not as title nor names but an altogether different system of signs to identify the album; the name of the band appears only on the actual label of the physical record within. Even as the album resists the written word, the inclusion of the lyrics to 'Stairway to Heaven' returns to the gesture of inscription. This representation as a system of signs lends the album its mystical aspect, something that the music echoes, especially when Robert Plant sings a line such as 'the magic runes are writ in gold to bring the balance back' in the Tolkien-soaked 'The Battle of Evermore' (*Led Zeppelin Complete* 1973: 169). As Chuck Eddy (1991: 12) says, 'The fundamentalists are right: This music, by any biblical standard, should be illegal. It is a golden calf. [. . .] *Zoso* is a jealous God, it will accept no competition, it demands that you devote your life to it.'

Erik Davis (2005: 10), in his exploration of this inscrutably titled album, while not devoting his entire life to it, looks through the lens of one 'once thoroughly enchanted'. Fully aware of Led Zeppelin's mythic status, he says,

148   *Ink on the Tracks*

> I write not as a believer but as an 'occulture critic', fascinated with esoteric love but convinced of no secret keys beyond the central revelation of the human imagination. So though I will take Led Zeppelin's magic seriously, I won't, I hope, be too serious about it. I am certainly not interested in sprinkling more pixie dust on a band already bloated with myth. (Davis 2005: 9)

The 'magic' Davis explores is not so much that of the individual members – except Jimmy Page's preoccupation with Aleister Crowley and the occult – but more the central role the supernatural plays in the image of the singular entity 'Led Zeppelin'.

Manufacturing myth is key to Led Zeppelin's success and one reason the band is considered one of the best rock bands ever. The myth-making is the product of, on the one hand, Jimmy Page's vision of the band, and on the other, the fans' vision of Page's vision. The idea of the group's complicated relationship with the rock press added to that mystique: the media's supposed antagonism that apparently engendered the band's notorious aversion to interviews contributed to enhancing the band's mythic status. Steve Waksman (1999: 356) argues that the band themselves played a significant role in perpetuating the notion of the press's antipathy, adding that 'research into 1970s rock journalism has shown little evidence that Zeppelin was vilified by critics', *Rolling Stone*'s lambasting notwithstanding. Davis's book is both apart from and very much a part of those mythical gestures, being a critical reading that broadens understanding in its unravelling of this notably arcane album even as it contributes to the very mysticism it sets out to reveal, the tone a blend of weighty contemplation and comic whimsy (sometimes in the same sentence) to match the suitably lucid yet labyrinthine disquisition. Davis's title adopts the same esoteric sigils as the album's, and the book is positioned as an extension of the mysticism of its subject.

Davis touches on Led Zeppelin's deliberate invocation and manipulation of mythic symbols, including the Tarot, Crowley's teachings and other of the occult arts. He also draws on the self-published *Fallen Angel: The Untold Story of Jimmy Page and Led Zeppelin Based on the Stairway to Heaven Album* by Thomas W. Friend, a 'born-again Christian' who wrote his book 'to warn other fans about the infectious diabolism that lurks at the core of Led Zeppelin's music' (Davis 2005: 31). Davis (2005: 31–2) says, 'The fellow is no scholar. He [. . .] quotes Faust as a source – the fictional character, that is, not the text. He makes much of synchronicities and numerology, and takes poetic language for supernatural fact, which makes the more imaginative passages in this book entertaining and occasionally illuminating.' He refers to one of Friend's interpretations as 'a doozy' (Davis 2005: 30), another as 'pretty silly' (2005: 59); however, rather than dismissing Friend outright, Davis (2005: 34) engages with the text, saying, for example, that 'there is a certain crazy charm to Friend's claim' about Crowley, even though facts contradict it. By acknowledging Friend's work on the occult and incorporating it into his own book, Davis follows through on his desire to take a light-heartedly serious approach to Led Zeppelin's magic; he also demonstrates that lines of thinking such as Friend's, misguided as they sometimes might be, are intrinsic to engaging with Led Zeppelin. The Led Zeppelin mystical aura is likewise enhanced by these interpretations, myth-making begetting myth-making.

In *Rock and Roll Hotels: Sex. Drugs. Fluffy Pillows*, Greg Simmons (2011: 57) foregrounds this propensity of rock to mythologize. He describes Robert Plant at the Continental Hyatt House (often dubbed the Riot House): "'I am a Golden God!" It is 1975, the height of rock music's heyday, and Robert Plant, Led Zeppelin's debonair vocalist, declares his rock-star status from his hotel room's balcony, overlooking the entertainment capital of the world.' Despite having had 'a multimillion-dollar renovation' (Simmons 2011: 57) and being renamed the Andaz West Hollywood, the hotel retains its importance as a locus for rock pilgrims because of its rock star haven status. As with the other forty-four places Simmons's book catalogues, its past has become very much a part of its present: 'The anarchic antics of the 70s may have disappeared with the decadent decline of that decade, but the staff at the Andaz are keen to uphold the legacy of the Riot House days and wax nostalgically about those heady times' (Simmons 2011: 58). The book also speaks of the various forms of 'rock gods' (Simmons 2011: 22). Where Robert Plant brazenly announced his own godhead, Kurt Cobain had to wait until it was bestowed upon him posthumously: Cobain's suicide '[cemented] his deification upon entry to the 27 Club' (Simmons 2011: 160). Simmons (2011: 54) also reports that West Hollywood's Sunset Marquis has 'walls [. . .] adorned with signed photographs of rock's deities' and that 'even the most discerning of deities will fail to pick out any fault with' Es Saadi Gardens and Resort in Marrakesh (Simmons 2011: 179). In his introduction, Simmons (2011: 1) writes about anticipating 'hearing more about the myth-making rock deities'. He also tackles a site so steeped in its own mythology of self-destruction that it has been erased: the Hotel Chelsea's Room 100 'in which Sid Vicious is said to have stabbed his girlfriend Nancy Spungen to death in 1978 [. . .] no longer exists' (Simmons 2011: 13). Simmons (2011: 13) contends that 'out of all the tragedies the Chelsea has encountered, it is only the Vicious/Spungen case that the hotel appears keen to eradicate from its chequered past'. This excising, though, adds to the mythology. In fact, in the end the Hotel Chelsea entry emphasizes the power of that myth by saying that the hotel is 'both a cultural institution and the haunting ground for the ghost of Sid Vicious, looking for his stabbed girlfriend' (Simmons 2011: 15). Key to Simmons's book, then, is not only rock history, but also the religiosity of rock, its myth-making and faith drawing devotees to these sacred sites.

As the book suggests, the three-headed spectre of rock history, myth and religion morphs into one generalized faith that pulls worshippers to these temples, with Simmons's language often calling on that of the spiritual or religious. Revelation, especially Rev. 6.8, is echoed when he says that the Es Saadi Gardens and Resort 'is perhaps the most obvious choice for someone trailing rock 'n' roll's pale horse of destruction, and yet Morocco's "red city" capital has welcomed the likes of Elton John and – if we're to stick with the apocalypse – the most venerated of rock music's pale riders, Led Zeppelin' (Simmons 2011: 177). The word *veneration* is often associated, in religious terms, with saints. Simmons (2011: 5) calling the leaving of roses outside Montreal's Fairmount The Queen Elizabeth's John Lennon and Yoko Ono Suite an 'act of veneration' beatifies Lennon; referring to the hotel room of Mötley Crüe's Nikki Sixx at New York's Le Parker Meridien as a 'reverential space' (Simmons 2011: 9) casts the room as shrine. This notion of shrine is reflected in other entries. He calls San Francisco's Phoenix Hotel 'a sanctum for rock stars' (Simmons 2011: 37) and speaks of the 'sacrosanct walls' of Liverpool's Parr Street Hotel (Simmons 2011: 120). Of the Joshua Tree Inn, Simmons (2011: 63) writes that he is thankful 'the entire hotel [has not been turned] into a shrine for Gram Parsons', previously noting that it 'has, in the main, lured pilgrims whose interest has been piqued by the tale of Gram Parsons' (Simmons 2011: 61). Simmons (2011: 33) also invokes the notion of pilgrimage in his comments on San Francisco's Mark Twain Hotel: 'having a debauched tale to tell usually means hoteliers hold onto decrepit furnishings in an attempt to hang onto the final breath that weakly left some rock star's lungs, thus entrenching their hotel's two-star status in annals of rock history and firmly on the pilgrims' rock 'n' roll map'. Fittingly, in his description of London's Sanctum Soho, a 'hideaway for rock stars' (Simmons 2011: 139), he states that this is a hotel that caters to rockers. Apart from being able to rent a guitar from the front desk, 'those who are really unapologetic about worshipping at the altar of rock 'n' roll [. . .] can also hire a Harley Davidson and rumble around the

West End in true "hog" style' (Simmons 2011: 140). Simmons positions hotels as being places of worship – the hotel as temple, shrine, reliquary or altar – and *Rock and Roll Hotels* as the guidebook for pilgrims to worship in these sacred spaces.

Underscoring this link between rock and religion, *The Rock Bible: Unholy Scripture for Fans and Bands* celebrates and lovingly mocks rock and roll. Matching its subject, it is appropriately cheeky, vulgar, offensive, funny and loud. Its content draws on the notion of a spiritual Bible, while its physical appearance recalls editions of the Holy Bible, the red leatherette cover reminiscent of versions published by Thomas Nelson, for example. The gilt-lettered words *The Rock Bible* are in gothic blackletter, a typeface echoing not only the Gutenberg Bible but also the King James Version (KJV), first printed in 1611. Gordon Campbell (2010: 90) says, 'The typeface of the [KJV] is blackletter (an imitation of Gothic script), and roman type is used for headers, chapter summaries, and words that have been supplied by the translators to make the text more intelligible.' According to Simon Garfield (2012: 187–9), this typeface 'today is largely confined to the confirmation of noble tradition [. . .] or as a measure of pastiche denoting pomposity [and] grandeur'. Indeed, Owings uses blackletter also in the headings, in red, perhaps parodying the red letter editions of the Holy Bible that highlight Jesus's words for easy reference. Garfield (2012: 189) also notes that gothic blackletter typeface is used in heavy metal. Metal bands' adoption of this typeface is ubiquitous and de rigueur. Marnie Sehayek (2016) argues that ever since the name Black Sabbath appeared in that typeface on the cover of 1973s *Sabbath Bloody Sabbath*, blackletter has become 'an established visual trope within the genre'. Playing with this trope, *The Rock Bible* conflates the KJV and metal, a genre often associated with Satan and the dark arts. The rest of the text is in P22 Franklin Caslon, a typeface replicating Benjamin Franklin's and having 'a timeless appeal' ('Franklin Caslon'). Combined with the cover's blackletter and the silk ribbon bookmark, this distressed typeface gives *The Rock Bible* gravitas and positions this irreverently amusing book as something venerable. The layout also invokes biblical comparisons. The King James Version of 1611 is an 11 × 16-inch folio with 'the two columns of text on each page [consisting] of fifty-nine lines enclosed within ruled margins' (Campbell 2010: 88); however, although *The Rock Bible*'s pages measure only 5 × 7 inches, with ruled margins, and have only thirty-nine lines, those pages are still divided into two columns like the 1611 KJV. Much of the book's humour rests on the content undermining its august facade, this disruption a characteristically rock and roll gesture.

152   *Ink on the Tracks*

The physical appearance of *The Rock Bible* anticipates its content. As Brian Teasley's introduction says, 'You can view this book as an all-purpose guide to how not to be in a crappy band or translate the Bible of Rock into your otherwise rockless civilian life' (Owings 2008: 10). Contributor Andrew Earles adds, 'Rock has lost something and needs a set of rules. Sadly, in this day and age the only true way to rock is to commit suicide on stage. [. . .] I hope that [*The Rock Bible*] changes the face of music, thus creating more music that actually does rock' (Owings 2008: 11). One aspect of this book, then, functions as a Bible in the sense of a codified set of laws, yet not necessarily spiritual ones. These rules are conveyed with vitriolic and sometimes puerile ironic humour, as several truths about rock style and attitudes are pilloried.

The Rock Bible's typography and layout suggest the KJV, but the content likewise echoes some biblical syntax and diction, as well as organization. *The Rock Bible* has a preface, an introduction, a 'Little Rock Bible Essay', nine main chapters imitating biblical ones and an appendix. Between 'Genesis' and 'The Book of Revelation' are seven 'Gospel' chapters: 'The Gospel According to the Drummer', 'the Singer', 'the Keyboardist', 'the Band', 'the Crew' and 'the Fan.' Within each chapter are headings for various 'Commandments', 'Psalms', 'Cardinal Rules' and 'Golden Rules', as well as 'Books' such as 'The Book of Live Performances', 'The Book of Mixing and Dubbing' and 'The Book of Bad Ideas', among others.

The Rock Bible incorporates elements of both Old and New Testaments. 'Genesis' invokes the KJV with the verbatim, 'In the beginning', but rather than saying that 'God created the heaven and the earth', this chapter launches into one long twelve-page sentence detailing rock's genealogy, starting with,

> In the beginning, Thomas Edison invented the phonograph, which begat the publishing of 'Memphis Blues' by Hart Wand in 1912 (often credited as the first blues title), which begat W. C. Handy writing 'St. Louis Blues' (often credited as the first real blues song) in 1914, which begat the Chicago Automatic Machine & Tool Company inventing the Jukebox in 1915, which begat the bluesman Leadbelly being imprisoned for murder in 1917. (Owings 2008: 14)

Apart from the phrases 'in the beginning' and 'begat', this long sentence is written in contemporary language. The litany is not always logical, the organization of the *begats* in this chapter suggests that people and events in rock history connect through something other than reason, and that events such as the phonograph's creation or Lead Belly's incarceration are as important as an album's release or

'The magic runes are writ in gold' 153

a band's formation. Titled 'Genesis' and reciting rock's lineage, the first chapter alludes to the Old Testament but also echoes the first sixteen verses of Matthew listing the genealogy from Abraham to Jesus and including the word *begat* thirty-nine times in twenty-five verses. Matthew's list ends with Jesus's birth and the conclusion that 'all the generations from Abraham to David are fourteen generations; and from David until the carrying away into Babylon are fourteen generations; and from the carrying away into Babylon unto Jesus are fourteen generations' (Matt. 1.17). In contrast, *The Rock Bible*'s litany ends with 'the Dead rising and every band that had ever been together uniting for one last reunion tour, well maybe not "the" last' (Owings 2008: 25), this 'rising' – of not only the aptly chosen Grateful Dead but all bands – a resurrection of sorts. The gesture of 'Genesis' of *The Rock Bible* invokes, then, both Old and New Testaments.

Counterpointing 'Genesis' in *The Rock Bible* is 'The Book of Revelation', which, as in the KJV, functions as prophecy. However, where the KJV Revelation speaks of 'things which must shortly come to pass' (Rev. 1.1) and says that 'Blessed is he that readeth, and they that hear the words of this prophecy, and keep those things which are written therein: for the time is at hand' (Rev. 1.3), *The Rock Bible*'s 'The Book of Revelation' has a markedly different voice, despite the KJV diction and syntax:

> And so the great rock prophet did set out to glimpse the yielding of his precious countenance through many a wise oracle of forgotten rock recordings and failed attempts at stardom and saw maddening disinterest in his plight to save the world of rock from utter folly. [. . .] And yea the prophet beheld the ten heralds of the Arockalypse and with narrow vision did name those beasts and foretold their wrath. (Owings 2008: 130)

What follows is a satiric excoriation of modern aspects that the 'prophet' deems anathema to rock, with portmanteau headings for each section, such as 'YouTuberius', 'The Myspacebook of Oblivion', 'Lord iTunia & His iPods' and 'Bonacoachapaloozavans'. Notable among the transgressions is the withering of rock journalism. The section 'The Scrolling Rune' says 'the scrolls' had once been long and detailed, but 'ALL rock criticism was, by millennium's end, reduced to the likes of eighteen full-color double-truck pictures and only three paragraphs spread across six pages' (Owings 2008: 133).

The Rock Bible celebrates rock and roll's essence and condemns the elements diluting it. With sardonic jocularity, this book presents doctrine while lambasting the transgressors. Tellingly, below the title on the cover is not a cross but an upright guitar in silhouette, flanked by stylized flames above the subtitle, 'Unholy Scripture for Fans and Bands'.

Notions of the holy and the unholy are also at play in Joan Jett and Greg Kihn's short story 'Bad Reputation', which represents rock as apotropaic, the authors trading Transylvania for San Francisco. After attending one of the unnamed narrator's concerts, vampires ambush the rock star in her limousine. Rather than defeating 'the undead' with garlic or the Christian cross, though, the narrator prevails over these soul-sucking entities with rock and roll. As the narrator says, 'Fuck the vampires. Rock and roll is bigger than that' (Jett and Kihn 2003: 33). When the 'lead vampire' Collum offers to make the narrator '"the ultimate rock and roll rebel until the end of time"' (Jett and Kihn 2003: 35), the rock star's rejection makes explicit the link between rock and faith: '"Listen, you unholy bitch. What I do takes a lot of soul. . . . If I didn't have soul, I couldn't do it. You think rock and roll is just going out there with a guitar and singing? Just posing and jumping around? That shows how little you know. The real connection takes place on a whole 'nother level"' (Jett and Kihn 2003: 35). The word *soul* appears elsewhere in the text. The second sentence of the story says that vampires 'got no soul' (Jett and Kihn 2003: 31); in the second paragraph, they are called 'soul suckers' (Jett and Kihn 2003: 31) and their victims 'all the lovely young souls who roam the streets' (Jett and Kihn 2003: 31). During her performance, the narrator sees the vampires and thinks, 'Don't give me the evil eye, you soulless blood junkies' (Jett and Kihn 2003: 33). The story links *soul* with rock's power and sound. On stage, the narrator '[gathers] energy from the amps and [shoots] back at them' (Jett and Kihn 2003: 33). Later, during the confrontation in the limousine, she feels 'the righteous courage of twin hundred-watt Marshall stacks' (Jett and Kihn 2003: 35). Rock's music is linked inextricably to volume, the strength engendered by this volume informing much of the faith. Throughout the story are nuances of the word *soul* in its connection to faith and rock and roll.

The story's tropes of the soulful rock star and the soulless vampire subvert those that depict the rock musician as vampire or other representation of evil. Many bands play on the idea of the evil supernatural, the bands themselves cast in the role of malevolence manifested. Black Sabbath's name and iconography are drawn from the dark arts. The Rolling Stones dabbled with the diabolic: as Simmons (2011: 177) says, they 'expressed sympathy for the devil', a phrase that conjures up the song title as well as their fleeting foray into part-time Satanism, embodied in the album title *Their Satanic Majesties Request* (but in none of the songs on it); as Keith Richards (1971) said, 'There are black magicians who

'The magic runes are writ in gold'

think we are acting as unknown agents of Lucifer and others who think we are Lucifer. Everybody's Lucifer.' The Sex Pistols used sacrilege to shock the system when John Lydon as the gleefully mischievous Johnny Rotten spat his opening blasphemous salvo in 'Anarchy in the UK', cackling, 'I am an antichrist, I am an anarchist' (Cook et al.), pronouncing this last word with the diphthong [ai] to create a wonderful rhyme that presents the singer as the ultimate threat of evil incarnate. Blasphemy is also celebrated in some other bands and artists invoking the satanic or the corrupt: Richard Hell, The Damned, Judas Priest, Coven, Lucifer, Lucifer's Friend, Corrupted and Vampire Weekend. Even as it repositions this conventional dichotomy of good and evil in rock, 'Bad Reputation' draws upon familiar tropes of the gothic vampire, though: fog, fangs, sucking, blood and vampires with no mirror reflections. Some diction, also taken from the realm of vampire lore, echoes the language of religion: 'undead' (Jett and Kihn: 31); 'unholy' (Jett and Kihn: 35); 'soulless' (Jett and Kihn: 33). The latter two words imply that the narrator – as well as rock itself – has the opposite traits of holiness and soulfulness. The first word, *undead*, as opposed to *alive*, suggests a liminal state, neither dead not alive. The opposite of *undead* is not *alive*; rather, it would be a word suggestive of not merely living but manifesting the ultimate state that rock and roll engenders: being un-*undead*, being more than alive. This is the exaltation that the narrator knows cannot be substituted by the vampires' offer of 'immortality' (Jett and Kihn 2003: 34) in exchange for her soul.

Disrupting this rock trope by situating the narrator as not perpetrator but target, Jett and Kihn offer an alternative view of rock's transcendental force, its 'raw power' stemming not from exerting violence but from resisting and rejecting it in favour of life-giving music and passion. To the violence against her soul, the narrator responds in kind, through both action and language. Fearlessly confronting the head vampire, the narrator draws her strength from her 'rock and roll blood [pumping] raw power through [her] veins' (Jett and Kihn 2003: 35). When Colum asks, 'You think you can resist me? [. . .] With just your faith? [. . .] Faith in what?' (Jett and Kihn 2003: 35), the narrator vehemently responds, 'Rock and roll, you asshole', before playing the cassette of her concert and entering a state of ecstasy in which she does not 'care about anything except the music' and is 'completely in the moment' (Jett and Kihn 2003: 36), the music both weapon and shield. She says, 'They didn't want the real me. They were only interested in the rock star, not that heart that beats behind it. As long as the music played, I was safe' (Jett and Kihn 2003: 36). The narrator's absolute faith in rock is the force protecting her from evil.

156   *Ink on the Tracks*

This 'raw power' alludes to the 1973 song and album by Iggy and the Stooges. Iggy Pop's lyrics (2019: 60) suggest that this 'power' is the source of rock itself: it 'got a son called rock and roll'. Although the raw power in the song has no gender, rock is positioned as masculine. In Pop's song, the pure unbridled energy giving birth to rock is both restorative and destructive, having 'a healin' hand' even as it 'can destroy a man' (Pop 2019: 60). By invoking this song, the story 'Bad Reputation' emphasizes the problematic dynamics of rock as faith, the power of the music being both balm and bomb. In Jett and Kihn's story, the cassette of the gig is the immediate revisiting of the rock experience; it is the *sound*, not the lyrics nor even the music, that defeats those who desire dominion over her soul. Whereas at the gig, the vampires stood removed from the crowd in its visceral embodiment of rock's essence, now in the enclosed limousine – a space in which the performance is reenacted and the relationship of the predators and their prey reinscripted and reconfigured – the vampires must bear witness to the noise that is rock and roll, as they hear the raucous offspring of the primordial raw power in all its purity.

An earlier title of the story, 'They Love Rock and Roll', complicates this relationship of the vampires to rock. Anthologized as 'Bad Reputation' in *Carved in Rock*, edited by Greg Kihn, the story is listed in the credits as 'They Love Rock and Roll', with Joan Jett as sole author (Kihn: 329). Just as the story's title 'Bad Reputation' alludes to Jett's homonymous song, so too does 'They Love Rock and Roll' draw from her music, this time from Jett's cover of Alan Merrill's song 'I Love Rock and Roll', a title she used for her second album. In the context of the story's title, the pronoun *they* refers to the vampires rather than to the narrator. The retitling of the story corrects this imbalance, since while it is true that the vampires in the story are somehow drawn to rock concerts, they only 'float on the fringes of the rock movement' (Jett and Kihn 2003: 31) and stand 'stock still' at the narrator's show (Jett and Kihn 2003: 33), indicating that they do not in fact love rock and roll. They are interested not in rock but in the rock star, the surface glamour. The vampires' misunderstanding of the spirit – the soul – of rock and roll leads to their destruction through 'the power of rock and roll' (Jett and Kihn 2003: 36), the narrator's faith.

This faith, along with the energy stemming from it, beats in the heart of rock and roll. These four texts writing about rock are also writing about the beliefs it engenders. However, to paraphrase Davis, writing about rock's religion and mythology means taking rock and roll's magic seriously without being too serious about it. Documenting the dens of various rock deities,

Simmons waggishly mocks that deification even as he reinforces it. While Simmons provides an accurate and useful guidebook in chronicling some of these saints and sacred sites, Owings offers irreverent wisdom about rock and cloaks it in the guise of scripture. These texts write rock and roll's raw power and transcendence. At the height of rock's reign in 1975, William S. Burroughs said (2014: 155), 'Rock music can be seen as one attempt to break out of this dead soulless world and reassert the universe of magic.' Each of these texts is an attempt to reassert the universe of the magic – and the magic runes – of rock music.

References

Burroughs, William S. (2014). 'Rock Magic: Jimmy Page, Led Zeppelin, and a Search for the Elusive Stairway to Heaven', in Hank Bordowitz (ed.), *Led Zeppelin on Led Zeppelin: Interviews and Encounters*, 150–64. Chicago: Chicago University Press.

Campbell, Gordon (2010). *Bible: The Story of the King James Version 1611–2010*. Oxford: Oxford University Press.

Cook, Paul, Steve Jones, John Lydon, and Glen Matlock. 'Anarchy in the UK', *Sex Pistols Official*. https://www.sexpistolsofficial.com/nmtb-lyrics/ (accessed 25 February 2023).

Davis, Erik (2005). *Led Zeppelin [Four Symbols]*. New York: Continuum.

Eddy, Chuck (1991). *Stairway to Hell: The 500 Best Heavy Metal Albums in the Universe*. New York: Harmony Books.

'Franklin Caslon', *P22 Type Foundry*. https://p22.com/family-Franklin___s_Caslon. (accessed 25 February 2023).

Garfield, Simon (2012). *Just My Type: A Book About Fonts*. New York: Gotham.

Jett, Joan and Greg Kihn (2003). 'Bad Reputation', in Greg Kihn (ed.), *Carved in Rock: Short Stories by Musicians*, 31–6. New York: Thunder's Mouth Press.

Kihn, Greg (ed.) (2003). *Carved in Rock: Short Stories by Musicians*. New York: Thunder's Mouth Press.

Led Zeppelin Complete. New York: Superhype Publishing, 1973.

Owings, Henry H. (2008). *The Rock Bible: Unholy Scripture for Fans and Bands*. Philadelphia: Quirk Books.

Pop, Iggy (2019). *'Til Wrong Feels Right: Lyrics and More*. New York: Clarkson Potter.

Richards, Keith (1971). 'Keith Richard: The Rolling Stone Interview'. Interview by Robert Greenfield, *Rolling Stone*, 19 August, https://www.rollingstone.com/music/music-news/keith-richard-the-rolling-stone-interview-238909/ (accessed 13 June 2023).

Sehayek, Marnie (2016). 'These Fonts Shred: A Typographical Survey of Heavy Metal', *Vice Magazine*, 15 October. https://www.vice.com/en/article/9anp93/heavy-metal-typographical-survey-fonts (accessed 25 February 2023).

Simmons, Greg (2011). *Rock and Roll Hotels: Sex. Drugs. Fluffy Pillows*. London: Punk Publishing.

Waksman, Steve (1999). *Instruments of Desire*. Cambridge, MA and London: Harvard University Press.

12

Paul is dead . . . long live Paul

Reinventing Eden in rock and roll writing

Charles Holdefer

'When legend becomes fact', observes a newspaper editor in John Ford's *The Man Who Shot Liberty Valance*, 'print the legend'. And lo, a version of the 'American West' was born, a place of larger-than-life heroes and villains.

Historically speaking, it's a dubious account, ideologically driven and in some respects, morally suspect. But such caveats miss the point. The 'American West' is not history but rather a powerful narrative that influences and shapes future retellings and performances of itself. What gets said about the past informs the present and becomes a part of the culture. A shaky relationship with facts does not detract from its seductive charm. On the contrary, it is probably a necessary ingredient.

The story of rock and roll follows a similar trajectory. What we know (or think we know) about the music, and the way we speak and write about it, has been shaped by folklore, legend and myth. Our language expresses desires that go beyond a specific artist or musical performance and seeks out a place, not unlike the 'American West', where we are free to indulge in fantasy projections. We want to go *there*, even if *there* is not and has never been, literally, there.

Fans, like so many Huckleberry Finns, want 'to light out for the Territory' and escape the restraints of home, the predictability, the standards and judgement, and replace obligation with possibility. As Greil Marcus has observed about Elvis Presley: 'reviews of his concerts, by usually credible writers, sometimes resemble Biblical accounts of heavenly miracles' (113). For better or worse, imaginative subjectivity is brought to the fore.

To acknowledge this tendency is not to make light of the work of historians. On the contrary, this discussion is indebted to their work, which by way of contrast sheds light on myth. In recent decades, the writing of rock and roll history has blossomed. Once the province of ephemeral journalism or fanzines, it has been professionalized to a degree that would have been unimaginable two generations ago. University professors write learnt tomes of musicology (Moore 2001) and compile historiographies of major figures like the Beatles (Torkelson Weber 2016) while scrupulously annotating their findings, for instance, tracking three different versions of how Marc Bolan came to use glitter on *Top of the Pops* (Auslander 2006: 196n).

Methodological rigour is a good thing, to be sure: rock and roll deserves a serious history. But rock and roll writing is not (or not only) writing about the music from a historical perspective. Nor is it reducible to a style, which is another possible – and difficult – avenue of inquiry. (Is it the style of the Bob Dylan of *Chronicles Volume 1* or of *Tarantula*? The Patti Smith of *Just Kids* or *A Useless Death*? Does it set itself apart from other kinds of writing in a manner analogous to *l'écriture féminine*? Thorny questions, these.)

My discussion will emphasize another approach, which addresses a seemingly unruly welter of folklore, legend and foundational myth in search of common narratives. These narratives arguably constitute a form of rock and roll writing, even if their sources are sometimes oral or impossible to trace, or enter the written realm through the back door, so to speak, when they are debunked by historians. Not always writing in the literalistic sense, they nonetheless leave their imprint on the culture. This focus on myth-making is more typically associated with literary scholars like Northrop Frye, structuralists like Claude Lévi-Strauss or writers like J. R. R. Tolkien and Joseph Campbell, and at first blush, it might seem a stretch in regard to the world of rock and roll, where the word 'myth' is often employed in the service of hype. But saying as much doesn't mean that a more probing attempt to trace foundational narratives might not serve our understanding of the music.

My purpose is not to seek an academic lever to ratchet up the cultural status of the subject, since rock and roll requires no such special pleading. Nor should an emphasis on myth be reduced to an exercise of spotting and decoding literary allusions. How much does it really tell us that Leonard Bernstein referred to the Beatles as 'these Four Horsemen of Our Apocalypse' (2004: 333) or that Horace Engdahl of the Nobel Prize Committee compared Bob Dylan to 'the oracle of Delphi' (2016)? Not very much, I would say. A certain kind of fan doesn't scream or faint but finds other ways to hyperventilate.

Rather, myth-making will be construed here not as mere allusion but as replication of a pattern. I'll concentrate on a particular myth, in this case the

Paul is Dead . . . Long Live Paul　　　　161

story of Eden, and how it is renewed and repeated in multitudinous forms, and how the existence of this common narrative or hypotext informs the story that rock and roll tells about itself. This story is a collaborative narrative, shared by artists and audiences. Despite its romanticized facts, distortions or ambiguities, the Eden myth, and its necessary reinvention in the face of death, also points to continuities, to coherence.

In the beginning, take one

'We record anything – anywhere – anytime.' Sam Phillips put up these words on a small rented shopfront in Memphis, Tennessee. And lo, in through his door walked Elvis Presley, Johnny Cash, Carl Perkins, Roy Orbison and Jerry Lee Lewis.

So goes the legend. And it is factually true that such a sign existed at Sun Records. It is also true that these artists, then unknown, appeared at his door and changed the course of musical history. It is a truly remarkable story, so compelling that it easily slides into a more beguiling myth: 'In the beginning, Sam spoke over the void: "Let there be rock and roll". And there was rock and roll. And it was good.' The myth resounds with echoes of Genesis: 'There were giants in the earth in those days' (6.4).

On the other hand, historians helpfully remind us that Memphis, though not a capital or entertainment centre, was hardly a void: it was a crossroads of cultural influences, Black and white, city and country. With hindsight, maybe it's not so surprising that these influences could coalesce and create a new art form along the banks of the Mississippi River. Perhaps Memphis was the perfect place for such a flowering. In any case, Sun Records did not mark exactly the *beginning*: the pre-Sun recording of young Ike Turner and his Kings of Rhythm, recommended to Phillips by B.B. King, resulted in 'Rocket 88' which is often hailed as the first rock and roll record (credited to 'Jackie Brentson and His Delta Cats'). This 1951 single helped finance Sam Phillips's creation of Sun Records the following year. Nor were all Sun artists giants (Tex Weiss also recorded – where's his Wikipedia entry?). Moreover, with performers like Howlin' Wolf and James Cotton, they certainly were not all white. According to Rufus Thomas, 'Me and Sam Phillips, we were tighter than the nuts on the Brooklyn Bridge, but when Elvis and Carl Perkins and Johnny Cash came along, no more blacks did he pick up at all' (Wolff Scanlan

162   *Ink on the Tracks*

2016). Meanwhile, in New Orleans, Little Richard cut groundbreaking singles for Specialty Records, and Big Mama Thornton (the first to record Leiber and Stoller's 'Hound Dog') and Sister Rosetta Tharpe (who wrote 'Ball and Chain') were recording and touring throughout the South and beyond, leaving their mark on this era.

All of this is now well documented, but parallel to the historical narrative, the story of ex nihilo creation retains a hold on popular imagination. In the most stripped-down form, it is the myth of an individual, in this case a young man from Tupelo, Mississippi, who walked into Sun Records to record a song as a birthday gift for his mother and then went on to change the world. Enter Elvis – as Adam.

As history, it is nonsense, and for all the charm of its simplicity, need it be said one more time that simplicity does not equal innocence, when one considers the historical erasures? On the other hand, just because it isn't true doesn't mean it doesn't *matter*. It is no disrespect to history to recognize the potency of myth, especially since the two are often in dialogue. As Greil Marcus also observed, 'History without myth is surely a wasteland; but myths are compelling only when they are at odds with history' (Marcus 1975: 115).

The power of myth is nothing if not tenacious. And this might be the place for a few words about terminology, since standard reference works admit to a 'bewildering variety of applications of the term "myth" in contemporary criticism' (Abrams 1981: 112). Often a 'myth' refers to a symbolic narrative rooted in a distant past, involving gods or supernatural events, whereas 'legends' concern real historical figures or events, but with embellishment or exaggeration to amplify their deeds. When Marcus refers to 'myth' in regard to Elvis Presley, it is not, I think, a matter of sloppy usage but rather a recognition of how deeply the narrative resonates. Yes, Elvis is the source of legend, but for the purposes of this discussion, particularly in regard to a symbolic Memphis Eden, he participates in myth, too.

A certain type of purist (unlike historians, who are generally attune to ambiguities, to difficulties of categorization, to 'problematizing') would like to be rid of myth altogether, usually in defence of an idea of authenticity (Holdefer 2019). This authenticity supposedly underpins aesthetic practices. Critics like Iain Chambers have pointed out how 'the most arbitrary distinctions [are] rapidly drawn up into fiercely controlled aesthetic boundaries' (1985: 21). Such internecine arguments are not the focus here, nor will I limit myself to an exclusively text-centred approach to myth. For instance, although I will occasionally refer to song lyrics for their explicit content, it is the mythic pattern that interests me most.[1]

However one values myth (or not), there is no denying its ubiquity and reiteration. Similar narratives get told again and again. Early 1950s Memphis is only the tip of the myth-berg.

In the beginning, take two

Beyond Sun Records, there are many Memphises, many beginnings, venerated sites with musical scenes where, we are told, new sounds were born. Rock and roll is awash in Edens. Chronologically, a partial list would include early 1960s Merseyside, or 1967 San Francisco with its 'summer of love',[2] or mid-1980s Seattle or late 1980s 'Madchester'. During the Beatles' last tour in 1966, a controversy arose in the United States concerning John Lennon's remarks about Christianity, prompting a city commission in Memphis to issue a public statement: 'The Beatles are not welcome in Memphis' (Wiener 1984: 165). But by then, mythically speaking, it was too late. Eden had moved on.

By the time a notion of a 'Woodstock nation' had emerged, there was a self-awareness of a positive fluidity, in which the name of a place was a mere marker for an extra-geographical state of mind. Joni Mitchell's song lyric, popularized by Crosby, Stills, Nash and Young's anthemic rendition, proselytizes that 'we've got to get ourselves back to the garden' (1970). Images of naked youth in the Michael Wadleigh documentary (1970) about the rock festival convey not only a bacchanalia but also the innocence of Adam and Eve. 'Woodstock' enjoins a project-in-the-making that looks *backward*. For all its celebration of youth, rock and roll mythology is also prone to nostalgia.

Sometimes the garden is construed as a more intimate venue, a hothouse of creativity like the Cavern or Crawdaddy Club, the Whisky a Go Go or Max's Kansas City or CBGBs, the Blitz or the Hacienda nightclub. Each has its

---

[1] A *partial* list of songs that participate in a prelapsarian narrative includes Chuck Berry's 'Johnny B. Goode' (1958); Scott McKenzie's (written by John Phillips) 'San Francisco' (1967); The Velvet Underground's 'Rock and Roll' (1969); Joni Mitchell's 'Woodstock' (1970); Led Zeppelin's 'Rock and Roll' (1971); Don McLean's 'American Pie' (1971); The Who's 'Long Live Rock' (1974); Bob Seeger's 'Old Time Rock and Roll' (1978); The Ramones' 'Do You Remember Rock 'n' Roll Radio?' (1980); Billy Joel's 'It's Still Rock and Roll to Me' (1980); Carl Perkins' 'Birth of Rock and Roll' (1985).

[2] For Paul Kanter of the Jefferson Airplane, the real summer of love was the less mediatized previous summer of 1966, where 'for about a week [...] anything you wished would come true'. In *Fly Jefferson Airplane*, DVD 2004, Dir. John Sarles.

particularity, its acolytes and lore. Or conversely, it can be a nondescript place like a garage, whose beauty derives from the absence of particularity. You don't have to live in a capital or cultural centre or have access to a locale which is hip: your Eden is still within reach. The 'garage band' is the group for the aspiring Everyman, whose Sun Records is right where he is.

As Edens go, the garage-as-play-space is probably more of an American phenomenon, a product of automobile culture. But it is not exclusive to the United States. The label 'garage band' has also been applied in Australia to the Easybeats or in Britain to the Troggs (Hicks 2000: 36). The Clash also celebrated it in their song 'Garageland' (1977). As with 'Woodstock Nation', the literal place is less important than the liberating possibilities of an assumed creative attitude. The Memphis is not in the state of Tennessee but in your state of mind.

The most fluid Eden of all exists on the road, where renewal is possible at every stop. For instance, the highly mythologized Route 66, dubbed 'the Mother Road' by John Steinbeck in *The Grapes of Wrath* (1939) and popularized in song by Bobby Troup and Nat King Cole (1946). Rock and rollers were quick to latch on to this sense of promise. In Bob Dylan's first radio interview, broadcast in New York in 1961 before Columbia Records released his first song, the then-obscure twenty-year-old from Minnesota invented out of whole cloth a mythical past for himself, claiming he was raised in Gallup, New Mexico, a railroad town on Highway 66, where he learnt cowboy songs and 'Indian songs' before pursuing an itinerant life, travelling with carnivals. He goes the full Huckleberry, and his interviewer, Oscar Brand, unquestioningly goes along for the ride (Yakas 2021). A short time later Dylan spun a similar tale to Izzy Young at the Folklore Center in Greenwich Village. Young was a well-established, savvy figure in music circles, yet he, too, was seduced and supported the young artist's career. Afterwards he remarked, 'I should have figured out right away he was bullshitting me. [. . .] I was a set-up, a very easy set-up, but I'm proud of it, because the guy wrote good songs' (Scorsese 2005). Young, in effect, collaborated with the myth, participating in the writing of a story that enabled the artist. As early as 1963, Dylan's version of his past was debunked by *Newsweek* magazine but the myth had staying power, as journalists for the *Albuquerque Journal* were still reporting in 2012 that 'People of a certain age can tell you about spotting him here or there in the 1950s when Gallup was a bustling little border town' (Linthicum 2012).

Dylan shrewdly tapped into his listeners' desire to believe. Janis Joplin, according to her biographer Holly George-Warren, used similar tactics after leaving Texas for the liberating open space of the San Francisco music scene:

Paul is Dead . . . Long Live Paul

Janis's self-mythologizing – emphasizing her troubled youth and downplaying her ambition and years of work to become a great singer – had begun. She quickly perfected the art of the interview, giving journalists outré quotes and feeding them exaggerated stories of tortured adolescence and accidental success. She learned quickly that she could wow them in print just as she did onstage. (2019: 233)

Other artists have taken a more mocking approach to this hunger for myth, for instance a young John Lennon in 1961 telling *Mersey Beat* that the Beatles' unusual name 'came in a vision – a man appeared on a flaming pie and said unto them, "from this day on you are Beatles with an A"' (Sennett and Simon 2010: 232). The language register of his joke implies a disdain for the affectations that can accompany mythic retellings. Later, during the recording of 'You've Got to Hide Your Love Away', when he mistakenly sang 'two foot small' instead of 'two foot tall', he laughed and said, 'Leave that in, the pseuds'll love it' (MacDonald 1994: 312n); in 'Glass Onion', he devotes an entire song to misinformation directed at enthusiasts of Beatles' lore ('And here's another clue for you all / the walrus was Paul' (*The Beatles* 1968)). According to Ian MacDonald, the changing sartorial poses in the promotional video for 'Hello, Goodbye' were an 'attempt to debunk their own escalating mythology' (312n).

Of course not everyone was keen to play such games. Frank Zappa, though no stranger to poses and mockery (one is hard-pressed to find 'straight' song lyrics in Zappa's work), made clear in the liner notes of his debut album *Freak Out* (1966) that he had no truck with romanticizing his past or his influences. Amid the jokes or ironic asides about the recording industry and pop music he offers a very earnest account of himself and his beliefs, his divorce and his heroes. He berates America's educational system and admonishes his youthful listeners, 'Forget the Senior Prom and go to the library and educate yourself if you've got any guts' (Green and Black 2017).

But Zappa is a cranky outlier; more representative of later rock and roll self-mythologizing is Martin Scorsese's documentary *The Last Waltz* (1978), which centres on the 1976 farewell concert by The Band. Interviews with Robbie Robertson return several times to the theme of life on the road, a place of unparalleled camaraderie and unforgettable encounters with legends like Sonny Boy Williamson. Scorsese splices intimate footage of the band improvising the song 'Old Time Religion' and Robertson remarking with a rueful laugh, 'It's not like it used to be' before segueing directly to the live concert performance of

'The Night They Drove Old Dixie Down', a song imbued with nostalgia for an irrecoverable past.[3]

The Last Waltz is a fond tribute to some of rock and roll's grizzled veterans. It's worth remembering, though, that Robertson was only thirty-three years old at the time of these interviews. More than forty years later, it is easy to find recent interviews of him on YouTube repeating the same anecdotes. In fairness, Robertson *did* start young, touring from the age of sixteen, so by 1976, he had reason to be weary – but a casual viewer could be forgiven for seeing him as a much older figure, a witness to the time when giants walked the earth, which is an image that Robertson, a gifted raconteur, encourages, and that Scorsese, as a film director, collaborates with and augments by his editing choices, which emphasize a lost Americana, a rock and roll Eden to which we cannot return. If it's the last waltz, we'll never hear the music again.

For the record, The Band's farewell concert, which Scorsese lovingly preserves, took place on 25 November 1976, the day before the release of the Sex Pistols' debut single, 'Anarchy in the U.K.' In the beginning . . .

Hip cats have more than nine lives

Memphis is finished, and you can't afford to go to the big city, and your local club doesn't rock, and your parents won't let you use the garage, and you're unsure whether Route 66 still leads to a garden. What to do? It's hard not to sympathize with the fictional British rock band Spinal Tap, the subject of Rob Reiner's 1984 fake documentary, which, during a disastrous American tour that will see the band implode, makes a pilgrimage to Elvis's gravesite at Graceland, in the hope of recovering the old magic. After struggling unsuccessfully to harmonize on 'Heartbreak Hotel', group member Nigel Tufnel remarks, 'It really puts perspective on things, doesn't it?' to which his unhappy bandmate David St. Hubbins replies, 'There's too much fucking perspective now.'

How long can the myth go on? How many deaths can rock and roll endure? Doesn't it get harder and harder to rewrite the tale of fresh creation, of another endless Saturday night, when you have too much fucking perspective?

---

[3] History tells a different story. Ta-Nehisi Coates has described the persona of Confederate soldier Virgil Caine in this song as 'the blues of Pharaoh' while adding, 'The Band has their myths. I have mine.' Coates, 'Virginia', *The Atlantic*. 18 August 2009, https://www.theatlantic.com/entertainment/archive/2009/08/virginia/23415/

Paul is Dead . . . Long Live Paul

These questions will not go away. Neil Young's 1979 grunge anthem 'Hey Hey, My My (Into the Black)' tries to sound a hopeful note, claiming that rock and roll will 'never die' while also acknowledging that 'the King is gone'. Young, too, is in a questioning mode, asking: 'Is this the story of Johnny Rotten?'

Here is an inescapable flip side of rock and roll beginnings. Death goes with the territory. In fact, it is inscribed in the process of renewal, which supposes the demise of what preceded. It's easy to hear the beginning of 'Anarchy in the U.K.' where John Lydon declares, 'Right! Now!' laughs ominously and snarls, 'I am an antichrist' as a part of this pattern. In response to Greil Marcus's 'Presliad', which explores Elvis mythology, John Hansen floats the idea of Nietzsche's Eternal Return (Hansen 2015), which might offer a philosophical framework for the process of renewal, not just for Elvis and the various stages of his career, but for his inheritors, too. Still, even if Johnny Rotten makes a plausible Übermensch, the pattern of these musical Edens does not, I think, require such all-encompassing conceit to include the return of 'every pain and every joy and every thought' (Nietzsche 2008: 194). Rock and roll is more focused, localized and above all, performative. There is no guarantee that the show will go on. It's up to performers to make it happen, if they can.

Occasionally history intervenes to test the myth with a dramatic stroke, for instance the 1959 plane crash in Clear Lake, Iowa, that took the lives of Buddy Holly, Ritchie Valens and The Big Bopper. For many fans, it wasn't unreasonable to see the event as a watershed, the end of a rock and roll era, later mythologized by Don McLean in 'American Pie' as 'the day the music died' (1971). The lyrics to this eight-minute single are long on allegory, a rock and roll fan's Pilgrim's Progress, and while the symbolism is heavy-handed, the song ironically contradicts its message by breathing new life into its subject with a tune that is undeniably catchy.

Premature deaths have become a commonplace in rock and roll, notably the '27 Club' of figures like Robert Johnson, Jimi Hendrix, Brian Jones, Janis Joplin and Jim Morrison, who all died suddenly at the age of twenty-seven. When Kurt Cobain joined their ranks in 1994 with a self-inflicted gunshot wound, leaving a suicide note which mentioned the lessons of 'punk rock 101' and his dissatisfactions with success and 'faking it', referring also to Neil Young's 'Hey Hey, My My' lyrics, 'It's better to burn out than to fade away' (1979), it seemed to admirers an embrace of a notion of purity, a choice to stay in the garden and never sell out. Of course, parsing the motives for a suicide is risky, and it must be noted that heroin use and depression were also a part of the potent mix; still, it's not implausible that Cobain was acting on a belief in the prelapsarian aspect of the myth. He stayed true to his love and left life like a rock and roll Werther. Not everyone, though, was impressed. Cobain's mother, Wendy O'Connor, took a decidedly different view: 'Now he's gone and joined that stupid club' (Norton et al. 1994).

Given the circumstances, this is no glib remark. To rock and roll myth's aforementioned qualities of being ahistorical, nostalgic and seductive, can we also add stupid? (At least in regard to the risks of jejune romanticism?) The cycle of death and renewal can encourage morbid fascinations. In addition to the '27 Club' and other young casualties who could be described as tragedies, there has sometimes been a perverse readiness to seek death where it is not. After his 1966 motorcycle accident, Bob Dylan withdrew from the public eye and soon rumours began to circulate that he was dead. It would be terrible, after the release of the massive *Blonde on Blonde*, for the artist to be cut down in his prime, but wouldn't it also (so ran the undercurrent to the rumour) be poetic? Wouldn't it be *cool*?

Thanatos can be a source of adolescent titillation, even among those who aren't adolescents. In the 1970s, when drug abuse had left Keith Richards looking skeletal and ravaged, you could place a bet in his 'death pool' (Chiasson 2011); sensational accounts circulated about his trips to Switzerland to get his blood changed until, defying the odds, Richards became rock and roll's favourite zombie, stumbling through the decades to provide comic survival memes on social media. ('When death came to get Keith Richards, he chopped death up and snorted it' (Thomson 2023)).

The most elaborate death wish projection concerned Paul McCartney. A complete description of this urban legend exceeds the bounds of this chapter – it could, in fact, be fodder for a book, and, considering the exhaustive treatment of the Beatles and their legacy, it's surprising that the book hasn't already been written. There were various versions of the narrative, which included the theory that the deceased McCartney had been replaced by a lookalike. This substitution supposedly explained why the Beatles had stopped touring. Radio DJs and college newspapers found 'evidence' of McCartney's death in the Beatles' recording and imagery, sometimes via secret messages and backmasking, so the myth was accidentally encouraged by the Beatles' themselves with their cryptic pranks in songs like 'Glass Onion' and 'Revolution 9' (Noden 2003). Some of the 'Paul is dead' critical exegesis is ingenious; all of it is daft. The appearance of McCartney in late 1969 on the cover of the American

Paul is Dead . . . Long Live Paul

mass-circulation weekly *Life* magazine with the title 'Paul is still with us' helped dispel the rumours.

Looking back, the interest of this extended episode of nuttery is not that it happened, but rather the likelihood it could not have been otherwise. Philip Larkin, whose music criticism usually focused on jazz, speculated about the price of the Beatles' rock and roll 'hagiolatry'.

> So gigantic a success as theirs seems like the tapping of some unsuspected socio-emotional pressure that when released swept them completely away from their natural artistic context to perish in the rarefied atmosphere of hagiolatry. The four tiny figures [. . .] destroyed [. . .] by their own legend. (1983: 421)

Put another way, if the Beatles' retreat from touring into the studio was for them a quest to regenerate themselves anew, it was also a kind of death. The literal versions of the rumours, for instance that McCartney was killed in an automobile accident on the M1, hardly mattered. Paul *had* to die, in order to be resurrected again. Or, inversely, when Elvis actually did die, in 1977, it was inevitably followed by a spate of Elvis sightings, which writers like Gail Brewer-Giorgio cashed in on by writing conspiracy-driven books such as *The Elvis Files: Was His Death Faked?* (1990). Of course the King lives, even if he doesn't.

In the end, the result of rock and roll myth-making can be fascinating or banal; it is a constant work-in-progress which, at its best, in spite of its shaky relation to historical truth, offers insights and above all, synthesis. At its worst, as Ian MacDonald reminds us, it can be incoherent, even psychotic, for instance in the case of diehard Beatle fan Charles Manson, who concocted a song-based apocalyptic narrative to justify his murderous actions. In rock and roll, unlike less popular art forms, 'stars have often found themselves harassed by demented individuals among the millions following their careers' (2007: 313).

The value of a collaborative effort between artists and audiences is ever in flux and negotiable. In the 'American West' according to *The Man Who Shot Liberty Valance*, you 'print the legend'; in rock and roll, you repeat the myth, and thereby reinscribe it in the collective Eros.

A hope for Eden and its regeneration, omnipresent in the story that rock and roll culture has told about itself, provides coherence as well as a promise of new possibilities. This promise is not ancillary to the art but a part of it. Rock and roll myth does not record history, but it helps make history. And future performers will test if this myth still has something to tell us.

References

Abrams, M. H. (1981). *A Glossary of Literary Terms*. New York: Holt, Rinehart and Winston.

Auslander, Philip (2006). *Performing Glam Rock*. Ann Arbor: University of Michigan Press.

Bernstein, Leonard (2004). 'Introduction to the Beatles', in Mike Evans (ed.), *The Beatles Literary Anthology*, London: Plexus (1980).

Brewer-Giorgio, Gail (1990). *The Elvis Files: Was His Death Faked?* New York: Shapolsky Publishers.

Coates, Ta-Nehisi (2009). 'Virginia', *The Atlantic*. 18 August. https://www.theatlantic.com/entertainment/archive/2009/08/virginia/23415/ (accessed 20 February 2023).

Dylan, Bob (2004). *Chronicles: Volume One*. New York: Simon & Schuster.

Chiasson, Dan (2011). 'High on the Stones', *The New York Review of Books*, 10 March. https://www.nybooks.com/articles/2011/03/10/high-stones/. (accessed 24 February 2023).

Dylan, Bob (1971). *Tarantula*. New York: Macmillan.

Engdahl, Horace (2016). 'Award Ceremony Speech'. https://www.nobelprize.org/prizes/literature/2016/ceremony-speech/ (accessed 22 February 2023).

George-Warren, Holly (2019). *Janis: Her Life and Music*. New York: Simon and Schuster.

Hansen, John (2015). 'The Myth of Elvis Presley', *Pop Matters*, 7 July. https://www.popmatters.com/194967-the-myth-of-elvis-presley-2495513476.html (accessed 17 January 2023).

Hicks, Michael (2000). *Sixties Rock: Garage, Psychedelic, and Other Satisfactions*. Champaign: University of Illinois Press.

Holdefer, Charles (2019). 'From "Discourses of Sobriety" to Deadpan Comedy: Christopher Guest's Musical Trilogy', *Angles*, 1 November. http://journals.openedition.org/angles/2216; https://doi.org/10.4000/angles.2216 (accessed 16 February 2023).

Larkin, Philip (2004). 'Fighting the Fab', in Mike Evans (ed.), *The Beatles Literary Anthology*. London: Plexus (1983).

Linthicum, Leslie (2012). 'Did Dylan Roots Really Reach Gallup?', *Albuquerque Journal*, 13 September, A1. https://www.abqjournal.com/130451/did-dylan-roots-really-reach-gallup.html (accessed 19 January 2023).

MacDonald, Ian (1994). *Revolution in the Head*. New York: Henry Holt and Company.

Marcus, Greil (2015). *Mystery Train: Images of America in Rock 'n' Roll Music*. New York: Plume (1975).

Moore, Allan F. (2001). *Rock: The Primary Text: Developing a Musicology of Rock*. New York: Routledge.

Nietzsche, Friedrich (2008). *The Gay Science*. Trans. Josefine Nauckoff. Cambridge: Cambridge University Press (1882).

Noden, Merrell (2003). 'Dead Man Walking', in *Mojo Special Limited Edition: 1000 Days of Revolution (The Beatles' Final Years – Jan 1, 1968 to Sept 27, 1970)*, 144. London: Mojo Publishing.

Norton, Dee, Peyton Whitely, Dave Birkland, and Barbara Serrano (1994). 'Nirvana's Cobain Dead – Suicide Note, Shotgun Near Body of Musician at His Seattle Home – Mother: "Now He's Gone And Joined That Stupid Club"', *The Seattle Times*, 8 April. https://archive.seattletimes.com/archive/?date=19940408&slug=1904521 (accessed 21 February 2023).

Reiner, Rob, dir. (1984). *This is Spinal Tap*. Embassy Pictures.

Sarles, Bob, dir. (2004). *Fly Jefferson Airplane*. DVD.

Scorsese, Martin, dir. (1978). *The Last Waltz*. United Artists.

Scorsese, Martin, dir. (2005). *No Direction Home*. Paramont Pictures.

Sennett, Sean and Simon Groth (eds) (2010). *Off the Record: 25 Years of Music Street Press*. ([Online-Ausg.]. ed.). St Lucia: University of Queensland Press.

Smith, Patti (1972). *A Useless Death*. New York: Gotham Book Mart.

Smith, Patti (2010). *Just Kids*. New York: Ecco.

Thomson, Kim (2023). 'Keith Richards Memes', *Pinterest*. https://www.pinterest.com.au/kimthomson5/keith-richards-memes/ (accessed 28 February 2023).

Torkelson Weber, Erin (2016). *The Beatles and the Historians: An Analysis of Writings about the Fab Four*. Jefferson: McFarland & Co.

Wadleigh, Michael, dir. (1970). *Woodstock*. Warner Brothers.

Wiener, Jon (2004). 'First Steps Toward Radical Politics: The 1966 Tour', in Mike Evans (ed.), *The Beatles Literary Anthology*, London: Plexus (1984).

Wolff Scanlan, Laura (2016). 'The Birth of Rock 'n' Roll is Found at Sam Phillips's Sun Records', *Humanities* 37(1). https://www.neh.gov/humanities/2016/januaryfebruary/statement/the-birth-rock-%E2%80%98n%E2%80%99-roll-found-sam-phillips%E2%80%99s-sun-records (accessed 17 January 2023).

Yakas, Ben (2021). 'Sixty Years Ago Today, Bob Dylan Kicked Off His Career with a Made-Up Backstory for WNYC', *Gothamist*, 29 October. https://gothamist.com/arts-entertainment/sixty-years-ago-today-bob-dylan-kicked-his-career-made-backstory-wnyc (accessed 25 January 2023).

Zappa, Frank (2017). 'Frank Zappa and the Mothers of Invention: The *Freak Out* Gatefold', *Green and Black Music*, 2 May (1966). https://greenandblackmusic.com/home/2017/05/02/frank-zappa-the-mothers-of-invention-the-freak-out-gatefold/ (accessed 19 February 2023).

13

Something up their sleeve? The doubtful art of liner notes

Andrew McKeown

'Before you proceed any further, ask yourself why you are reading this' (Aldred 1965).[1] So begin Michael Aldred's liner notes to the Kinks' 1965 album, *The Kink Kontroversy*. What matters, Aldred goes on, is surely the music, not the publicity puff on the back of the cover, which, as he puts it, 'is, after all, only the designer's fill-in'. Contrast this self-deriding pith with Bob Mehr's ninety-page sleeve-writing opus accompanying the 2022 twelve-disc re-release of Wilco's *Yankee Hotel Foxtrot*, for which he won the 2023 Liner Note Grammy and in which he says things like:

> In the wake of 9/11, *Yankee Hotel Foxtrot* would be burdened with unintended meaning. The disc had originally been scheduled for a September 11 release. Its cover – a Sam Jones – shot image of Chicago's twin Marina Towers angled in looming fashion – bore an eerie resemblance to the felled World Trade Center towers. And the songs – with titles like 'Ashes of American Flags' and 'War on War', and lyrics about how 'tall buildings shake, sad voices escape' – took on a terrible new resonance. (Mehr 2023: 15)

Different strokes, to be sure. Nonetheless, Aldred, sometime co-host on 1960s pop TV showcase *Ready Steady Go!*, and Mehr, award-winning music journalist, are both doing the same job: writing about music on the back (or the inside) of the cover: a minor art we know as liner, album or sleeve notes.

So what do we, the readers, make of such writing? In the jazz world, liners have attracted a fair amount of critical attention. They've been anthologized and raised to status of serious prose; see Tom Piazza's *Setting the Tempo: Fifty Years*

---

[1]   I am most grateful to Maëlyn Marlière, a research student at the University of Poitiers, for compiling a database of one-hundred liner notes, from which this example is drawn and to which I refer in the course of this chapter.

of Great Jazz Liner Notes (1996). This focus is no doubt partly explained by the social importance of jazz in post-war America, where jazz was Black and political and where its champions believed it was and would be part of social change; where it was possible to equate jazz with classical music, as Oliver Nelson does in his notes to *The Blues and the Abstract Truth* (1961).

Regarding classical music, liner notes hark back to the composer's and/or conductor's programme notes for a concert performance. The advent of LP records (usually accredited to Columbia Records in 1948) saw this practice transposed, logically enough, to the record package, the intention being to reproduce the concert experience of music *with* notes in the home listening experience. In Colin Symes's discussion of classical sleeve writing, *Setting the Record Straight: A Material History of Classical Recording* (2004), the author suggests that liner notes 'occupy a modal universe different from that of the record', and goes on to affirm that the 'efficacy' of such texts 'depends on their capacity to accord with [the] contents and minimise any distortion that might flow from transferring between "modes of meaning"' (Symes 2004: 124). The possibility that sleeve writing might work *with* the music, that the *effect* of sounds and the *effect* of words might inform one another, is shooed away. Symes is prescriptive but his idea of distortion is an interesting one and I will return to this later.

As for rock and roll sleeve writing, while there is no critical anthology as with jazz, there is an online database, AlbumLinerNotes.com, though this offers primary sources with no commentary. Also, the coverage is patchy; of the hundreds of thousands of albums recorded and released in the history of the form, this website catalogues a mere thirty-one titles under 'n', including the Sex Pistols' 1977 release, *Never Mind the Bullocks* [*sic*].

In academe, we see the beginnings of critical interest. Dean L. Biron's essay, 'Writing *and* Music' (2011), for example, makes a case for liner notes as a form sui generis and raises the question of the relationship between words and music in sleeve writing; no hang-ups here about mixing one's modes. This essay aside, though, the field is thin, which is a surprise in some senses, given the interest in 'accessory' writing forms within the circles of lit crit. Witness Gérard Genette's *Paratexts*. Though the object of his discussion is literature, and not the blurb on the back of LPs, Genette's interest in literature's framing devices (titles, forewords, epigraphs, publisher's jacket copy, etc.) offers some useful parallels for our discussion of liner notes:

> More than a boundary or a sealed border, the paratext is rather a *threshold*, or – a word Borges used apropos of a preface – a 'vestibule' that offers the world at large

the possibility of either stepping inside or turning back. It is an 'undefined zone' between the inside and the outside, a zone without any hard and fast boundary on either the inward side (turned toward the text) or the outward side (turned toward the world's discourse about the text), an edge, or as Philippe Lejeune put it, 'a fringe of the printed text which in reality controls one's whole reading of the text'. (Genette 1997: 1–2)

Genette's image of a threshold is evocative: liner notes are definitely outside the music but they are also an access point into the music. Whether we follow the invitation to step inside, or draw back, return the record to the stacks and move on to some other product, the sleeve notes have placed us somewhere in between the music and the packaging, especially on a first reading. Now we all know the let-down that sometimes occurs between reading the blurb and listening to the actual recording; could Wilco's *Yankee Hotel Foxtrot* ever live up to the expectations of a ninety-page sleeve-spiel? Possibly not. This possibility is in part what lies behind Aldred's auto-derision in the opening sample of liner prose: to deflate unrealizable expectations before they get going. This isn't serious writing, Aldred seems to say, it's just commercial hype but it's also fun! At the same time, self-defeating liner notes may well be part of a broader take on sincerity and authenticity to be found in the music, too: see how Aldred's put-down of naive credulity matches up with the Kinks' sarcastic dig at nostalgia and nostalgics in 'Where Have all the Good Times Gone?', feature track of the album he is introducing: two tricks up the same sleeve.

Stimulating though the threshold image may be, it doesn't address the question of the nature of the transaction between words and music. We may recall Colin Symes's belief that when words make contact with (classical) music there should be minimal 'distortion'. But what if distortion – unavoidable anyway – were given its head? It could be argued that sleeve writing takes distortion between the two modes as a given and exploits precisely that fact. It takes the idea that music is affecting and seeks to anticipate/reproduce that experience, the effect, in words. Those words then *re-affect* the music they describe. The idea of distortion then is a second useful tool for our discussion of sleeve writing: it reminds us that written words and recorded sound are constantly transacting; *affect* (that which moves) and *effect* (the movement) are indistinguishable in the experience of the entire record product package.

So, if liner notes are a noisy threshold, what kind of noises do we hear? Let me begin with a style of cover copy which we might call retrospective. Bruce

Springsteen's notes to 1987s *In Dreams*, a re-recording of Roy Orbison hits by the Big O himself, is a transcript of his speech given at Orbison's induction into the Rock and Roll Hall of Fame, 21 January 1987. In his notes, Springsteen recalls hitching a ride to Nashville in 1970 where he was booked as a support act for his idol. He remembers too listening to Orbison's songs alone in the dark and the power they had to speak 'right to the heart of what you were livin'' (Springsteen 1987). Springsteen was and remains a fan, and his concluding thoughts describe that sometimes disarming mixture of admiration and emulation that is the fan's lot:

> I carry his records with me when I go on tour today, and I'll always remember what he means to me and what he meant to me when I was young and afraid to love. In 1975 when I went into the studio to make *Born to Run*, I wanted to make a record with words like Bob Dylan that sounded like Phil Spector, but most of all I wanted to sing like Roy Orbison. Now everybody knows that nobody sings like Roy Orbison. (Springsteen 1987)

Springsteen's tribute is sentimental, with a touch of humble self-irony in its closing joke which does much to render the whole modest and credible.

Other retrospective approaches are a little less personal and start out at least from an archivist's point of view. Step forward Mark Paytress and his account of Buzzcocks' UK 7" releases compiled on an album for the US market in 1979: *Singles Going Steady*. Paytress's notes were written in 2001 and were lifted from *Mojo* magazine to accompany the remastered CD re-release of the compilation. His account of the record and the band is at first historical and chronological, setting Buzzcocks within the 1970s punk scene, but also stressing frontman Pete Shelley's affinities with glam superstars Marc Bolan, David Bowie and Gary Glitter and of course transatlantic inspiration from the Velvet Underground and the Stooges. From here Paytress goes on to offer his opinion of why Buzzcocks matter:

> While the years have not been kind to the blank generation of one-chord wonders, it's Buzzcocks' instinct for great pop melodies, their mastery of the bittersweet love song, and the unstoppable energy that emanates from Martin Rushent's bright, buoyant productions, that gives their work the veneer of timelessness. (Paytress 2001)

Pop accessibility wasn't one of punk's signature tunes, Paytress acknowledges, which makes Buzzcocks' achievement all the more significant: 'A hits collection to rival those by The Kinks or The Beach Boys, *Singles Going Steady* is a crucial cornerstone of pop per se' (Paytress 2001).

Paytress's liner notes, though retrospective, are in part aimed at the Britpop generation coming of age in the noughties, for whom punk may well have been *another music in a different kitchen*. So, in a sense they're pedagogical. They're also part of a wider picture of remastering and re-release – rehashing, some might say – that may well suggest the rock and roll wheel has turned a full circle and is now in a nostalgic spin. The second demographic that early noughties music magazines traded on was of course the generation that were now looking back: kids from the 1960s and 1970s. And Paytress's liner notes, crisp and convincing though they are, are part of that kick.

Let's switch sides of the Atlantic – and eras – and see if there isn't another side to retrospection. In 1975, a selection of the much-bootlegged home recordings by Bob Dylan and The Band dating back to 1967 was finally released commercially under the title *The Basement Tapes*. To mark the occasion music journalist Greil Marcus wrote the sleeve notes. While Marcus is technically looking back at a pre-existing – and obscurely extant – set of recordings, there is little if any sense of the record as a thing of the past. Or, to be more precise, the past that Marcus hears from Dylan's basement is a bigger issue than the one usually broached in tribute, over-the-shoulder sleeve notes. Marcus's claim is that *Basement's* past is in fact America's past, what he dubbed 'The Old, Weird America' in the book that he worked up from these liner notes and which was published first in 1997 (under the name *Invisible Republic*) then later in 2001 under its now historic title.

Marcus asserts that Dylan's recordings of traditional music on *The Basement Tapes* are 'a testing and a discovery of roots and memory' (Marcus 1975). Like the liner photographs that accompany the release – dwarf, magician, strongman, fire-eater and belly dancer resembling a cast from Hubert's famous freak museum in New York – Dylan's songs are a tangible presence of the old, weird past projected into contemporary America:

> The spirit of a song like 'I Wish I Was a Mole in the Ground' matters here not as an 'influence', and not as a 'source'. It is simply that one side of *The Basement Tapes* casts the shadow of such things and in turn, is shadowed by them. (Marcus 1975)

It is also true that Marcus's notes indulge in some of the classic impression-mongering that seems to be, in varying degrees of palatability, a staple of liner writing. Witness the 'slow, uncoiling menace of "This Wheel's On Fire"', or indeed the 'patented mixture of carnal bewilderment and helpless delight in "Don't Ya

Tell Henry"' (Marcus 1975): words which re-enact the *effect* of the *affect*. But the real significance of Marcus's notes is this interest in history, working backwards and forwards in American song. Not bad for the minor art of sleeve-spiel.

If retrospective sleeve writing provides an opportunity for composers and critics to restate (or re-imagine) the significance of what has gone before, agitprop liner notes have no such truck with the past. Writing in this vein is where Genette's threshold see-saws towards the inside. You must believe, says agitprop; there is no truth outside our gates. And here of course the distortion between *affect* and *effect* is pretty noisy.

In 1979, Gang of Four brought out the album *Entertainment*, the jagged, leading edge of post-punk, announcing and confirming the marriage of angles and rhythms that would define the otherworldly danceability of the 1980s underground. The liner notes to *Entertainment* offer three, roughly distinct narratives: a cowboy greeting an Indian; overweight people being photographed; and a series of grainy TV screens depicting an assortment of what looks like street violence, celebrities meeting, war scenes, a surgical intervention, an equestrian statue and British policemen. The first narrative says that the cowboy exploits the Indian; the second says that the fat people spend their money to stay fat while those who 'who decide what everyone will do grow rich' (Gang of Four 1979); while the third storyline takes aim at 'mass communication' and concludes 'People are given what they want' (Gang of Four 1979). *Entertainment*'s cover copy has that oblique antsiness that characterized much of the cut-up/ defacement/xerox ethos of punk, as deployed and defined in fanzines like *Sniffin' Glue*. No thank you, say the unlovely collages, we'll have no more of your consumer society schtick. These are broken liner notes that perform the demise of promotional wording, at least for the space of this album: words of music are (es)chewed up and spat back at the industry.

Of course, it's an easy point to score to say that such agitprop happens (self-defeatingly?) within the boundaries of that same industry. Then again, do any liner texts ever achieve 100 per cent authenticity and disinterestedness? As Michael Aldred noted with regard to the Kinks, the endgame of cover copy, whatever its topsy-turvy ways, is to make the buyer buy. While this might be so, it shouldn't be assumed that agitprop liner writing can be easily dismissed as vain gesturing. Some sleeve texts have unnerving propagandist connections with real historical movers.

Allow me to introduce Funkadelic and their, in several ways, memorable LP, *Maggot Brain*. 'Fear is at the root of man's destruction of himself' (Funkadelic

1971), the liner notes begin. Nothing especially controversial there. Man may indeed be a timorous critter, fair enough. But jump forward to the next paragraph and the tone changes:

> [Fear] can be seen in the fantasy world of escapism known as entertainment. It can be seen in riot torn streets and campuses. It can be seen on another level in the mammoth build up of war machines in every corner of the world. It can be seen in the squalor of ghettos and the pretentious elegance of 'civilised' society. (Funkadelic 1971)

And keeps on changing: 'Afraid to step down into the darkness of his lower self or to rise up into the light of his higher self, he hangs suspended in between, stultified into an alien pattern of nothingness' (Funkadelic 1971). It doesn't take much of a diet of cod Nietzsche to detect the baleful shadow of an Übermensch lurking behind these sleeve notes; nor do we have to look hard to find echoes of real-life violence the notes might point to: Altamont, Kent State, Attica and so on. Funkadelic were no doubt playing with fire, and the clincher to this is to be found in the text's authorship: 'Taken from Process Number Five on Fear. The Process-Church of the Final Judgement' (Funkadelic 1971). This organization was a Satanist cult (at least that was the rumour) and was mixed up (so another rumour has it) with the Manson Family. The Manson connection might be a tenuous one in terms of hard facts. Counterculturalist Ed Sanders was indeed forced to retract the claim he'd made in an earlier version of his book on Manson, *The Family* (2002), that Manson was a Process member. But precisely in terms of rumour and paranoia, in terms of the fear it fed and fed off, the Process Church and Funkadelic's derivative liner notes were no anodine stunt: the overcoming of fear that they imply and the class/race war that they talk up were exactly the sort of glib litany that the Manson Family peddled (and that the Tate and LaBianca circles died as a result of).

If we move back a little in time to another set of agitprop liner notes, this time from MC5's debut LP, *Kick Out the Jams* (1969), the difference between revolution and *talking* about a revolution becomes a little clearer. The notes for *Kick Out the Jams* were supplied by John Sinclair, the group's manager, who signs the sleeve and announces himself to be 'Minister of Information. White Panthers' (Sinclair 1969). Sinclair believes 'separation' is society's fundamental affliction; its solution, the MC5:

> We say the MC5 is the solution to the problem of separation, because they are so together. [. . .] They live together to work together, they eat together, fuck

together, get high together, walk down the street and through the world together. (Sinclair 1969)

While some might say you can have too much of a good thing like togetherness, for Sinclair it's the key to the revolution:

> We are a lonely desperate people, pulled apart by the killer forces of capitalism and competition, and we need the music to hold us together. [. . .] The MC5 is that force. The MC5 is the revolution, in all its applications. There is no separation. Everything is everything. (Sinclair 1969)

Sinclair's sentences strike a familiar note: the callow overconfidence in one's own beliefs, the incontrovertible faith in *the* revolution, that characterized parts of late 1960s and early 1970s counterculture. Sinclair and the MC5 were often linked, for example, with the so-called Yippies, or Youth International Party, famed for anti-establishment street theatre, pranks and smoke-ins, and, perhaps unfairly, once dismissed on ABC news as 'Groucho Marxists'.

Of course Sinclair and his liner notes are an easy target: 'Everything is everything.' Quite. That being said, Sinclair's liner notes just don't ring true. The MC5 were not the revolution; their musical legacy didn't turn rock and roll (or society) around. The puff on the cover (deemed controversial and withdrawn from releases subsequent to that of 1969) doesn't match the music, at least not in this critic's estimation. Sinclair's notes overreach and fall down – perhaps the real reason why they were pulled – unlike the Funkadelic screed which did play with *real* fire. And unlike the Stooges, Elektra stablemates who also released a debut in the same year and whose cover has no copy (beyond the credits) but whose music eschewed *talking* about a revolution and – Iggy take a bow – got on with bringing one about instead.

Agitprop liner notes are downright noisy; a threshold that brooks no turning back. Literary sleeve writing is another example of demanding *paratext*, though perhaps with its volume control set a little lower. Patti Smith's *Horses*, released in 1975, comes equipped with a concise, poem-shaped text on its back cover, signed by the singer herself. Written all in lower case, with suspension dots punctuating noun groups and snatches of sentences, the writing is immediate, impressionistic and obscure: 'compacted awareness . . . gems flattening . . . long streams of resin tools ' (Smith 1975). Its most obvious debt is to Burroughs (and Gyson) and their cut-ups: slashed consciousness spread out like a patient etherized... well, you get the picture. There are odd borrowings of French ('mer', 'histoire'), too, nodding to other, kindred decadent/romantic conspirators:

Rimbaud, Verlaine, Baudelaire. If there are threads to be followed through Smith's maze, they are music, drugs and horses: music, in the 'drums tongue' and the 'system of wax'; drugs in the 'veins filled' and the 'arm of the needle'; and of course the eponymous 'horses', the 'feel' of them 'groping for a sign, for a breath' (Smith 1975). Smith's symbolist figure of the horse is both drug (heroin) and deceased artistic forebear – Brian Jones, Jim Morrison or Jimi Hendrix to whom the album track 'Elegie' is dedicated. As liner notes go, Smith's exploding-semantic-intangible is high-calorie fare. Not for her the light-hearted quip cum plug. As a threshold text, it performs the same degree of seriousness to be found in the music. In other words, it weds itself to the record so as to make the parts of the whole indivisible. It is a text which could very well be a lyric from the songs. This is art, say the liner notes to *Horses*.

And so they may be. But there is a broader picture of literary sleeve writing which takes itself a little less seriously. Cue Andrew Loog Oldham's notes to the Rolling Stones' second LP, released in 1965. Oldham delivers a narrative which, very roughly, describes the Stones' journey from Richmond's Crawdaddy Club to their first US tour under the helmsmanship of his good self and co-manager Eric Easton. But what the text really does is recast the Stones' story as ersatz *Clockwork Orange*. Thus, we have the Stones as 'malchicks' roaming London's tower block land. Halfway through Oldham drops in a commercial break: go buy this LP, he commands, and 'if you don't have bread, see that blind man / knock him on the head, steal / his wallet and low [*sic*] and behold you have / the loot' (Oldham 1965).

It's probably safe to assume most readers from 1965 would have picked up on the reference Anthony Burgess's 1962 novel and taken it as a joke, possibly in poor taste, but a joke nonetheless. In any event, the literariness of Oldham's pastiche is, because it's a pastiche, unpretentious. One could make an argument that what divides Oldham and Smith's texts (in addition to the fact that Smith is the artist, whereas Oldham is the manager) is drugs: one pre, the other post. And while that may sound simplistic and reductive, it is true that liner writing with a literary bent after the 1960s drug tsunami hit – for argument's sake, let's say circa-Pepper – becomes significantly *different*: think of Hendrix's 'Letter to the Room Full of Mirrors' on the US *Electric Ladyland* (1968).

Someone who sits perhaps on both sides of the literary fence is Bob Dylan. His liner notes to *Highway 61 Revisited* introduce White Heap and a cast of assistants, the 'Inevitables', with names like 'Savage Rose' and 'Fixable'. There is no narrative as such; instead, Dylan throws together a mishmash of occurrences, ideas, places

Something Up Their Sleeve?   181

and things which seem intent on *not* making sense, with comicbook absurdity, like the character Cream Judge who is writing a book on 'the true meaning of a pear' (Dylan 1965). Dylan avers in conclusion that the subject matter of the record these notes enfold is 'meaningless' but nonetheless has something to do with 'beautiful strangers' (Dylan 1965). If anything were to be extracted from the notes it would be just that: the meeting of the strange and the beautiful, with an important caveat: Dylan declares no meaning in that meeting. That, we must assume, is our job.

Highway 61 Revisited's sleeve text reads a little like Whitman among the Marvel Comics. The setting is recognizable, as familiar as the Western, or *West Side Story*, and as American as Robert Frank *The Americans*. But it's also off-kilter, as misshapen and uprooted as Diane Arbus's freaks and just as unsettlingly captivating. That ability to mix and match the absurd and the everyday is Dylan's signature and bespeaks his undeluded realism wedded to his romantic insights. While it's not my aim here to say whether or how much Dylan's writing is indebted to drugs, the point is that he was moving in and was a mover of a world that was popping pills and smoking pot, and would soon hit the harder stuff. The *otherness* of these notes bears testimony to a certain riff-rapping, drug-hat touching style. That style was busy being born as 1965 turned into 1966 turned into 1967, while perhaps simpler types of liner writing (of the Michael Aldred sort we saw earlier) were busy if not dying, at least going out of fashion. Dylan's notes are part of that shift.

To finish my tour of sleeve notes, let me isolate a final category: comedy. Introducing the Small Faces and their first LP, music publicist Tony Brainsby has this to say: 'How did they get their name?' to which the answer comes: 'Just one look at them is sufficient to see that they do indeed have small faces' (Brainsby 1966). A pretty crummy gag, I think you'd agree. If agitprop sleeve notes see-saw inward towards the music, then throwaway lines like this and comic notes in general see-saw outward: one pumps up the balloon, the other punctures it. At times the fooling around can be pretty groan-inducing. Witness Brian Sommerville's mock manifesto on the Kinks' first LP:

> The letter K has been sadly neglected in the English language for centuries. The Kinks, when they are knot making records or doing one-knight stands, are kampaigning to restore the K to its rightful and knoble place. [. . .] To help this kampaign on its way some simple rules have to be observed. First the letter K should never be silent in words such as knee, know and knockout;

secondly, where possible K should be substituted for C in pronunciation. (Sommerville 1964)

And so it continues. This type of humour is perhaps a British thing. Sommerville was also the Beatles' press agent and no stranger to a certain type of absurdist humour, the so-called satire boom of the early 1960s, beginning on the radio with the *Goons*, moving to the stage show *Beyond the Fringe* before graduating to TV in *That Was the Week That Was*. In a sense, fun liner notes in the Sommerville or Brainsby style were tie-ins with satire in the wider entertainment world and as such were also *buy-ins*. It is no surprise that the people behind such pitches were first and foremost businessmen: publicist and press agent.

Parts of satirical liner writing from the 1960s had a harder edge, however, mirroring the aggressive styles of print publications such as *Private Eye*, or, perhaps most aggressive of all, *Oz*. Part of that *Oz* bent was Bonzo Dog Doo-Dah Band, led by Vivian Stanshall. The sleeve copy to *Gorilla*, released in 1967, picks up on the nascent psychedelic *mode* and offers a series of hand-drawn statements concerning the art of 'Doo-Dah', delivered in speech bubbles issuing from a microphone held by a bespectacled academic type on a rostrum. 'Dog Doo-dah' suggests perhaps dog faeces but it's also close to Dada, so that the combined effect is a scatalogical debunk of art, or artiness. But there are other hints linked to doo-dah: 'During my school days I sometimes gave in to the impulse. Teachers responded inflicting agonizing blows to my body' (Vivian Stanshall 1967). Masturbation? Castigation? The notes throw out these sexual suggestions but offer no overt connection between art, the scatological and sex. The text ends (if indeed there is such a thing as a linear sentence here) or starts (depending on your point of entry) on 'bah, blub, bore', while credits go to 'Prof. R. Spread (more potty fun) University of Acne, Eng' (Vivian Stanshall 1967). Maybe the speech bubbles were fart bubbles, after all.

Comic liner notes have what Richard Neville, editor of *Oz*, would have called 'playpower'. They are part of another version of revolution – adversary to the one we've seen touted on agitprop record sleeves – and pick up on another 1960s vibe that is sometimes lost in the din of drugs and psychedelia:

If you make a revolution, make it for fun,
don't make it in ghastly seriousness,
don't do it in deadly earnest,
do it for fun. (Lawrence 1994: 430)

Something Up Their Sleeve?　　183

Comic liner writing takes the idea of unseriousness and exploits it in the belief (propagandists excepted) that liner writing isn't serious anyway. A double-yoked joke, you might say.

Let's fast forward to the 1980s to my final sample of comic liner writing produced by the improbably named Half Man Half Biscuit. With a penchant for shouting out loud that the Emperor's got no clothes on ('Venus in Flares') and a knack for seeing the other side of conventionality ('National Shite Day'), these merry punksters have pranked their way through the recorded sound industry for the last four decades. Their debut release, *Back in the DHSS* (1985), has liner notes that offer a roll call of what look like jokes: 'Matthew Kelly: housewives' favourite. Should've been a racehorse', 'Lionel Blair: TV's first emetic', 'Jesus Christ: Right arm, over the wicket' (Half Man Half Biscuit 1985). Those jokes obviously speak to a UK readership familiar with television entertainers (and cricket and anyone who's ever heard of Christianity), and they are very much in the stand-up comedy vein. Maybe they don't travel well across the Atlantic or outside of the 1980s, but they are a sign that mock album cover copy has persisted beyond the 1960s.

And they have carried that vein over into the twenty-first century, era of the ninety-page liner 'booklet'. Half Man Half Biscuit's most recent LP, *The Voltarol Years* (2022), offers a reverse cover with pasted-on cut-outs, drawings and old-time photos. Under a messy sketch of a group of people queuing somewhere we read the following caption:

> Goya smuggling his beloved Gadwall past suspicious types using a colleague's Pronghorn as a decoy (on the exact spot where the Bernabeu stadium would later be built). (Half Man Half Biscuit 2022)

Quite so. Now I don't intend to suggest that there is anything significant about this foregoing 'text'. Absolutely not. But as a parody of the genre to which it belongs, it only needs *not* to make sense to be effective. Its silence as a threshold is its noisiness.

My discussion of liner writing is clearly drawn from a small sample. That said, I have tried to pick writing and writers that are exemplary in a certain field or are thought-provoking, ideally both. Essentially, I have selected material that I like, for one reason or another. I hope those reasons have become evident in the course of the chapter.

Another caveat should also be offered regarding the categories. They are of course only suggestions and others might feel that different emphases are merited by liner writing: the journalistic, or the philosophical, for example. Furthermore, the categories overlap – agitprop and literary are obvious bed hoppers – and are in no sense meant to be read as exclusive boundaries. Again, the choice of labels was dictated by taste, rather than a desire for absolute objectivity.

From Michael Aldred's quip about liner writing being nothing more than the designer's 'fill-in' to the absurdist captions on Half Man Half Biscuit's latest LP: we have come a long way and yet we're still in pretty much the same place. Sleeve-spiel has that gratuitousness that seems to go with commercial copy writing, which is really what it is in the last analysis. This is not to say that some of the products for sale (such as revolutions) aren't serious. Nor is it to say that other products (such as poems) *are* serious. Liner notes leave the buyer free to decide, poised somewhere between the trite and the truth.

References

AlbumLinerNotes.com

Aldred, Michael (1965). https://kindakinks.net/discography/showrelease.php?release =51 (accessed 4 July 2023).

Behr, Bob (2022). Quoted in: *Tinnitist*, 30 September.

Biron, Deal L. (2011). 'Writing *and* Music: Album Liner Notes', *Portal* 8(1), January, Terpsichorean Architecture Special Issue. Tony Mitchell (ed.).

Brainsby, Tony (1966). https://www.discogs.com/master/304383-Small-Faces-Small -Faces/image/SW1hZ2U6ODM1ODE3NjM= (accessed 4 July 2023).

Dylan, Bob (1965). https://www.discogs.com/release/4028730-Bob-Dylan-Highway-61 -Revisited/image/SW1hZ2U6Mjg0MzQ1NjI= (accessed 4 July 2023).

Genette, Gérard (1987). *Paratexts: Thresholds of Interpretation*. Trans. Jane E. Lewin. Cambridge: Cambridge University Press (1997).

Half Men Half Biscuits (1985). https://www.discogs.com/release/985903-Half-Man -Half-Biscuit-Back-In-The-DHSS/image/SW1hZ2U6MjkyNzU1OTM= (accessed 4 July 2023).

Half Men Half Biscuits (2022). https://www.discogs.com/master/2727173-Half-Man -Half-Biscuit-The-Voltarol-Years/image/SW1hZ2U6ODE4ODA0NzU= (accessed 4 July 2023).

Hendrix, Jimi (1968). https://www.discogs.com/release/2492300-The-Jimi-Hendrix -Experience-Electric-Ladyland/image/SW1hZ2U6NDk1MDE2Mw== (accessed 4 July 2023).

Lawrence, David Herbert (1929). 'A Sane Revolution', in David Ellis (ed.), *The Complete Poems of D.H. Lawrence*, 430. London: Wordsworth Editions (1994).

Marcus, Greil (1975). https://theband.hiof.no/albums/basement_tapes_ln.html (accessed 4 July 2023).

Morrison, Jim (1968). https://www.discogs.com/master/45365-The-Doors-Waiting-For-The-Sun/image/SW1hZ2U6Nzc1ODkwMg== (accessed 4 July 2023).

Nelson, Oliver (1961). https://www.discogs.com/master/56196-Oliver-Nelson-The-Blues-And-The-Abstract-Truth/image/SW1hZ2U6NDI4MTczMDU= (accessed 4 July 2023).

Oldham, Andrew Loog (1965). https://www.discogs.com/master/54105-The-Rolling-Stones-No-2/image/SW1hZ2U6NzU4OTgyMTE= (accessed 4 July 2023).

Paytress, Mark (2001). https://www.discogs.com/release/571576-Buzzcocks-Singles-Going-Steady/image/SW1hZ2U6NjAxOTUwNQ== (accessed 4 July 2023).

Piazza, Tom (ed.) (1996). *Setting the Tempo: Fifty Years of Great Jazz Liner Notes*. New York: Anchor.

Process-Church of the Final Judgement (1971). https://www.discogs.com/release/773587-Funkadelic-Maggot-Brain/image/SW1hZ2U6NzUzMTA0MA== (accessed 4 July 2023).

Sinclair, John (1969). https://www.discogs.com/release/1310994-MC5-Kick-Out-The-Jams/image/SW1hZ2U6MjMzODgwOTg= (accessed 4 July 2023).

Smith, Harry (1952). https://www.discogs.com/master/339200-Harry-Smith-Anthology-Of-American-Folk-Music-Volume-One-Ballads/image/SW1hZ2U6NjA3OTY5OTA= (accessed 4 July 2023).

Smith, Patti (1975). https://www.discogs.com/master/40109-Patti-Smith-Horses/image/SW1hZ2U6NDc4MzI2OTE= (accessed 4 July 2023).

Sommerville, Brian (1964). https://www.discogs.com/release/13676933-The-Kinks-Kinks/image/SW1hZ2U6NDAzMzIyMTA= (accessed 4 July 2023).

Springsteen, Bruce (1987). https://www.discogs.com/master/137148-Roy-Orbison-In-Dreams-The-Greatest-Hits/image/SW1hZ2U6NDQxMDQxNjU= (accessed 4 July 2023).

Stanshall, Vivian (1967). https://www.discogs.com/master/69317-Bonzo-Dog-DooDah-Band-Gorilla/image/SW1hZ2U6MjIxMTY0NDA=?query=liner+notes (accessed 4 July 2023).

Symes, Colin (2004). *Setting the Record Straight: A Material History of Classical Recording*. Middletown: Wesleyan University Press.

General Bibliography

Anonymous. *Album Liner Notes*. http://albumlinernotes.com.

Armitage, Simon (2008). *Gig: Rock and Roll Dreams in a Northern Town*. Harmondsworth: Penguin.

Auslander, Philip (2006). *Performing Glam Rock: Gender and Theatricality in Popular Music*. Ann Arbor: University of Michigan Press.

Bangs, Lester ([1987] 2014). *Psychotic Reactions and Carburetor Dung*. New York: Vintage.

Barthes, Roland (1978). *A Lover's Discourse: Fragments*. Trans. Richard Howard. New York: Hill & Wang.

Berthomier, Maud (2019). *Encore Plus de bruit: L'âge d'or du journalisme rock en Amérique par ceux qui l'ont inventé*. Paris: Tristram.

Boyd, Patti with Penny Junor (2008). *Wonderful Tonight: George Harrison, Eric Clapton and Me*. New York: Three Rivers Press.

Bradley, Lloyd (2000). *Bass Culture: When Reggae Was King*. London: Viking.

Brennan, Matt (2017). *When Genres Collide: Downbeat, Rolling Stone and the Struggle Between Jazz and Rock*. London: Bloomsbury.

Brennan, Matt (2020). *Kick It: A Social History of the Drum Kit*. Oxford: Oxford University Press.

Burchill, Julie and Tony Parsons (1980). *The Boy Looked at Johnny*. London: Pluto Press.

Carducci, Joe (1991). *Rock and the Pop Narcotic*. New York: Redoubt Press.

Carson, Tom, Kit Rachlis, and Jeff Salamon (eds) (2002). *Don't Stop 'til You Get Enough: Essays in Honor of Robert Christgau*. Mount Pleasant: Nortex Press.

Christgau, Robert (2000). *Any Old Way You Choose It: Rock and Other Pop Music 1967–1973*. Lanham: Cooper Square Press.

Christgau, Robert ([1998] 2000). *Grown Up All Wrong: 75 Great Rock and Pop Artists from Vaudeville to Techno*. Cambridge, MA: Harvard University Press.

Christgau, Robert (2018). *Is It Still Good to Ya? Fifty Years of Rock Criticism 1967–2017*. Durham: Duke University Press.

Christgau, Robert (2019). *Book Reports: A Music Critic on His First Love, Which Was Reading*. Durham: Duke University Press.

Clapton, Eric (2007). *The Autobiography*. London: Arrow Books.

Clarke, John Cooper (2020). *I Wanna Be Yours*. London: Picador.

Cohn, Nik ([1969] 1996). *Awopbopaloobop Alopbamboom: The Golden Age of Rock*. New York: Grover Press.

Daltrey, Roger (2018). *Thanks a Lot, Mr Kibblethwaite*. London: Blink.

DeLillo, Don ([1973] 1999). *Great Jones Street*. London: Picador.

Des Barres, Pamela ([1987] 2005). *I'm With the Band: Confessions of a Groupie*. Chicago: Chicago Review Press.

Dettmar, Kevin J. H. and William Richey (1999). *Reading Rock and Roll: Authenticity, Appropriation, Aesthetics*. New York: Columbia University Press.

Douglas, Tana (2021). *Loud: A Life in Rock'n'Roll by the World's First Female Roadie*. Birmingham: ABC Books.

Doyle, Roddy ([1988] 1993). *The Commitments*. London: Minerva.

Dylan, Bob (2005). *Chronicles: Volume One*. London: Simon and Schuster UK Ltd.

Dylan, Bob ([1971] 2005). *Tarantula*. New York: Daedalus.

Faithfull, Marianne (1995). *Faithfull*. Harmondsworth: Penguin.

Frith, Simon (1981). *Sound Effects*. New York: Random House.

Frith, Simon (1988). *Music for Pleasure*. London: Polity Press.

Frith, Simon (1990). *Facing the Music*. London: Mandarin.

Frith, Simon (1998). *Performing Rites: Evaluating Popular Music*. Oxford: Oxford University Press.

Frith, Simon, Matt Brennan, Martin Cloonan, and Emma Webster (2013, 2019, 2021). *The History of Live Music in Britain*. 3 vols. London: Routledge.

Frith, Simon and Andrew Goodwin (1990). *On Record: Rock, Pop and the Written Word*. London: Routledge.

Frith, Simon and Howard Horne (1987). *Art into Pop*. London: Routledge.

Goddard, Simon (2013). *Ziggyology: A Brief History of Ziggy Stardust*. London: Ebury Press.

Golson, G. Barry and David Sheff (eds) (1982). *Playboy Interviews with John Lennon and Yoko Ono*. New York: New English Library.

Goss, Nina and Eric Hoffman (eds) (2018). *Tearing the World Apart: Bob Dylan and the Twenty First Century*. Jackson: University Press of Mississippi.

Goss, Nina and Nick Smart (eds) (2011). *Dylan at Play*. Newcastle Upon Tyne: Cambridge Scholars Publishing.

Grafe, Adrian (2003). 'Presences of Rock in Contemporary Literature', in *Recherches Valenciennoises n° 13, numéro spécial sur Loisirs et société britannique au XXe siècle, études réunies par Simone Kadi*, 9–24. Presses Universitaires de Valenciennes.

Grafe, Adrian (2005). 'The Poetic Voice and the Voice of Popular Music in Poems by Philip Larkin, Paul Muldoon and Hugo Williams', in Pierre Iselin and Elisabeth Angel-Perez (eds), *Poétiques de la voix*, 141–54. Paris: Presses de l'université Paris-Sorbonne.

Grafe, Adrian (2006). 'Bob Dylan. *Chronicles* Vol. 1', *Etudes anglaises* 59 (4): 490–3.

Guralnick, Peter (1999). *Lost Highway: Journeys and Arrivals of American Musicians*. New York: Back Bay Books.

Guralnick, Peter (2000). *Careless Love: The Unmaking of Elvis Presley*. New York: Abacus.

Guralnick, Peter (2002). *Sweet Soul Music: Rhythm and Blues and the Southern Dream of Freedom*. Edinburgh: Canongate Books.

Guralnick, Peter (2020). *Looking to Get Lost: Adventures in Music and Writing*. New York: Little, Brown.

Hebdidge, Dick (1979). *Subculture: The Meaning of Style*. London: Routledge.

Heylin, Clinton (1992). *The Penguin Book of Rock and Roll Writing*. Harmondsworth: Penguin.

Hines, Barry ([1998] 1999). *Elvis over England*. London: Penguin Books.

Holmstrom, John (2013). *The Best of Punk Magazine*. New York: ItBooks.

Hornby, Nick ([1995] 1996). *High Fidelity*. London: Indigo.

Hudson, Mark (1999). *The Music in My Head*. London: Vintage.

Hunter, Ian (1974). *Diary of a Rock and Roll Star*. London: Omnibus.

Inglis, Ian (ed.) (2006). *Performance and Popular Music: History Place and Time*. Aldershot: Ashgate.

Jones, Steve (2016). *Lonely Boy: Tales from a Sex Pistol*. London: Windmill Books.

Kent, Nick (2007). *The Dark Stuff*. London: Faber and Faber.

Kent, Nick (2010). *Apathy for the Devil: A Seventies Memoir*. London: Faber and Faber.

Kent, Nick (2021). *The Unstable Boys*. London: Constable.

Kureishi, Hanif and Jon Savage (eds) (1996). *The Faber Book of Pop*. London: Faber & Faber.

Landau, Jon (1972). *It's Too Late to Stop Now: A Rock and Roll Journal*. San Francisco: Straight Arrow Books.

Larkin, Philip ([1964] 1971). *The Whitsun Weddings*. London: Faber & Faber.

Larkin, Philip (1985). *All What Jazz: A Record Diary*. London: Faber and Faber.

Long, Pat (2012). *The History of the NME*. London: Portico.

Lydon, John (2003). *Rotten: No Blacks, No Irish, No Dogs*. London: Plexus.

Macdonald, Ian (2003). *The People's Music: Selected Journalism*. London: Pimlico.

Macdonald, Ian ([1994] 2005). *Revolution in the Head*. London: Pimlico.

Marcus, Greil ([1975] 2000). *Mystery Train*. London: Faber and Faber.

Marcus, Greil ([1989] 2011). *Lipstick Traces*. London: Faber and Faber.

Matheu, Robert and Brian J. Bowe (2007). *Creem: America's Only Rock and Roll Magazine*. Glasgow: Collins.

McAslan, Simon (2017). 'Bob Dylan Is the Most Important Literary Artist of Our Time', *The Globe and Mail*, 6 April. ww.theglobeandmail.com/arts/music/bob-dylan-is-the-most-important-literary-artist-of-our-ti me/article32360119/.

McDonnell, Evelyn and Ann Powers (eds) (1995). *Rock She Wrote: Women Write About Rock, Pop and Rap*. London: Plexus Publishing.

McLeod, Kembrew (2001). '"★½": A Critique of Rock Criticism in North America', *Popular Music* 20 (1): 47–60. http://www.jstor.org/stable/853694.

McNeil, Legs and Gillian McCain ([1996] 2016). *Please Kill Me: The Uncensored History of Punk*. London: Abacus.

Melly, George (1970). *Revolt into Style: The Pop Arts*. London: Faber & Faber.

Monk, Noel E. and Jimmy Guterman (1990). *12 Days on the Road: The Sex Pistols and America*. New York: William Morrow and Company.

Negus, Keith (1996). *Popular Music in Theory: An Introduction*. Cambridge: Polity Press.

Parsons, Tony (1981). *Platinum Logic*. London: Macmillan.

Perry, Mark (2009). *Sniffin Glue and Other Rock and Roll Habits*. London: Omnibus.

Richards, Keith (2010). *Life*. London: Phoenix Paperback.

Ricks, Christopher (2003). *Dylan's Visions of Sin*. New York: HarperCollins.

Rolling Stone Editors ([1997] 1998). *Bruce Springsteen: The Rolling Stone Files*. London and Basingstoke: Pan Books.

Rushdie, Salman (1999). *The Ground Beneath her Feet*. London: Jonathan Cape.

Sampson, Mark (1999). *Powder*. London: Jonathan Cape.

Savage, Jon (2005). *England's Dreaming*. London: Faber & Faber.

Sculatti, Gene (2016). *Tryin' to Tell a Stranger' Bout Rock and Roll*. NewYork: CreateSpace Publishing.

Shaar Murray, Charles (1991). *Shots from the Hip*. Harmondsworth: Penguin.

Skinner Sawyers, June (ed.) (2006). *Read the Beatles: Classic and New Writings on the Beatles, Their Legacy and Why They Still Matter*. New York: Penguin Books.

Smith, Patti (2012). *Woolgathering*. London: Bloomsbury.

Springsteen, Bruce (2016). *Born to Run*. New York: Simon & Schuster.

Sutherland, Steve (ed.) (2002). *NME Originals: Punk 1975–1979*. London: IPC Ignite.

Toop, David (1984). *The Rap Attack: African Jive to New York Hip Hop*. Boston: South End Press.

Toynbee, Jason (1993). 'Policing Bohemia, Pinning up Grunge: The Music Press and Generic Change in British Pop and Rock', *Popular Music*, 12 (3): 289–300.

Townshend, Pete (2013). *Who I Am*. London: HarperCollins Publishers.

Weberman, Alan Jules (1969). *Dylanology*. New York: Whitepress.

Wenner, Jann (1972). *Lennon Remembers*. Harmondsworth: Penguin.

Wenner, Jann (2017). *50 Years of Rolling Stone: The Music, Politics and People that Changed our Culture*. New York: Abrams.

Whiteley, Sheila (ed.) (1997). *Sexing the Groove: Popular Music and Gender*. London: Routledge.

Wilson, Mary (1986). *Dreamgirl: My Life as a Supreme*. New York: St Martin's Press.

Wolfe, Tom ([1965] 2018). *The Kandy-Kolored Tangerine-Flake Streamline Baby*. New York: Vintage Classics.

Wood, James (2010). 'The Fun Stuff: My Life as Keith Moon', *The New Yorker*, 29 November. https://www.newyorker.com/magazine/2010/11/29/the-fun-stuff.

Wood, Ronnie (2007). *Ronnie*. London: Macmillan.

Young, Neil (2012). *Waging Heavy Peace: A Hippie Dream*. New York: Blue Rider Press.

Zappa, Frank (1990). *The Real Frank Zappa Book*. New York: Simon and Schuster.

Index

Adorno, Theodor W. 2, 35–48, 72
'American Pie' (song) 163, 167
autobiography 121, 123, 130

Bangs, Lester 1–2, 11, 24–34
Barthes, Roland 1, 5
Beatles, The 26–8, 38, 42, 54, 65, 68, 70, 74, 93, 95, 97, 109, 119, 129, 160, 163, 165, 168–9, 182
Bible, The 36, 91, 151–3
biography 4, 121, 142
Bowie, David 54, 108, 114, 175
Burgess, Anthony *A Clockwork Orange* 180
Burgess, John 17–18
Burgess, Melvin 94, 100–1
Burroughs, William 143, 157, 179

canon 119–32
Chbosky, Stephen 94–6
Clash 16
Clash, The 36, 164
Cobain, Kurt 139–41, 143–4, 149, 167–8
Cohn, Nik 2, 66–75
Cohn, Rachel 93–4, 98
concert, as rock and roll writing 49–63
Creem 135–6

Disc & Music Echo 12
Dury, Ian 94
Dylan, Bob 42, 56, 60, 109, 119, 141, 160, 164, 168, 175–6, 180–1

elegy 4, 133–45
Eliot, T. S. 135

Face, The 16
Facebook 3, 82–4, 89–90
fanzines 12, 14, 17, 122, 160, 177

feminism 67, 69, 110, 119–20, 125, 130
Foucault, Michel 3, 94, 102, 104
Frith, Simon 3, 51–2, 70–5

Genette, Gérard 49, 173–4, 177
Godard, Jean-Luc 133
Gracyk, Theodore 39, 41–4, 46–7, 49
Grammy Awards 5, 172
Gramsci, Antonio 73–4
Grateful Dead, The 3, 81–92, 153
Guralnick, Peter 1

Hendrix, Jimi 35–6, 39, 48, 137–9, 141, 143–4, 167, 180
Hinton, S. E. 93–4
history/historic/historical 1, 3, 10, 20, 24, 26, 28–33, 41, 43, 46, 49–50, 52, 54, 56, 60, 64–77, 82–9, 91, 93, 99–100, 103, 106–19, 121–2, 125, 130, 133, 150, 152, 159–62, 166, 167, 169, 173–4, 176–7
Hoggart, Richard 74–5
Holiday, Billie 123
Holly, Buddy 84, 167

internet 9, 12–15, 20, 81–3, 85–9, 98, 119–20
interviews 1, 3, 11, 13–14, 17, 38, 52, 99, 106–14, 116, 125, 129, 137, 139–40, 148, 164–6

jazz 31, 35, 37–8, 40, 65–6, 123, 169, 172, 173
Jett, Joan 146, 154–6
Johnson, Robert 167
Jones, Brian 133–6, 138, 140–2, 144, 167, 180
Jones, Grace 3, 106, 108, 116
Jones, LeRoi 65–6
Joplin, Janis 137–8, 141, 164, 167

Index

journalism 1, 9–23, 73, 106, 125, 148, 153, 160
Joy Division 10, 97

Keats, John 133
Kent, Nick 2
Kerrang! 16
Kihn, Greg 146, 154–6
Kinks, The 172, 174–5, 177, 181
Kureishi, Hanif 9

Landau, Jon 1, 11
Larkin, Philip 169
Led Zeppelin 146–50, 157, 163
legend 138, 159–62, 165, 168, 169
Levithan, David 93–4, 98
literature 14, 17, 24, 28, 60, 74, 93, 94, 96, 101, 105, 121, 124, 170, 173
Lydon, John (Johnny Rotten) 155, 157, 167
lyrics 4, 56, 60, 71, 95, 113–15, 117, 121, 145, 147, 156, 157, 163, 165, 167, 172

McLuhan, Marshall 13
Mahon, Maureen 107, 109, 118
Mapplethorpe, Robert 134, 139
Marcus, Greil 11, 33, 68, 69, 77, 109, 159, 162, 167, 170, 176
Marsh, Dave 1, 11, 145
MC5 178, 179
media, digital 1, 3, 9, 13–15, 17, 20, 21, 81–3, 87–92
Melody Maker 9, 12, 13
memoir 4, 10, 16, 119–27, 129–31
Middleton, Richard 53, 62, 73, 74, 76, 77
Mojo 16, 144, 171, 175
Morrison, Jim 135–41, 143, 167, 180
myth/myth-making 1, 3–5, 24, 25, 27–9, 31–3, 52, 56, 63, 73, 74, 92, 108, 138, 146–50, 156, 159–70

Neuwirth, Bobby 134
New Cue, The 13
New Musical Express (NME) 11–13, 15, 16
New Statesman 10, 16, 21, 22

Paddison, Max 35, 39, 40, 48
Paytress, Mark 175, 176
Phillips, Sam 42, 161, 171
Piazza, Tom 172
Pitchfork 12, 14, 19
Pop, Iggy 28, 29, 32, 33, 156, 157
Portman, Frank 94, 102, 105
Presley, Elvis 5, 9, 54, 73, 93, 159, 161, 162, 170

Q 1, 9, 10, 12, 13, 15, 16

Radiohead 39, 53, 59, 60, 96, 119
Record Mirror 12
religion 4, 105, 150, 151, 155, 156, 165
Ricoeur, Paul 90, 92
Rimbaud, Arthur 135, 138
Rolling Stone 9, 12, 16, 110, 148, 157
Rolling Stones, The 42, 56, 64, 65, 106, 108, 128, 138, 154, 180

satire 182
Sawczuk, Tomasz 124, 131
Scorsese, Martin 164–6, 171
Sex Pistols 155, 157, 166, 173
Shank, Barry 118
Shelley, Percy Bysshe 133
Smith, Patti 4, 54, 120, 131, 133–45, 160, 171, 179–80
Smiths, The 95
Sounds 12, 14, 17
Springsteen, Bruce 11, 23, 117, 175
Stanshall, Vivian 182
Steinbeck, John 164
Symes, Colin 173, 174

Thorn, Tracey 119, 120, 131
Turner, Tina 106, 131
27 Club 141, 149, 167, 168, 171

Winehouse, Amy 57, 141
Wiseman-Trowse, Nathan 74, 77

young adult (YA) fiction 3, 93–6, 99
Young, Neil 167

Zappa, Frank 3, 39, 165, 171, 190

www.ingramcontent.com/pod-product-compliance
Lightning Source LLC
LaVergne TN
LVHW011952201224
799619LV00003B/135